Leadership in Career Services: Voices from the Field

Emanuel Contomanolis, Ph.D.

Trudy Steinfeld, M.A.

Editors

CONTENTS

*This book is dedicated to our profession
and the many talented, committed and passionate individuals who do
so much to meet the needs of our clients and stakeholders.*

Introduction
and Acknowledgements

We are fortunate in holding career services leadership positions we love but also, through our consulting practice, in being able to assist other career services leaders in enhancing the performance of their offices and programs. It occurred to us, after we conducted a review of a career services office, that an untapped opportunity existed to contribute to the preparation of the next generation of career services leaders beyond the many training programs and professional activities already being offered and in which we were actively involved.

Our idea was to write a book – a resource that directors and aspiring directors could reference for advice and perspective. We were convinced, however, that any such book written by any one person could never effectively account for all the diverse experiences, insights and perspectives which are so valuable and necessary to today's practicing professionals.

So we turned our attention instead to a different approach – an *edited* book that, in lieu of formal chapters, would include essays on a wide variety of leadership topics. We were certain that many of our colleagues shared our passion for serving the next generation of leaders in our profession and would be willing to participate in this effort. We were not wrong.

We quickly determined we could make even more of a contribution to the profession we love if the NACE Foundation, whose mission is to advance the knowledge and learning of the profession, could utilize the royalties from the sales of this book to further its many worthy initiatives particularly in the area of leadership development. Our colleagues were quick to embrace the idea and eager to contribute in this generous way.

We wish first to acknowledge those essay contributors to this book who shared our passion for this project and gave so generously of their time in providing their experience and knowledge. We are indeed fortunate to have such great colleagues and such great friends.

We also wish to thank those colleagues who shared their words of advice within the challenging constraints of 100 words or less.

Finally, we wish to acknowledge those individuals who contributed to the production of this book. The cover design is by Courtney Hirsch of New York University. Format and layout assistance was provided by M'Chelle Ryan, also of New York University. Editorial assistance was provided by Mimi Collins of the National Association of Colleges and Employers.

Finally, we wish to thank the National Association of Colleges and Employers and all the regional and related professional organizations that together serve the needs of our profession and its practitioners with such commitment and excellence.

Here then is the first edition of a book we plan to continue to enhance and expand in subsequent versions always, we hope, responsive and timely in supporting the needs and interests of career services leaders today and tomorrow.

Manny Contomanolis, Associate Vice President, Rochester Institute of Technology

Trudy Steinfeld, Assistant Vice President, New York University

Foreword

As I read through the chapters of this book, I am reminded of the hundreds and hundreds of voices I encountered this past year at NACE *Face2Face* events across the country, all seeking to understand fully the conditions and trends we are facing in our profession, to anticipate and predict what lies ahead, and finally to lead the way with responsive and relevant actions to prepare us for the future.

Just consider some of the issues in front of us: a volatile and uncertain global economic context as many organizations expand education and recruiting activity to a global scale; rising costs of higher education along with increased demand for accountability, definitions and measures related to value proposition and attention to ROI; legislative and social issues that impact graduating students, higher education institutions and employers; expansion of mobile technology and social media and their direct impact on delivering career development and access to employers; population and enrollment demographics impacting workforce diversity as well as supply/demand issues related to skills and knowledge preparation. Simply put, being a career services practitioner today is not easy.

Yet, despite the range of issues and difficulties, we must also acknowledge that some of these very considerations place career services professionals at the center of value and impact for our institutions and stakeholders – employers, administrators and faculty, alumni, parents, and of course, our students. They look to career services offices as the primary resource and facilitator for students to plan for and achieve their career goals. This is no small expectation when we consider the outcomes expected from acquiring a college degree in today's world.

So what does it take to be a successful career services leader? There is no single or simple answer; our editors are wise to engage contributors with a range of leadership experience, knowledge and insight to inform us on topics of critical import to our profession. Whether you run a one-person office or a large decentralized operation, want to strengthen your understanding of ethical issues or budget management, are starting a new job or considering how to increase innovation in your existing framework – you will find guidance and new ideas to consider in the chapters of this book. What a great compendium of the practical and philosophical, of the "true and proven" alongside challenges for risk-taking and a willingness to pursue the untried.

And more than that, we have a resource here that is organic in nature and will continue to be expanded even more as we evolve this book of insights on new topics and issues over time. Perhaps some of the readers of today will be the contributors of tomorrow.

My challenge to the reader is this: do not think of this book as just a shopping list of topics to be read as though you are doing a Google search or learning from a Wikipedia entry. While we all can benefit from such efforts and there is indeed significant information to be garnered in these pages, there is so much more here – look for that which is thought-provoking and open-ended to help expand our thinking and capabilities as leaders.

Marilyn Mackes, NACE Executive Director

Career Services Leadership: Some Guiding Principles

Emanuel Contomanolis and Trudy Steinfeld

This is a book for leaders but not necessarily about leadership.

The leadership development field is vast, with an enormous array of theoretical constructs, philosophies, assessment tools, research literature, and strategies for the would-be leader. A concise survey of the current state of thinking in this field is neither practical nor appropriate for our purposes. In this introductory essay, we want instead to provide an overview of some basic guiding principles of leadership that we believe are particularly appropriate to higher education in general and career services organizations specifically. We believe, in fact, that the most highly effective and successful career services organizations are most often led by directors who embrace and apply the 12 principles we describe here.

These principles are practical in nature and grounded in experience. You will also find that many of them are affirmed and elaborated upon in other essays in this collection, and in the insights offered by professionals in the "In 100 Words or Less" section of the book.

Always remember the difference between leadership and management

The terms "leadership" and "management" are often used interchangeably, prompting the question as to whether there is a difference between the two concepts. Michael Useem of the Wharton School of Business offers this perspective in distinguishing between leading and managing:

> The distinction is between *running* the office and adding *value* to it, between *discharging* our responsibilities and *exceeding* them. Leadership is a matter of bringing more to the office than we were given, of adding greater value to

the organization than it would have achieved without us. (Useem, 2011)

While the concept is a valuable one, we suggest a simpler distinction between leading and managing—*you lead people, and you manage things.* You can manage your time, you can manage a project flow schedule, and—if you're lucky—you might even be able to manage your checkbook, but if it involves people, it is always about leadership. No one comes to the office every day eager to be "managed," but everyone benefits from and is energized by effective leadership. We believe the distinction is important because working effectively with others in a leadership role will be one of the most challenging yet rewarding experiences you'll ever have.

Know where you want to go and make sure everyone else knows as well

One of the most critical roles for leaders is setting the vision and direction for the office. Regardless of the process that is used to establish this vision and direction, or the goals and activities that the office undertakes in pursuit of it, as a leader you must know where you want to go with your organization. Codifying that office direction with a vision and mission statement, as well as a set of the broad goals you are trying to achieve, is incredibly important to everyone in your organization and to your clients, constituents, and stakeholders outside of it. The vision, mission, and goals of your organization come alive when a statement of your office values and operating principles accompanies them. Together, these help define and articulate the organizational culture you want to develop in your office.

Disseminating appropriate versions of these documents to key individuals and organizations throughout the campus community helps in communicating consistently the important strategic elements of your office plan and in setting performance expectations for your organization and staff.

Know the field but reflect the institution

Despite what some people characterize as the straightforward nature of career services work, there are many differing philosophies, organizational models, strategies, and approaches in undertaking that work. Keeping up to date on current thinking, alternative approaches, best practices, and future trends in the field is a vital task in your role as office leader. While you need to understand the field broadly, you must *apply* what you have learned in a way that will be most effective in *your* institution. A common mistake made by leaders when establishing the direction, focus, and organization of their career services office is to neglect to connect clearly the office direction with the vision, mission, and values of the institution. Always test the direction of your office against that of the institution: In what ways does career services support the specific mission, values, and culture of the institution? The connection should be clear and obvious to any observer, and it should go beyond words to reflect the shared perceptions, beliefs, and actions of the institutional community.

There are many diverse and effective career services delivery models. The "best" one is the one that fits your institution.

Know yourself and what you need to be successful

Critical to your leadership success is self-awareness, yet this is often one of the most difficult tasks to accomplish for any leader. Always try to be honest with yourself—about your strengths and weaknesses, skills and abilities, and likes and dislikes. A mentor and trusted colleagues—both inside and outside of your office and institution—can be very helpful to you in gaining that valuable insight and self-awareness. Nurture those relationships, and be open to the feedback you receive.

If you are truly self-aware, you are in a much better position to consider strategically and honestly the ways in which you can craft your leadership role to best contribute to the success of your office. That self-awareness also provides the necessary foundation to building and developing the team of people that will be working with you. It will also help you and your team establish trust and a shared vision of success.

Think twice and hire once

As the leader of your career services organization, you are an essential component of its success; however, no leader can truly be successful without others. Making the best hiring decisions for your organization is a critical task for leaders. In doing so, keep in mind the following considerations:

- Be clear in what you are looking for—in the role and in potential candidates—and make sure any others involved in the sourcing and selection process know that as well.

- When in doubt over a hiring decision, always give greater weight to the interests and skills of candidates over their experience. You want the appropriate balance in all areas, but passion for this work and the right skill set will always serve your organization well over the long term.

- Involve others in sourcing, vetting, and interviewing candidates, but remember—even if you delegate the final choice to others, the final responsibility and accountability for that hire will always be yours.

Invest in people

As a leader, your office team is your greatest asset and your greatest responsibility. Jeff Haden (2012), in an Inc.com blog post, shared what he believed was the best answer he ever heard to the question: What is the key to leading people?" The answer? "No one cares how much you know until they first know how much you care about them." He went on to elaborate:

> Yeah we're in charge and yeah we talk about targets and goals and visions, but our employees don't care about any of that stuff for very long…When an employee knows— truly knows—that you care about them, then they care about you. And when they know you care, they will listen to you…and they will do anything for you.

While bordering on hyperbole, the sentiment is an important one. People perform best when they feel needed and respected and their individual goals and interests are accommodated. This might not always be possible, but the effort to do so can be enormously important to the members of your team. Always keep in mind the following:

- Be clear in what you expect from people, and always relate those expectations to the needs of the office and your institution.

- Take time to get to know your team members, leveraging their strengths and abilities and supporting their interests and goals.

- Invest in their professional development and make use of the new skills and experiences they acquire.

- Always be positive and constructive with people, whether that is in dealing with problem situations or coaching them for success.

Make good decisions

Making timely and effective decisions is a staple of effective leadership. In a career services leadership role, you will make countless decisions—important, routine, or trivial—and deal with any number of potentially challenging situations, including budgetary (staff layoffs, budget cuts, difficult negotiations for fiscal support); human resources related (terminations, staff performance improvement plans, staff conflicts), employer related (problem recruiters, inappropriate employer demands, student lawsuits against employers), student related (student deaths, complaints about service, students with problematic and hostile behaviors), and institutional politics related (problem faculty and deans, efforts to decentralize services, unreasonable demands for service and outcomes) to name a few.

These are some simple yet powerful lessons to help guide you in working through those diverse yet equally challenging situations:

- Always make sure you understand the problem and the situation. Too many people are too quick to take action or fail to consider the situation from all angles and perspectives. Take the time to fully explore the problem and circumstances focusing on the broader context and implications of different courses of action.

- Problem-solve thoughtfully. Invite diverse perspectives and insights. Seek the help of others with more experience or specialized knowledge appropriate to the circumstances. Be open to different ideas and ways of looking at things. Effective leaders surround themselves with smart people and have the good sense to listen to them—even when they don't like what they hear.

- Be decisive. When you're ready to make a decision or chart a course of action, do so decisively and confidently. When in doubt about what to do—and you will be because there are different, yet equally effective, ways to handle things--always remember this guiding principle: If you believe your decisions and actions are consistent with your values and those of your institution and are in the best interests of your clients and stakeholders, then more often than not you will have done the right thing.

Value collaboration over confrontation

Collaboration and collegiality, as a rule, are highly valued in higher education, which lacks much of the hierarchical structures and control systems of the corporate world. It is not unusual, however, for "turf-dom," personality style clashes, miscommunication, or competition to spoil that spirit of collegiality. Career services work--never more so than today—relies on partnerships and collaboration. The ability to achieve those things with, among others, faculty, administrators in alumni relations and advancement, student clubs and organizations, senior institutional administrators, and even trustees often is characteristic of effective career services organizations and their leaders.

The key to collaboration is building relationships—reaching out to key individuals and organizations, understanding their needs and interests, and finding common ground. Based on that foundation of trust and knowledge, joint initiatives are more likely to reflect the interests of both parties and enhance the chances for success. Collaboration can be more challenging when there are differing opinions by well-intentioned people as to how best to achieve a common goal. In those instances, always emphasize the interests and needs of the clients and stakeholders you are trying to serve. If you can always keep client satisfaction first, it is easier to work back to a common ground. Just remember: Collaboration does not mean that everything will always work the way you want. There is always some measure of compromise. This is much easier to accept when you put the needs of clients and stakeholders first.

Effective collaboration can be a significant factor in extending a leader's *referent authority*. By that we mean the influence an individual extends beyond the administrative authority that accrues to his or her title and position. Referent authority is highly prized because it can both strengthen administrative authority and extend it significantly to the benefit of the leader and the career services organization.

Never lose touch with your clients and stakeholders

Effective leaders should never lose sight of the mission and desired outcomes of their organization and should never lose touch with the needs, desires, and expectations of their clients and stakeholders. Through both formal means (e.g., advisory boards, focus groups, feedback surveys) and informal means (e.g., cultivating relationships with key decision-makers, potential confidantes, mentors, and trusted colleagues), it's vital that as a leader you are constantly testing the assumptions you and your office team have concerning the effectiveness of your efforts. It's the natural instinct of professionals in every field, but fight the urge to assume you always know what's best for your clients and stakeholders and that they are always open and transparent concerning their perceptions of your office and staff.

It's vital that as a leader you are constantly aware of how your office is viewed by your clients and stakeholders and that you are conscious of the extent to which you are addressing their needs and expectations.

Be cautious of the "comfort zone"

There's a natural tendency in individuals and organizations to reach a "comfort zone"—the point at which everything appears to be running smoothly and according to plan. In these circumstances, there is also the strong inclination to "coast" for a bit and savor the success of your efforts. We urge you to be cautious about the seductive nature of the "comfort zone." It is important to recognize that in today's fast-paced world with such extraordinarily high expectations for higher education, there is no such thing as a "comfortable status quo." *An organization is either moving forward or moving back.* Too much time in the comfort zone often means missed opportunities or being forced to react to changing circumstances and priorities rather than strategically driving them.

Key to avoiding the comfort zone is being open to change and innovation. While any change or new innovation demands some degree of risk taking, embrace the notion that the future can be better than the present. Your openness to change and encouragement of new ideas and new ways of doing things can be immensely powerful in driving the success of your office.

As a leader, always keep your eye on the next step and never underestimate the longer-term implications of the actions you take. The focus on moving the organization always forward helps to foster a more energetic and creative work environment and sends strong signals to your institutional community that there is thought leadership and a drive for excellence in your organization.

"Lead up"

The natural emphasis for leaders is to focus on the team of people and the organization we're responsible for. As such, there is the understandable tendency to focus attention on those that work for us and with us. Truly effective leadership, however, also requires the ability to "lead up." "Leading up" refers to the on-going process of building a relationship with your supervisor to obtain the best possible results for your organization, your supervisor, and you. All leaders have a certain style and approach, and it's critically important you understand that of your supervisor. While there are no shortcuts to building that effective partnership with your supervisor, there are certainly some helpful strategies to employ:

- *Know what matters to your supervisor.* Determine what's important to your supervisor, what the person values and expects from you and your organization. Align your efforts accordingly or at least make every attempt to address those preferences and values consistently and sensitively

- *Fill in the "gaps" your supervisor may have.* Focus on doing things that your supervisor may not be particularly good at or enjoys doing. If your supervisor, for example, is a "big picture" strategist, emphasize your ability to execute plans and handle the details.

- *Do more than is necessary.* Productivity and performance go a long way in any professional relationship, but always strive to exceed expectations. Seek new responsibilities and assignments and always demonstrate your interests and knowledge beyond career services. Strive to understand the bigger organization of which you're a part, as well as the institutional landscape and field of higher education broadly.

- *Commit to being a problem solver.* Always try to bring solutions to your supervisor rather than problems. When you need direction from your supervisor, identify the issue or problem, offer your analysis and interpretation, and present some possible solutions including the one you would recommend based on your analysis.

- *Always protect your supervisor.* Inevitably, at some point, you will find something to criticize in your supervisor. There is nothing to be gained by expressing your frustrations to anyone else—especially others in your institution. The old adage "If you have nothing good to say, say nothing at all" is wise counsel for those circumstances.

- *Accept that you will not always get your way.* There will always be circumstances when you and your supervisor will disagree or, at least, see the situation and potential options differently. Understand that, in most instances, your supervisor's decision will carry the day. Accept it gracefully, support it appropriately, and learn from the situation.

Learn to live with the loneliness of leadership

The demands, pressures, and expectations for leaders of career services organizations today are formidable. The "distance" that by necessity exists at times between leaders and the rest of the office team can make those challenges even more daunting. Leaders often have to make difficult decisions. At times, those decisions may not please everyone in the organization, or they may add to the stress and challenge team members are already feeling. Often it is problematic or impractical to maintain the same kind of personal relationships with colleagues when the responsibilities of supervision necessarily intrude. Some office team members may find it more difficult to fully disclose how they are truly feeling to leaders because of perceived and actual differences in authority and influence.

So what's a leader to do? The answer is not always simple or easy. The best advice we can offer is to prepare for and accept the "loneliness" that often comes with the role. Accept that some professional and personal "distance" is necessary and healthy for your organization. It becomes especially important, consequently, for leaders to form other professional and personal networks as a support system. Often these networks will include trusted members of the institutional community as well as other career services leaders, professionals, and friends.

Leaders need to seek information, solicit diverse opinions and perspectives, and apply their best thinking to any situation. They must also have the courage of their convictions and beliefs in making decisions—especially the most difficult ones where no easy answer is evident. Effective leaders will understand and accept that the final responsibility is theirs, but also will have the courage and integrity to revise a decision if new knowledge, insights, or circumstances demand new approaches.

A concluding thought

Leadership is an art *and* a science. As you survey the national and global landscape of career services, you will observe, as we do, that there are leaders of different styles, in different kinds of offices, at different types of higher education institutions. While we believe the principles we have shared here are universal, the art and science of applying those principles allows for the tremendous variety that makes our work in career services leadership so challenging *and* so rewarding.

References

Useem, M. (2011). *The leader's checklist, expanded edition: 15 mission-critical principles.* Philadelphia: Wharton Digital Press.

Haden, J. (2012). The Only Management Strategy You'll Ever Need. Inc.com. Retrieved from http://www.inc.com/jeff-haden

Leaders in Career Services—The Exploration of "Self" and Supportive Interventions

Ryan M. Herson

Responsibility and impact

Higher education career services leaders hold significant responsibilities that come with a high degree of visibility as critical institutional metrics are directly influenced by their performance. To be successful in this role, one must possess advanced skills that include communication, listening, presenting, report-writing, data analysis, and negotiation. These skills are then to be combined with, in equal measure, competencies of management, creativity, and emotional intelligence.

This position requires the need to manage complex business-related matters while empowering their teams to achieve professional and personal goals. This is not easy to orchestrate in an environment where there are frequent changes to strategic priorities and organization readiness (e.g., opportunities, demands, and limitations). Therefore, complacency is not an option and is certainly not sustainable even in the short term.

Awareness of self

I often push leaders to be self-aware of their own strengths and skill gaps so they can be more effective in managing the current and future work force and drive strategic priorities. Therefore, it is vitally important that university career services leaders actively seek both formal and informal developmental opportunities aligned with business objectives. Simple ways to assess one's effectiveness can include instituting a process that enables staff members to provide anonymous feedback, seeking feedback from a trusted advisor, or even receiving real-time feedback from a high potential over coffee in a local café. Each assessment can provide relevant data points that allow a given leader to obtain a pulse on how things are operating within the university career services center he or she manages and determine what requires attention.

However, more often than not, leaders pick the path of least resistance and are more interested in compliance, taking the required training as opposed to seeking out more robust and comprehensive continuous developmental opportunities. Most leaders I speak to say they simply don't have the time. In these instances, leaders take part in training programs where only vague notions of "development" and "high performance" are applied as opposed to initiatives that transfer concrete skills relevant to that level of management. If a lack of time is the issue I would challenge them to delegate some tasks to direct reports who have the desire to expand their skill set. If that is not an option, then go back to the basics. Take action in being more efficient by drafting a prioritized list of activities at the beginning of the day that need to be completed before the close of business. These leaders must be realistic about what they intend to complete so every minute of the day can be attributed to matters of importance.

When leaders don't focus on their own training and self development, they are heading down a slippery slope where they run the risk of diminishing their own authority and credibility. In these situations, I have observed several consistent behaviors that serve as early warning signs to include a leader possessing a high degree of complacency, isolation, selfishness, and arrogance; such leaders are often disengaged and not interested in receiving constructive feedback. Furthermore, fact-based evidence of talent gaps materialize which is typically a result of a leader's lack of interest in learning new skills. These gaps tend to emerge especially when individuals have been in a leadership position for an extended period of time and are not always as active in their own development. Simply stated, university career services leaders must continuously work to improve their cross-functional and technical capability so they can effectively manage programs and expand their leadership potential.

Key considerations

Before a leadership or coaching intervention is initiated, be sure that the investment is warranted, or at least make sure that you have identified the appropriate level of support required. Try to assess if an easier fix can be made. Perhaps the leader is stretched too far in time and effort or doesn't understand certain expectations or what constitutes success. If these are not well understood, try to align the meaning to their interests, and reassure them that they are supported through both formal and informal mechanisms. When all else fails, it may be time to take specific action.

Leadership and coaching interventions will enhance the performance of the learner by further developing their leadership competencies. This results in the improved ability to inspire and not just manage, to be accountable to both supervisors and subordinates; and to continue to develop their skills in core leadership responsibilities and characteristics. However, real progress cannot be made unless they remain focused on being more self-aware, engaged, and proactive and posses the desire to continuously improve. In order to support this behavioral shift, I help the leader understand how these interventions fit within the bigger picture of his or her professional and personal development. In doing so, these individuals will understand that the intended benefits will only be realized if they actively apply the key concepts and adopt the new strategies learned to support continuous improvement.

When selecting a leadership or coaching intervention, decision makers should understand that improvements will take an investment of time, resources, and patience. These interventions are a worthy investment considering they build enhanced leadership capacity for the future. The value of promoting a culture of leadership development and coaching should be visible across the institution in order to improve overall operational effectiveness, work force motivation, performance, and aptitude for change.

Leadership and coaching intervention

Leadership and coaching practitioners are trained to listen, observe, reflect, and customize their approaches to the unique needs of the learner in order to facilitate transformational and sustainable individual, team, and organizational results. However, based on the popularity of coaching, I have observed unqualified and ill-equipped practitioners deploy their own haphazard leadership and coaching techniques. Therefore, seek interventions whose results are backed by research or credible institution. If not, it may be hard to establish a causal link to suggest that any improvements made were a result of the intervention. Tested methodologies that can be embedded in the culture are attractive to stakeholders and serve as a strategic organizational asset generating greater return on investment.

Reinforcing a point made earlier, leadership and coaching interventions should always lead in with a vision-centered approach highlighting the strategic goals of the university so a deeper connection and sense of impact of what they influence is well understood. Don't overlook importance of taking this approach. Leaders often need this reinforcement early and often, which is why it serves as a great starting point.

Methods of interventions need to be practical, easy to understand, and easy to apply so key concepts are validated to help build the foundation for subsequent activities. Furthermore, I find it necessary to create learner-specific interventions, scenarios, and materials to support learning methods that are engaging, create an active learning environment, and encourage participation, openness, and fun. This allows the achievement of learning objectives and makes a significant difference in the overall learning experience. Learning objectives can include but are not limited to obtaining a clear understanding about what you should work on for maximum impact on your team's top goals; becoming a more valued leader by focusing your work on the organization's highest priorities; learning how to use mechanisms to help you focus on key goals and stay on track to achieve them; bringing back innovative ideas to your teams with methods to help them execute with excellence; developing the habits to create high accountability within your team; exercising power and influence and attempting to affect significant change with multiple stakeholders; analyzing situations, their relationships to each other, and how to support the desired change; and weighing the costs and implications of key business decisions.

Rather than trying to transform a leader through a single learning event, deploying continual interventions that are coordinated in an integrated fashion creates more lasting and impactful change. In my experience, proposing a series of smaller, less-daunting recommendations for change are more easily accepted by a learner. Once these quick wins are realized and show demonstrable benefits, positive momentum for the remaining changes is generated and will lessen potential resistance. The interventions should reflect the day-to-day requirements of the leader's position and embed training solutions that are specific to job function so time to competency can be reduced. I also reinforce the need to apply interventions that address the learning styles, preferences, and needs of the specific leader receiving the intervention. Again, don't ignore the importance of using a learner-centered approach. If training is not learner-centered, the leader will not have the benefit of receiving candid feedback on his or her performance and will then be unable to apply new skills from the learning environment into life and the workplace.

Evaluation

Leadership and coaching interventions must retain a strong focus on performance improvement through rigorous and continuous evaluation overtime. The collection of these data will improve the effect of the interventions in an iterative process so subsequent trainings reflect evolving stakeholder needs and participant feedback. Evaluations need to assess the impact that these interventions have on addressing specific leadership gaps so resources applied to improve performance are properly allocated over time.

Closing

University career services leaders have significant responsibilities that directly affect the reputation of their institution. Their contributions are highly visible so they must be critical of their own development and always seek support when they are in need. Both measurable and observable improvements can be made through the application of well-coordinated leadership and coaching interventions that are backed by research and conducted by skilled practitioners. These interventions should help the leader learn through real business issues so new learnings are actively applied. If effective, and these leaders become more self aware, a higher performing and results-oriented culture can be sustained.

The First 100 Days

Kathy L. Sims

This era of career services is here to stay—the one in which accountability reigns supreme and expectations often exceed available resources and capacity. There is heightened scrutiny and focus on the appointment of new directors, as colleges and universities are recognizing the value proposition between effective career development services and the recruitment, retention, and success of their students and graduates. The importance of a director's first 100 days, when your early vision and direction for the longer term are formulated, has never been greater. The significance of this period in your new role is analogous to our message to students about having just one chance to make that first impression.

Whether you are a current director transitioning to a different campus, or you've just accepted your first directorship, the first three months in your new position will be formative, and merit deliberate and tactical planning. A flexible, disciplined approach to interacting with, listening to, and engaging your new stakeholders is essential to how they will perceive and respond to you in the short term, and it can result in long-term benefits throughout your tenure.

Preparing for the first 100 days

"Leadership onboarding" is the most descriptive label for defining the process you will undergo in the first three months. But unlike the onboarding of new employees that is managed by their bosses, as a new director you will craft your own onboarding program. Two fundamental keys to your success will be to have developed a strategy for this process *before* Day One, and to acquire an understanding of what pitfalls you should avoid during your first 100 days on the job. Joseph Kran, president and founder of OI Partners - Gateway International, aptly and colorfully captures the process:

Successful onboarding is a study in paradox. To be effective in your transition, you must focus on learning, rather than demonstrating your worth. Build alliances while not becoming overly political. Seek to improve the organization without devaluing what already exists. Gain the credibility to be allowed to enact decisions that should, by rights, be yours to make. Even, or perhaps especially, if your mandate is to bring about radical change, you must approach your onboarding with the sophistication of an anthropologist studying a foreign culture (and the caution of someone who is unsure whether the natives are armed and dangerous). (2009).

As you contemplate how you will approach your first 100 days, balancing your intellect and emotions can be challenging. Do not underestimate the impact of the excitement, anticipation, fears, and personal transitions on your ability to concentrate on your plans to efficiently optimize those early weeks in the new position. It's wise to seek the support of a trusted and experienced external colleague for the modest support you may need to focus. The colleague should be someone who can candidly react to your ideas, observations, and tactics without bias.

Your frame of mind in approaching the new directorship is an essential key to how successful you will be. Remember that you are no longer a candidate; you have already earned the job. Don't try to provide a lot of answers in this period. Alternatively, provocative and measured questions will go far to impress others while eliciting the information you seek. Likewise, no matter how dire the situation may be for your new career center, you'll want to avoid the "savior syndrome." During the recruitment process you may have been told you are just what the career center needs to solve all issues, but don't fall into the trap of believing that yourself. Your first 100 days is a time to be humble, to acknowledge the learning curve, and to engage your new colleagues, staff, and bosses in your experience. The onboarding process should be a time for reflective introspect; with that vote of confidence you received in the form of the job offer, you can afford to check your ego at the door. Prepare yourself to listen—intently, with focus and with respect.

Content and context: Where to focus

By the end of your first 100 days, you should be able to lay out a blueprint for your leadership going forward, a preliminary strategic plan that outlines core themes you have identified during this time frame. Of course, many new appointments are accompanied by explicit charges from senior leadership, often with the expectation that you will make swift and momentous changes to set a new course. In this situation, you must exercise your leading up skills to negotiate time to source, collect, and assess the intelligence required to develop an informed plan. It is as important for you to make your intentions and expectations clear to your superior(s) as it is for you to understand theirs.

In formulating your plan for your first 100 days, you should devise the methods you will use to target seven core spheres that will advise your ultimate blueprint for leadership of the career center.

1. Data, Data, Data: Gather the numbers and records you need to be informed and clear about the career center's budget, services usage, outcomes, recruitment, and staffing.

2. Identify Operational Strengths and Weaknesses: Study available documentation such as program reviews, annual reports, and evaluative summaries. Interview staff, campus partners, faculty, students, senior administrators, employers, and alumni to learn about your career center's operational strengths that can be leveraged, and its weaknesses that may require remedial attention.

3. Understand the Career Center's History: Learn about the scope of the career center's mission over time, and how events have impacted reporting lines, operational and staffing structures, service offerings, and the customer base. This context will be crucial to better understanding your staff, constituents, and campus politics.

4. Get to Know the Career Center's Stakeholders: Who are they? Strategically select representatives of these groups to meet with and interview about their needs, expectations, interests, and concerns. How have they been accommodated, and how have they

contributed to the career center's current status? Investing your time here creates a solid platform toward establishing your personal credibility and political capital.

5. The Campus Culture: Immerse yourself in campus activities and programs beyond those in career services. Study the governance structures for the administration, the faculty, and the student body. Ask new colleagues for their insights into the culture of the campus. Digest staff and student media; participate in selected campus events—the arts, athletics, and convocations, for example. Investigate the politics that influence decisions about your career center, and learn how these decisions evolve.

6. Appreciate Your New Boss(es): What is their existing perception of the career center, and how would they describe the ideal operation? Where would they like the organization to go, and what do they want to avoid happening?

7. Cultivate Staff Relations: As crucial as your first 100 days are in shaping others' perceptions of you, the first **20** days with your new staff can define your working relationships for years to come. It is during this time that you should display your leadership style in not-so-subtle ways, offering staff a clear understanding of your expectations, while overtly demonstrating your interest in them, their work, and their expectations. Don't hesitate to pitch into team projects or events to get a feel for their work and to show that you appreciate every staff member's contribution to accomplishing the mission of career services. This tactical approach will engage the staff in your journey, expand their awareness of your thinking, and build their appreciation for the priorities you will ultimately identify.

If you haven't figured it out already, you will be working some long hours during your first 100 days! Don't worry. With your adrenaline in high gear and the realization that you will be leading this career center into the future, you'll find the effort exhilarating, and time will pass with seemingly record speed.

A blueprint for your leadership

Reflecting on the vast wealth of information you'll collect could be daunting, but your seasoned, professional judgment, one of the reasons you have reached this leadership level, will serve you well in these first 100 days. Technical, expert analysis is critical, but your intuitive perceptions cannot be underestimated. Your discerning insights can contribute significantly to your assessment of your new center, of its existing and potential positioning within the institution, and of the individuals who can or cannot play a role in advancing your ultimate vision.

As you analyze what you are learning about your new organization, you should be looking for emerging themes that will shape your blueprint for the future. Within the first 80 days, the intentional research, acute observation, thoughtful interviews, and inquisitions should be contributing to your foundation of knowledge as well as setting your course of direction. Plan to use those final four weeks of your first 100 days to synthesize all that you've learned into three to five broad-sweeping themes that will offer clarity and focus for your staff and bosses. For example, one theme may focus on the integration of advanced technology, while another on the model(s) of service delivery. At this stage, you are not offering operational strategies to pursue the core themes, but describing the overarching concepts that will become the career center's priorities. Recipients of your blueprint should include the stakeholders you've engaged in your onboarding process, accompanied by your insights to how they are important to the center's successful future.

New career center directors are positioned to move their organizations to greater heights. With a solid game plan for those impressionable first 100 days, you lay the ground work for engaging the campus community in the career center's work. Through early consultation, research, and introspection, you will optimize your leadership effectiveness, align your center's goals with the institutional mission and priorities, inspire your staff and colleagues, and create collaborative teams to advance your blueprint. Michael Watkins (2009), in *Why the First 100 Days Matter* for the Harvard Business Review Blog Network, makes the case quite succinctly:

> "The first hundred days mark is not the end of the story, it's the
> end of the beginning... And that's why the transition period

matters so much."

References

Kran, J. (2009). Nailing It: How to Cement Your Success in a New Leadership Role. OI Partners- Gateway International. Retrieved from http://joekran.com/nailing_it.html.

Watkins, M. (2009) Why the First 100 Days Matters. Harvard Business Review Blog Network. Retrieved from http://blogs.hbr.org/watkins/2009/03/why_the_first_100_days_matters.html.

Recommended Readings

O'Keeffem, N. (2011). *Making the First 100 Days Pay Off.* Source: Special to CNN.

Torres, R. and Tollman, P. (2011). *Five Myths of a CEO's First 100 Days.* Source: Harvard Business Review Blog Network.

Bradt, G., Check, J., Pedraza, J. (2006). *The New Leader's 100-Day Action Plan.* Source: John Wiley & Sons, New York.

Watkins, M. (2003). *The First 90 Days: Critical Success Strategies for New Leaders at All Levels.* Source: Harvard Business Press Books.

Smith, D. (2011). *Leadership Onboarding: A Short-Term Solution for Long-Term Success.* Retrieved from besmith.com.

Toward Strategic Thinking: Identifying and Addressing Challenges For the 21st Century Career Center

Timothy B. Luzader

Introduction

A conundrum is defined as a paradoxical, insoluble, or difficult problem. We as career center directors often encounter confusing and intricate issues that present us with our own conundrums.

Do any of the following challenges seem familiar?

- Fulfilling the role of educator and seizing upon teachable moments in a climate where students regard themselves as customers with unwavering support as such from their parents and other career center stakeholders.
- Recruiting candidates as career services generalists requiring contrasting skill sets—impeccable organizational abilities with attention to detail, a strong sense of public relations, and theory-based counseling skills in support of student career development.
- Providing recognition and convenience to a major corporate donor to the institution that is not specifically a corporate partner of the career center.
- Attempting to participate in timely direct service delivery to students while effectively addressing the multiple demands required of the career center director.

The world within which career services directors operate involves conflicting expectations. Actions taken in support of service delivery to *all* students may be viewed by some campus administrators as directors being territorial and trying to make a power play. Career services staff that abide by federal legislation and the National Association of Colleges and

Employers (NACE) Principles for Professional Practice when responding to employer or trustee requests can be perceived as being inflexible and not customer-friendly.

In an atmosphere of open communication, the rationale for difficult decisions can be explained and understood. The problem is that such communication channels are often flawed or non-existent. As a result, perception is reality.

Without a strategic direction, the career center will be bogged down with putting out daily fires and being reactive to urgent needs that are handed down. In doing so, relatively little else will likely be accomplished.

Given the tough challenges that face career center directors, a strategic plan provides a framework for reference when hard decisions are made and accompanying actions are implemented. This context for strategic decision-making can promote greater understanding among internal and external parties. In other words, a good strategic plan will help place stakeholders and career center staff members on the same page relative to the expectation for resource and service delivery. Career services staff members will also greatly benefit from having a better understanding of the career center's direction and focus.

Establishing direction

A core component of a career center's strategic plan is vision—the destination to which the career center aspires. According to strategy consultant Glenn Tecker (2012), "A strategic plan is about where you want to go, not where you are." (p. 31). When considering the process for engaging in strategic planning, the career center director may wish to consider how a mountaineer plans her journey. She starts by looking at the mountain peak—that precise location where she envisions standing at the end of her climb. Then, the mountaineer works her way backwards and takes into account the conditions and barriers that she will encounter along the way. Her presence at the mountain peak represents the vision.

Another approach to launching the strategic planning process and communicating to stakeholders is to establish a mission statement. Whereas the vision identifies where the career center wants to be, the mission defines what it does. The mission is a statement of purpose that is often laid out with broad, overarching goals. Note the differences between vision and mission in the fictional university examples provided below:

Vision Statements

- The Trumann University career center aspires to be an international leader by establishing new synergies, providing outstanding career development services, and using state-of-the-art technology to empower students to make informed choices that lead to lifelong career fulfillment and contribution in a global society.
- The vision of the Trumann University career services center is to counsel and support Trumann students to become the nation's most market-ready applicants in the global workplace.

Mission Statements

- The CSI University career center prepares CSI students to launch successful careers by providing them with career development processes, job-search services, and resources.
- The CSI University career center provides students with career counseling and assessment, experiential learning programs, and career library resources. We also facilitate relationships with students and employers to foster a community of learning and engagement to advance students' career development.

In addition to establishing a vision and/or a mission statement, some career centers opt to include values in their strategic plan. Values represent commonly held beliefs among career services staff and reflect the center's culture and priorities. As part of a strategic planning document, value statements are declarations about how career services values students, employers, and other constituents.

Values also govern the actions that career centers implement on behalf of its stakeholders. An example is the well-known proverb attributed to Confucius: "Give a man a fish and he eats for a day, teach him to fish and he eats for a lifetime." This value statement promotes self-sufficiency over dependence.

Finally, value statements provide a framework for directors in their selection of new employees. Candidates chosen for hire are typically those regarded as having consistent values with career services staff. Subsequently, they're perceived as being a better fit for the career center.

Analyzing the landscape

In the spirit of the mountaineer that considers the conditions and barriers that she may face in her journey, a career center is also advised to take environmental conditions into account and to work through a thoughtful assessment. A tried-and-true method for conducting strategic planning activity is to build context for an eventual action plan through group process. Often included among these context-building activities are the following:

- Assessing needs: The needs of stakeholders to career services (i.e. students, employers, faculty and staff, senior administration) are identified and considered. This information may be collected through surveys or focus groups. In some cases, a facilitated discussion of experienced career services practitioners and campus stakeholders will surface relevant needs sufficient for helping to build a needs-based foundation for a strategic plan.

- Scanning the environment: The focus in this exercise is to build a common understanding of the current environment within which the career center operates. The objective is to produce informed responses to strategic questions relating to social, technical, economic, and political environments. While there are common themes relevant to all colleges and universities (e.g. students seeking individualized assistance, social media trending, tight budgets and greater accountability), each institution is different. This is especially true for economic and political realities. In-depth knowledge of these areas is a critical component of this process.

- Aligning with the NACE Principles for Professional Practice and Professional Standards for College and University Career Services – career services directors have significant resources available to them through NACE. Experienced career services produce and periodically update professional standards that reflect dimensions of career services that affect program performance and quality. To provide practical application convenience, a companion evaluation notebook can be used internally to gauge how the career center's existing staffing, facility, resources, and delivery of service correspond to multiple categories of standards.

- Conducting a SWOT analysis: This process of identifying strengths, weaknesses, opportunities, and threats is accomplished by peering through a magnifying glass at the career center's current operations and considering the center's role within the framework of stakeholder needs and existing environments. When completed, career services directors and their staff should have a greater understanding of the center's strengths and weaknesses, as well as the opportunities available and the threats that could affect the reputation of the center.

- Conducting external reviews: The aforementioned activities could be conducted internally contingent upon the size and experience of the career services staff. However, in most cases, a better option is to employ external reviewers. It is often difficult for directors and their career services staff members to spot flaws in their own service delivery or fully grasp the best practices conducted at peer institutions. An opportunity for improvement or greater efficiency may be more obvious to an experienced colleague who looks at it with fresh eyes. The authors of the articles in this text all have the depth and breadth of career services experience to be good choices for an external review team. NACE also maintains a list of trained reviewers along with their biographies.

Translating knowledge into action

Some organizations put forth great effort to draft vision, mission, and values statements and conduct activities to assess themselves and their stakeholders, but then stop. They place their strategic planning-related documents on a shelf to gather dust, or on a remote part of their website to be rarely accessed. In the same way that a student's career development does not end with the acceptance of a job, strategic planning has not been accomplished when the process has been documented and published.

As strategic planning author John Bryson (2004) has pointed out, it is not enough to simply adopt a strategic plan. "Without effective implementation, important issues will not be adequately addressed, and lasting, tangible public value will not be created." (p. 32). The strategic plan is far more meaningful when the knowledge gained from the process directly impacts the future actions of the career center.

There are numerous ways to implement changes and affect the strategic direction of the center. As a starting point, directors are encouraged to give full consideration to strategic planning processes that are currently occurring on campus or will soon be launched. It is not unusual for colleges and universities to align S.M.A.R.T. goals with action plans that chart progress based on scorecards or dashboards. Doran (1984) describes such goals as specific, measurable, attainable, relevant, and time-bound. Adopting an existing campus process could give career services' strategic planning efforts greater credibility among campus colleagues and make progress reports more visible to important internal stakeholders.

If the campus does not offer a satisfactory framework for conducting an internal process to identify and follow through with strategic action items, then a number of existing models are available for your consideration. Bryson (2004) conceptualized *The Strategy Change Cycle*, which is designed to "organize participation, create ideas for strategic interventions, build a winning coalition, and implement strategies." This model offers a deliberate and thorough approach for making positive, systematic change. The opportunity for success will be greatly enhanced if strong leadership is in place to sponsor and champion the strategic planning initiative and to facilitate each step of the process.

Another approach entitled *Strategic Market Planning*[i] was specifically adapted to career services by Peter and Julie Rea (1990). While several issues that confront today's career center have evolved since this article was published, the constructs offered for implementing a strategic plan continue to be relevant and timely. Specific to matching the career center's mission to external trends, the Reas introduce and describe an evaluative matrix model within a framework of career services implementation.

By its very nature, strategic planning can be a time-intensive and disruptive process. It is not unusual for offices to involve staff in a full-day retreat along with periodical sessions as a follow up. Not all career centers have the time to invest in such a protracted process. La Piana Associates (2008) worked to generate alternatives to traditional strategic planning with a particular focus on reducing time spent on strategic planning and the pursuit of strategic thinking versus following a specific process. Through these efforts, they conceived the *Real-Time Strategic Planning Model.* Like the Bryson model, it was not established with career services in mind, but it offers practical and useful tips for implementation.

Final thoughts

No matter which approach is chosen for implementing a strategic plan, the outcome will be dependent on the leadership provided and follow-through efforts. Our persistence as career services directors to ensure that our career centers plan, operate, and think strategically will ensure a high quality of service delivery. In doing so, the distinctive competence that career services practitioners possess will be validated within our respective accountability structures and visible among our stakeholders.

When we made the decision to enter the career services field, we embarked upon a profession that truly makes a difference in peoples' lives. It is a privilege to participate in and help steer a young person's developmental process as she or he enters into adulthood. To serve in a facilitation role to help college students successfully transition to professional society is to help launch future leaders who will make a difference in the world.

References

Bryson, J.M. (2004). "Implementing Strategies and Plans Successfully", *Strategic Planning for Public and Nonprofit Organizations, 3rd Edition*, San Francisco: Jossey Bass, 2004, pp. 262.

Bryson, J.M. (2004). "The Strategy Change Cycle", *Strategic Planning for Public and Nonprofit Organizations, 3rd Edition*, San Francisco: Jossey Bass, pp. 32.

Doran, G. T. (1981). "There's a S.M.A.R.T. way to write management's goals and objectives." *Management Review*, Volume 70, Issue 11 (AMA FORUM), 1981, pp. 35-36.

La Piana, D. (2008). *The Non Profit Strategy Revolution: Real-Time Strategic Planning in a Rapid-Response World*, St. Paul, MN: Fieldstone Alliance.

Luzader, T.B. (1994). "Negotiations Considerations, Ethics and Other Practical Considerations." In J.P. Downey (ed), *Choices and Challenges: Job Search Strategies for Liberal Arts Students*. Bloomington IN: Tichenor Publishing.

National Association of Colleges and Employers (2009). *Professional Standards for College and University Career Services*, Bethlehem, PA.

National Association of Colleges and Employers (2012). *Principles for Professional Practice* Retrieved from: www.naceweb.org/Knowledge/Principles/Principles_for_Professional_Practice.

Rea, P.J. and Rea, J.S. (1990). "Strategic Market Planning: A Useful Tool for Career Services and Recruiting Offices," *Journal of College Placement*, Fall 1990, pp. 41-46.

Tecker, G.H. (2012). "The Future of Planning for the Future" *Associations Now*, April/May 2012, pp. 31.

Motivating Staff Performance: Challenges and Opportunities

Emanuel Contomanolis

One of the greatest challenges for leaders in career service organizations—and in any organization for that matter—is motivating staff performance. The greatest asset of any organization is the staff and ensuring the team is maximizing their efforts in the achievement of office goals and objectives is a distinctive characteristic of the most effective career services offices.

How is this high level of performance best achieved, however, given the enormous differences between individuals and in what motivates them at different points in their personal and professional lives? Creating an office environment that motivates performance requires that we:

- Define workplace motivation.
- Understand the key principles essential to motivating others.
- Apply specific strategies that help motivate performance.

Defining workplace motivation

Sometimes to best understand what something is, we need to understand what it is not. Motivation is not the result of inspiration slogans, posters, and logo coffee cups. It is not the exclusive bailiwick of energetic and charismatic leaders, nor mandated by organizational declaration. Perhaps most importantly it is *not* a "one-size-fits-all" strategy.

For our purposes, motivation is best defined as the process of mobilizing and sustaining individual behaviors in support of office goals and objectives. Emphasis in this working definition should be placed on the notion of a *process* and of focusing on *individual* behaviors.

There is a significant array of theoretical constructs about motivation and many offer overlapping concepts and principles. Some of the seminal work in this area includes the work of B. F. Skinner (1974) who determined that behavior results from the anticipated consequences of actions, introducing the ideas of positive reinforcement, avoidance, extinction, and punishment. In his conceptualization, people are motivated to do things because it's in their best interests to do so, i.e. to receive positive rewards and avoid "punishment."

Mazlow (1943) theorized that individuals are motivated to do things to meet their needs, which he categorized in a hierarchy of needs ranging from physiological, safety, social and love, esteem, to self-actualization. McClelland (1976) also theorized that individuals are motivated by needs that, in his model, were specific to the areas of achievement, power, and affiliation.

Latham and Locke (2002) expanded the thinking on motivation to introduce the concept of goals. In their conceptualization, individual behavior is goal driven. Individual motivation is maximized when those goals are specific; challenging, yet realistic; set and accepted by the individual; learning-oriented; and linked to performance and rewards.

Vroom and Yetton (1973) placed great importance on personal values in determining what motivates individuals. Their expectancy theory suggests that individuals make deliberate choices to engage in activities in order to achieve worthwhile and desirable outcomes in accordance with their values, needs, goals, and preferences.

Social learning theory, introduced by Bandura (1977), places great weight on the fundamental desire of individuals to seek approval and suggests that individuals are motivated by observing and consequently imitating the behaviors of others whose actions are being recognized and rewarded.

Boggiano and Pittman's (1992) theory of self-determination or intrinsic motivation suggests people are intrinsically motivated to do interesting work especially when they have a choice in initiating and regulating their work. Herzberg, et al (1959) also considered motivation within the context of work in their two-factor theory that suggests there are two sets of job factors: one set that motivates and the other set that is either neutral or causes dissatisfaction.

So how can we make the most useful sense of these varying theories and perspectives? Together, these theories inform leadership practice by suggesting some key principles that can be applied in motivating performance.

Key principles essential in motivating performance

Clearly everyone has individual needs, interests, and values. When thinking about the work environment, however, there are certain things that are important to everyone. The experience of many leaders in career services suggests that team members in any office value the following:

A sense of purpose

Everyone wants to understand and value the purpose of their role and that of the organization in which they work.

A sense of pride and respect

Everyone wants to feel the work they're doing is important and in some way contributes to something greater and more meaningful. Along with this comes a sense of respect for that work.

Personal growth and development

Everyone wants opportunities to learn and grow as a result of their work, developing new skills and competencies and applying those to new tasks and responsibilities.

Recognition and appreciation

Everyone wants to be recognized for their contributions and accomplishments and appreciated for the skills, abilities, and commitment they bring to their work assignment.

Support and encouragement

Everyone wants to feel that the organization supports them and encourages them in the performance of their work in ways that are positive and helpful.

In assuming these common needs and interests, however, it is vital to remember that how they are manifested in individuals will vary widely. Individual preferences for appropriate recognition and appreciation, for example, can mean increased compensation for one person, a title change for another, and more prestigious or demanding projects or responsibilities for a third. It's clear then that motivation is an individual phenomenon influenced by both the many things that bring a team together and those that separate the individual members of that team.

Effective leaders consequently must be flexible and situational in motivating others. The key is not to treat people the way *you* want to be treated but rather the way *they* want to be treated. Recognizing the individual differences in your team members and responding to them is a powerful motivational principle. It's important to focus on your role of creating a motivating environment in which individuals understand and value their roles and in which the organization recognizes and supports the office team members as individuals. This concept is reflected in the difference between equity and fairness. Treating people *equitably* means treating them the same way; treating them *fairly* means understanding that the differences between people require that we should appeal and respond to them in different ways.

Keys then to creating a motivating office environment, based on the theories and principles we've identified here, requires leaders do the following:

- Create a compelling office vision that focuses on possibilities and opportunities rather than problems and obstacles.
- Determine what levels and kinds of performance are needed to achieve the goals of your organization and share those expectations.
- Be goal-oriented but flexible about how to get there. This allows greater freedom for individuals to find ways to contribute collectively and through their individual efforts.
- Help team members feel fully engaged. Don't just ask for feedback; use it, and help people understand why some suggestions are implemented and others are not.
- Foster a learning environment by encouraging staff training, continuing education, and further skill development.

42

- Support team members when they make mistakes. Always be positive and constructive in your critiques and advice.
- Understand and respond to individual differences and needs.

Strategies that help motivate performance

Certainly one could argue that, in principle, there are as many motivational strategies as there are individuals that respond to them. There are, however, some particular strategies that may be more applicable and effective in the higher education environment.

Recognition programs

There are many such programs typically based on the accomplishment of specific individual or team goals or exceptional service or achievement. Actually, recognition can often come in the way of certificates, plaques or written statements, congratulatory events, or media publicity. The most effective programs take into account staff input concerning what is being recognized and how. Recognition programs that factor in peer, client, or stakeholder assessments and input can be especially valued. Be thoughtful about these types of programs since they can often have a very limited shelf life and can easily lose their appeal over time. Also be sensitive to the differences in how people value the nature of the recognition. An individual team member may appreciate most a personal note and quiet word of praise while another team member prizes a very public acknowledgement and visible symbol of their achievement.

Job enrichment/job sculpting

Absent clear career ladders and regular promotions, staff members can often become entrenched in their roles. While generally satisfied, they may feel "stale" and eager for new challenges and projects. Job sculpting or job enrichment provides the opportunity to take an existing role and add to it or refine it in such a way that it creates new challenges and opportunities. A career advisor position, for example, can be enhanced by allowing the individual greater control over office resources or personal scheduling, or by providing responsibility for a special student group, program, or for the management of a particularly important employer recruiting relationship. The individual, of course, could also be provided with new training opportunities and subsequent projects that take advantage of newly developed skills. New responsibilities, projects, and tasks can re-shape a position in such a way that keeps the essential responsibilities in place but adjusts them to better meet the changing needs and interests of the team member and ultimately the office.

Self-managed work teams

Strategies similar to those in job enrichment/sculpting can also be applied to groups of office staff through the use of self-managed work teams. Self-managed teams are assembled and formally recognized as responsible for an entire work process. A group of office team members could, for example, be charged with organizing a major career fair, or redesigning all office-marketing materials, or managing all employer outreach and partnership development activities. Key to self-managed work teams is making them responsible for achieving the desired outcomes but allowing them to set their own goals and review the performance of their team. Members should be empowered to share leadership and management functions specific to the team's work. If possible, members should prepare their own budgets and coordinate their work with others. The end result is a group of staff members that have developed new skills and gained valuable experience.

Financial incentives and rewards

While in the world of higher education this strategy is often the most difficult and meaningful to implement, it is important to recognize that many people claim financial rewards can be very motivating. Herzberg's (1959) two-factor theory, however, suggests that money is not a job factor that motivates performance but rather is either neutral or causes dissatisfaction (i.e. the absence of fair compensation for the work being done is the cause of dissatisfaction). It is important, consequently, to work with your institution and advocate for the appropriate compensation level for your team members. Benchmarking your office against other career services organizations and reminding your team that you're aware of and sensitive to those benchmarks goes a long way to assuring your team members that you're sensitive to this.

Beyond that, many organizations do allow for add-pay arrangements when new responsibilities are assigned or promotions are approved. Always be aware of how much flexibility you have in this area at your institution, and help your team members understand what the guidelines and opportunities are specific to your office, division, and institution.

Financial incentives and rewards, however, can also be of a more modest nature. Gift cards or office payment for fees and services can be effective in certain circumstances.

Concluding comments

Motivating staff performance is a vital leadership skill, and the principles outlined here provide a strong foundation for undertaking the various tasks associated with this effort. The strategies identified here, however, are by no means exhaustive. There is fertile ground for creativity and innovation when you understand that motivation is an individual phenomenon and that awareness of and responsiveness to the individual needs, values, and interests of staff members help to ensure a highly effective career services organization.

References

Bandura, A. (1977). *Social Learning Theory*. Englewood Cliffs, NJ: Prentice Hall.

Boggiano, A. K. & Pittman, T.S. (Eds.) (1992). *Achievement and Motivation: A Social-Developmental Perspective*. New York: Cambridge University Press.

Herzberg, F., Mausner, B. & Bloch Snyderman, B. (1959*). The Motivation to Work*. New York: Wiley.

Latham, G. & Locke, E. A. (2002) Building a practically useful theory of goal setting and task motivation. *American Psychologist, 57* (9), 707-716.

Maslow, A. H. (1943). A theory of human motivation. *Psychology Review, 50* (4), 370-396.

McClelland, D. (1976). *The Achievement Motive.* New York: Irvington Publishers: distributed by Halstead Press.

Skinner, B. F. (1974). *About Behaviorism.* New York: Knopf.

Vroom, V. H. & Yetton, P. W. (1973). *Leadership and Decision Making.* Pittsburgh: University of Pittsburgh Press.

Establishing Effective Employer Partnerships

Trudy Steinfeld

The last decade has been marked by a vast change in both career services and college relations work. Expectations for the types, levels, and volume of activities, service components, and programmatic efforts that career centers should provide have grown dramatically and often without additional resources. Much of this can be attributed to the rising cost of higher education during a time of economic uncertainty. Many students and their parents have adopted a consumer mentality that demands assurances of positive career outcomes in return for a significant investment of time and money in higher education. As colleges and universities articulate their brand proposition to prospective students and donors, the successful work of career centers is an increasingly critical element of that effort.

Recruiting organizations have also gone through a significant transformation over the last decade. Overall, they are much leaner organizations with less headcount to manage their campus recruiting relationships. Analytics are a major driver for employers and continue to have a huge impact on determining recruiting strategies and target schools. Many firms have adopted a core school strategy that concentrates recruiting efforts on campuses where they have demonstrable and consistent success in sourcing the right quantity and quality mix of new college talent for internship, cooperative education, and full-time opportunities. In an era of limited resources, increased social media capabilities, and virtual recruiting and interviewing technologies, organizations have greater challenges in justifying travel to smaller or more remote campuses for traditional recruiting and career fair attendance. Complicating these circumstances, key employer contacts have shorter tours of duty as recruiters, moving with greater frequency to other responsibilities within a company or to other opportunities outside of the organization. This regular turnover makes it more challenging to build deeper long-term recruiting partnerships.

Although all these factors create real challenges to establishing what were once considered traditional recruiting relationships, they also create opportunities for innovative and unique types of engagement. In fact, it is precisely because of all of these influences and demands on career services and college relations work that a strategic approach to establishing effective employer partnerships is more vital now than ever. Employer partnerships that are viewed as effective collaborations between both parties enhance the prestige of career services and help firmly establish an employer brand on-campus.

There are a number of important steps in establishing effective partnerships:

Work to dispel any semblance of an "us versus them" mentality when it comes to working with employers. There are some in our profession who take the view that employers don't really understand or appreciate the complexities of career services work. Many career services offices are under staffed, and they sometimes perceive the requests of recruiters to be too demanding, taking valuable time away from other more student-centric activities. Take the time to discuss with employers ways that you can work together effectively to reach or exceed goals, and appreciate and understand all the ways that employers can contribute to your office. Set the expectation for your career services operation that the employers you work with now and in the future must be considered your strategic partners.

Some career services professionals have seen themselves essentially as "counselors" and have traditionally left dealings with recruiters to very specific staff members tasked with that responsibility. Becoming familiar with employers and being able to discuss their available opportunities builds credibility with students, faculty, and other stakeholders on campus. Employer relations must be integrated into everyone's job responsibilities and should factor into future hiring plans. In this way, when new projects and services are being considered, everyone can be thinking about opportunities for increased employer engagement. Establish frequent opportunities for career services staff to interact with employers and get a greater understanding of their organizations and culture. Whenever possible, arrange visits for your team to employer offices and invite employers to campus to provide feedback, assist with ongoing staff training, and participate in information exchange. Being able to share with students and other stakeholders that you have visited specific employer offices and have deep relationships will only increase your credibility.

Even in a period of economic uncertainty, competition for the best and brightest students remains fierce. Recruiters are under increasing pressure to identify and create earlier talent pipelines, increase internship conversion rates, and create brand identity on campus. This often has resulted in employers' targeting first- and second-year undergraduates, and offering leadership and mentorship development programs to younger students. Consider the employer point of view and the pressures that influence their recruitment activities. Try to align your efforts accordingly. Supporting their work will only enhance the opportunities for the student and alumni clients you serve.

Benchmark with employer and career services professionals to identify best practices and be especially aware of any ethical considerations and current hot-button issues (e.g., unpaid internships). Always be prepared to adapt strategies and activities effective elsewhere to your own situation and circumstances.

Career services organizations must be flexible and work with employers in different ways depending on the employer's industry, size, needs, and interests. Attending a career fair, holding a campus presentation, or interviewing on campus may not always be the most effective way to drive students to a particular employer. Often a nontraditional approach, such as partnering on targeted social media campaigns, can be more productive, depending on the employer's interests and your capabilities and circumstances. Being able to say to an employer "yes" or "we have found a way to make this work" is always the preferable option.

Every career services operation should have a clearly defined employer relations strategy and corresponding activities that reflect the engagement principles outlined here. The following elements are critical to the development and effective implementation of that strategy:

1. Develop a strategic plan for employer engagement and partnership development. This should reflect a multi-faceted approach that engages employers by involving them in opportunities to interact

with students and other campus stakeholders as well as career services. Create buy-in by involving the career services team and key campus partners and develop a plan that can be disseminated with senior campus leadership.

2. As dedicated career services professionals, we sometimes think we know best. Although well intended, without obtaining feedback efforts can easily go off track. That's why it's important to assess your employer stakeholders' needs and goals. This can be accomplished by any combination of survey instruments, focus groups, formal employer advisory boards, and targeted conversations. Once you have the information, it's important to implement strategies that demonstrate your responsiveness to the feedback you received.

3. Engage your existing employer partners in assessing the effectiveness of your outreach and engagement efforts. Encourage employers to provide candid feedback and suggest activities that would better support both of your efforts. Employers will undoubtedly have thoughts on process improvement and partnership development that can be extremely helpful to your efforts. Make sure you listen to their suggestions, acknowledge their support, and be willing to try things that seem viable.

4. Conduct an audit of your current employer partner base and determine if there are other employer relationships that may exist with other units and individuals on campus that you can leverage for recruiting and hiring purposes. Focus on exchanging information with alumni affairs, institutional advancement and fundraising, academic departments, university research centers, and corporate training units.

5. Make sure to work closely with and strengthen your ties to individual alumni. Many are willing to serve as "recruiting champions" and may be in a position to advocate for their organizations to build or expand a recruiting relationship with your institution.

6. Determine your strongest institutional and career center branding

messages and be sure to consistently incorporate them into employer marketing materials, your office website, and other social media platforms. Institutional features that often attract the attention of employers include institutional student and academic program quality measures including appropriate rankings; the availability of co-op or internship programs especially if required; flexible recruiting options and activities; and demographics that demonstrate strong representation by underrepresented groups. Consistently integrate metrics and facts that will resonate with employers into your communications content and meetings. This can include diversity data, information on number of students enrolled in different academic programs, geographic representation, skills, and language competencies. Give your recruiting contacts strong justification for becoming more involved with your career services office and your campus.

7. Whenever possible, visit employer offices and always make it a point to talk with recruiters when they are on campus. Use conferences, professional meetings and expositions, and social media tools to network and increase your employer contacts. Try to combine activities whenever possible to maximize opportunities. If you are attending a conference, for example, make sure to schedule employer visits and meetings with alumni in the area.

8. Identify and develop short- and long-term goals and be realistic in targeting potential new employer partners. Employers committed to a "core school" strategy are often very limited in their ability to easily add new schools to their recruiting programs. Don't let this detract from proposing other methods of identifying candidates and getting your students into an employing organization's pipeline. Propose resume drops made more meaningful by marketing these job opportunities smartly and effectively. Take care to make sure that the candidates that are applying to opportunities online meet or exceed the qualifications that employers are seeking. Build upon initial successes and suggest incrementally sustainable efforts that will enhance your partnerships.

9. Leverage your existing partner base to connect you to new employers. Find out whom they know, what groups they suggest you join, and with whom you should connect. Everyone enjoys "talking shop," and if you have developed strong partners, they will most likely be willing to help connect you to colleagues.

10. Plan activities such as informational open houses and receptions to engage new employers. Deploy your staff and other campus partners to network with employers at these events, and make sure to follow up after by sending a thank-you e-mail correspondence and suggesting some activities that are relevant to your discussions and their recruiting needs.

11. Ask employers if there is any "value add" information you can provide to help them. These could include benchmarking data, salary, bonus and hiring trends, curriculum changes, and student perceptions in the recruiting process.

12. Conceive of ways to assist employers improve brand presence on your campus that also supports your student's ongoing career development. This could include niche presentations on field and career options, rather than specific company information sessions. Use employers as mentoring volunteers; in recruiter in residence programs; in career advisement meetings with students; as panelists on targeted career programs; and in special events, such as dining etiquette training programs.

13. Identify unique targets of opportunity for recruiting organizations that support new program initiatives, specialized populations, and corporate social responsibility objectives. This could include "naming" a small program or conference, sending speakers to a specialized career panel, participating in a specific school based networking program.

14. Understand the unique brand position and culture that each employer represents. Establish your career center as a strategic partner, tailoring and customizing advice to help each employer reach its hiring goals on your campus. If you have reason to believe that some of the employer's strategies are not working, don't be

afraid to share this information with the employer and offer alternatives. Be sure to factor in that different tactics and strategies are necessary for diverse types and sizes of employers on your campus, but that they are all important to build and sustain robust employer partnerships.

As you develop and roll out your employer relations strategy, it is critical that you build something that is scalable as you create demand and momentum, deliver on what you have promised, remain flexible, adapt efforts to changing conditions, and follow up with your employer partners. The benefits for your career services operation and your institution as well as for your employer partners are well worth your investment in these important partnership efforts.

Working With Employers: Winning Strategies

Marie Artim and Dan Black

Introduction

A professor in an introductory college marketing class once made a brief and poignant opening statement: "You have to know your product and you have to know your customer; if you can do both, the marketing will come easily." We've seen this principle applied to countless business situations, and we believe that it applies to the world of career services. On the one hand, there is the "product," which, for the sake of making this point, we equate to the students. Highly regarded career services offices do an excellent job of understanding students, what makes them tick, where their interests lie, and how best to prepare them for the job market. We have yet to meet an experienced career services professional who, if asked, couldn't expound on the merits of recruiting at his or her institution, or provide a seemingly endless list of complimentary attributes describing the students. If we determined how many schools to recruit from based on the passion of the career services representatives, we'd never spend a single day at home! The other side of the equation, however, is the "customer", which we equate to the recruiting employer. It is here we believe there is some room for improvement when it comes to marketing and understanding how best to approach the relationship for mutual benefit.

Forging effective partnerships between a college/university and an employer takes some work. While there are some obvious synergies—the high-tech company recruiting from a top technology program—others are less straightforward and will require a deeper understanding of what opportunities and constraints exist. We can recount dozens of instances over the course of our careers in which we've been approached by career services professionals who assured us we were "missing out on talent" by not recruiting at their institution, only to learn that the students there did not meet the minimum academic requirements and preparation for our entry-level positions. Consequently, we believe the first step in any new relationship is to get a good understanding of the company and what they are looking for. Similar to the advice that we give to students, this can be done in a number of ways, including online research, speaking with current or past employees, or reviewing recent job postings. Professional associations like NACE provide an excellent forum for exploring new relationships, and for leveraging best practices in this arena from other career services professionals. Just as important is gaining an understanding of an employers' recruiting model, and adjusting your "marketing pitch" accordingly. If, for example, an employer has limited or over-stretched recruiting resources, then asking the employer to visit campus in the early stages of the relationship might not be the best approach. Instead, offering to send resumes or facilitate phone or video interviews will likely lead to a better initial reaction and outcome. Of course, if there are alumni of your institution currently employed by the target company, that is an ideal "in" that you should take advantage of to start the conversation.

Developing new employer relationships and enhancing existing ones benefits most from a commitment to strategies that provide advantages for all parties.

Student programming

One of the easiest, most effective, and mutually beneficial ways to collaborate with employers is on joint student programming. In these scenarios no matter who asks "What's in it for me?" the answer will be a positive one. These programs can take on all different shapes and sizes and can be remarkably simple or very complex.

Some of the more common collaborations, such as opportunities for employers to offer resume critiques, conduct mock interviews, provide soft skill training, or participate in business etiquette dinners, for example, are quite valuable. Since the employers you work with may already find such options familiar, they offer an easy starting point for more advanced partnerships. In collaborating on resume critiques, the more you can allow the employer to target the student population that is of interest, the more value the employer will find in the program. If you are thoughtful in finding a diverse cross-section of employers, your student population will be better served. Depending on your institution and the clients you serve, you can focus on employer partners that recruit from most any major. Enterprise Holdings is just one example of an organization that is open to a wide cross-section of student majors and backgrounds.

The same considerations are true when planning mock interview programs. Again, the ability to involve students from the employer's target student audience will more likely gain you more interested employer participants. The mock interview experience is always more valuable to participating students when they are studying in fields that the participating employers normally target. We've participated in mock interviews where candidates were randomly selected as well as those that matched us with targeted candidates, and both have worked for different reasons. In the former, we feel as though we're "giving back" to the office and institution; actual recruitment is a secondary thought. In the latter instance, we're expecting a potential return for the investment of time and effort. It's important for you to recognize the difference and set the expectations accordingly with your employer partners.

With every instructional program for students, you're relying on the employer not only to contribute relevant content but also to bring credibility to the program as an "expert." Do realize, though, that not every representative a company sends to campus will be prepared to handle every potential challenge. Be sure to recognize the skill level and expertise of those coming to campus before putting them in front of your students. Plan carefully in advance of their participation by providing accurate and timely information about the desired goals and outcomes and setting expectations appropriately.

One of the student programming opportunities that many employers we know value and appreciate is being invited to hold "office hours" in the career center. This not only provides a chance to interact with students in different situations but also provides the time to develop deeper and more extensive relationships with the career center staff. A very desirable outcome of collaborating with your employer partners to develop specific, relevant programming for your students is the potential to enhance and expand the expertise of your staff members. It's a win for all parties.

Consult and assist with employer communications/interactions with students

We believe one of the most important services you can offer to employers is assistance with their targeted communications and interactions with your students. Whether it's supporting employer branding and messaging efforts or gathering candidate feedback to share, you are in a unique position to help organizations be more effective and more successful in their recruiting.

By offering to coordinate an employer's messaging through your office, you can help employers be more consistent and timely in their communications. By familiarizing yourself with the communication strategies of your employers, you can provide training to your students on appropriate efforts in their interactions with us. Your coaching will assist them in being more effective and more successful. If you are able to host a meeting to review employer existing and potential communication tools, you can provide incredibly helpful insights on the effectiveness of the employer's efforts in general and on your campus specifically. Employers must often work with third-party vendors or agencies to acquire these kinds of insights and feedback, and it's quite expensive and time consuming to gather information this way. Your willingness to provide assistance is extremely valuable and most helpful.

Providing learning opportunities for employers

Despite the fact that many employers have formal training programs, corporate universities, and/or a focus on learning and development, there are still many opportunities for career services organizations to provide educational opportunities to their employer partners. In our experience, the assumption is too frequently made that employers come to campus with all the skills, knowledge, and know-how needed to flawlessly execute on their recruiting strategy. If that were true, our lives would be considerably easier and much less stressful. The fact of the matter is that employers who come on campus stand to gain a significant benefit from their time spent interacting with career services professionals, both formally and informally. Several factors contribute to this environment being particularly conducive to learning opportunities. First and foremost, the vast majority of employer representatives who come to campus tend to either be full-time campus recruiters with less than five years of experience, or line managers who have had minimal training in candidate attraction and selection. In addition, there tends to be a relatively robust turnover rate for individuals involved in recruiting due to promotions, strategy changes, budget considerations, and so forth. As a result, campus recruiting managers are frequently faced with the difficult situation of having to train new team members on a very regular basis...in less time and with fewer resources. The savvy career services professional can provide an effective and efficient solution that will help the employer while strengthening the partnership and providing a unique consulting/teaching opportunity to his or her own staff.

One of the best examples of training that can be offered to employers by career services is interviewing and assessment skill development. Senior career services staff members are uniquely qualified to provide counsel based on their experiences with employers *and* students, a perspective that is not offered via other outlets or media. The added "bonus" of being able to offer content while employers are already on campus will appeal to both the budget-conscious and the travel-burdened, and offers the additional advantage of positioning your career services office in a very positive light compared to other institutions on the employer's target list. The career center that provides even one or two hours of learning can have a big impact on the participating recruiters and an equally big impact on its overall relationship with the employing organization.

Topics such as legal considerations in interviewing, assessment methods, and best practices in on-campus recruiting will appeal to most employers, and programs can be further tailored based on conversations with individual hiring managers or employer teams. Getting more-junior career services staff involved can also enhance the effectiveness of the learning. Several universities that we have relationships with offer to have junior- and mid-level career services staff play the role of students in "mock interviews" designed to build the skills of the recruiter. After conducting the interview, the recruiter receives immediate feedback on flow, style, and effectiveness of questioning techniques. The staff can also provide feedback on the appropriateness of the interview rating assigned by the recruiter and a summary of areas of development for review by the recruiting manager. Another effective learning/training forum provided by career services is the employer forum. Separate and distinct from meetings with individual employers, forums offer a unique opportunity to bring together *all* the key employers at a particular campus or university. Most forums that we've attended are structured in one of two ways: a) as a stand-alone event held in the "off" season for both the employer and career services (i.e., when school is not in session); or b) in conjunction with a campus event at which multiple employers will be present (e.g., a career fair). It has been our experience that the former is useful primarily in large metropolitan areas where employers have only a short distance to travel to attend the function, where the latter might be the best option for schools that are more remotely located. While there is no one "right" agenda for an employer forum, the most helpful and informative ones that we have attended typically include the following:

- Keynote speaker covering a hot topic or issue being faced by most employers,
- Remarks by the provost, dean, or other key university representative,
- A panel of current students and/or recent alumni to speak about their experiences and field questions from the employers, and
- Ample time for networking among employers and career services staff.

Although there can are costs associated with such events, those costs are more than outweighed by the benefit of providing valuable information to the employers, building relationships, and further branding the career services office both internally and externally. If you still can't find room in your budget, a call to a few of your employer partners to ask for their support could be another alternative worth exploring.

A final example of a valuable learning opportunity revolves around institution-specific topics that are of particular interest to a college or university's top employers. Regardless of size, most higher education institutions have a relatively small group of key companies that consistently provide support, resources, and - perhaps most importantly - job opportunities for students. It is with these key companies that career services has a unique opportunity to engage and further strengthen the relationship. We would recommend a two-tiered approach when it comes to this area of partnership. First, schedule strategic planning/learning sessions at least once a year that specifically cater to the unique needs of the *individual* employer on your *individual* campus. Generic information is helpful to a degree, but information that is pertinent to how, when, and who the employer is recruiting at your institution will be seen as invaluable.

To illustrate this point, we'd like to draw attention to the career outcomes statistics that many career services offices will provide to employers. While these are excellent indicators of macro trends at the university, they often fail to provide the level of specificity that employers would find most helpful. If a company is recruiting in the business school, it's likely it will find the nursing school employment statistics to be superfluous. Instead, seek out information specific to the employer, and spend time discussing the employer's unique needs and opportunities for the upcoming year. This discussion should include such items as changes in timing and curricula, major-specific trends and analysis, hiring statistics compared to similar institutions, and feedback from students that relates directly to the employer.

The second approach involves bringing all the employers from a particular industry or sector together to discuss recruiting results, guidelines, and strategy. We've participated in this type of session at just a small handful of institutions and found them extremely valuable. At the most basic level, they create an opportunity for all the relevant employers to address any concerns or issues that they may have experienced during the recruiting season. In our experience, most career services directors are adverse to this type of session, mostly because they don't like to play "peacekeeper" to the employers. But this is typically a very quick item on the agenda, and should not deter career services professionals from hosting such a meeting. The heart of the conversation should revolve around enhancing the development and recruiting experience of the students; topics that should, from the outset, be top priorities of all the parties involved. More often than not, we've experienced real collaboration and seen some real positive movement in the areas of programming, student education, hiring protocols, and feedback. At one institution, career services and the academic department from which most students were being recruited ran the meeting jointly. That kind of interdepartmental collaboration truly set the university apart, and made an immensely positive impression on the employers involved.

Gaining insight into the employer's model/strategy or student's experience at the company

Just as important as securing new employers to recruit on your campus is maintaining the relationship with existing employer partners. In addition to facilitating meetings specific to campus recruiting matters, there are many other venues through which you can build the connection and at the same time gain valuable insight into the employer's business. Chief among them are public or "semi-public" events hosted by the company. Most companies have open forums, discussions, meetings, or updates that are either open to the public or to strategic partners, vendors, and clients. As a supplier of talent, the university career services office is certainly a valuable partner that should inquire about the possibility of attending these types of functions. If there is no such opportunity, we recommend suggesting an on-site meeting at the company site, during which a portion of the agenda is dedicated to learning more about the company's business, industry, trends and recent developments. We know of several employers that have hosted such sessions, and have found that they are always mutually beneficial. More often than not, we learn about a program or offering with which we were not previously familiar that will assist in our recruiting or branding efforts. In fact, the insight we typically gain is so valuable that we once invited a career services director to a two-day recruiting strategy session to share her insights and opinions on how we could take our efforts to the next level; she was the only non-employee to attend. This can also be suggested at a more micro level; asking that you be involved in some way with the recruiting strategy meetings for your specific institution could be a good way to glean valuable information while simultaneously providing some in return. While companies in issuing such invitations often cover all or significant parts of the cost of attendance, in some cases this may not always be feasible or appropriate. In these instances, it would be worthwhile to add other employer visits to your trip to maximize the monies you are investing for trip. At institutions where career services has close ties with advancement or alumni affairs, these departments may be willing to help fund or share expenses for the trip.

Another great opportunity to connect with, and learn about, employers is to leverage internship or co-op programs more aggressively. There are many ways to engage, so finding one that will work for you and the employer is just a matter of deciding what works best for your situation. A few examples:

- Serve as an external advisor to one or more interns, with regular employer meetings to "check in" on progress, connections made, new skills, and so forth.
- Ask to attend any closing presentations or summaries being conducted by the interns at the end of the work site experience.
- Offer to have a debrief session with the employer recruiting team and student supervisors at the end of the internship to better understand any opportunities for program enhancement.
- Distance permitting, offer to host interns for a day at the career services office to conduct focus groups or discuss a hot topic (including interns from other schools).

Regardless of the approach, making an effort to be more actively involved should always be a give-and-take arrangement. Having a discussion with the employer to understand where the help is needed is a good place to start.

A last thought on this topic: The best strategy for enhancing your relationship with an employer might already exist—at another institution! There's no need to "recreate the wheel" if there is another career services office that is already doing something that works well for the employer. The best career services directors we work with frequently ask what we see at other colleges and universities that they could be doing better, or that they could start doing. Although not every program or initiative will be a fit for every campus, asking the question of your recruiting colleagues is good way to broaden your perspective and gain unanticipated insights.

Expand your network through your employers

To this point, we've focused on how you can work with employers to support your office and your programs, but a strategic relationship with employers can be beneficial beyond those services to students. As you are working to professionally develop yourself and your staff, your employer partners can offer valuable insight and connections.

When you meet with your employer colleagues, take the opportunity to ask about industry-specific meetings, training opportunities, or consortia gatherings that could help you to strengthen your knowledge of our field or the recruiting landscape as a whole. They can also provide insight for you on the credibility of those resources from their perspective that will help you to prioritize your efforts. We have taken advantage of this on several occasions and, thanks to our career center partners, we've have learned of some training and vendor offers that weren't all that they'd seemed but also some that turned out to be hidden gems.

We would also recommend that you gain knowledge and broaden your network by partnering with employers to work together via organizations such as NACE, DirectEmployers, the regional associations, and other similar organizations. We've found that the relationships we've developed through these professional associations are some of the deepest and most fulfilling in our professional roles. You learn about each other and the importance you play in each other's business, but you also gain insight into the individuals involved and how you can best work to support each other. This is, of course, in addition to the many other benefits of professional association membership.

An added bonus of these relationships is also that established and highly networked employers can introduce you to other career services professionals and other employers and serve as a conduit for you to build partnerships and learn from them. In a world where networking, whether through social media or the old-fashioned personal kind, is so critical, it always helps to have people in your circle willing to help.

Important networking can happen on your own campus, as well. It is quite possible that the employers visiting your career center already have established strong relationships with other campus constituents such as faculty and members of the administration. Leverage this goodwill by allowing employers to serve as your advocate with those institutional colleagues as a way to enhance the credibility of your office and of you.

In working with employers, the key to success is in consistent execution. They are typically juggling multiple colleges and universities, other functions, and teams of people who support their efforts, so planning in advance, providing critical details, and setting clear expectations are critical. Once involved, quick, concise instructions and follow up must come next. Ideally, as you work to establish and maintain these deep and valuable relationships, you will identify new opportunities specific to your campus and the needs of your clients.

Customize

With ever-increasing reliance on—and preference for—"self-service" among students and professionals alike, career services professionals will need to be increasingly nimble and flexible to effectively meet the needs of all their constituents. Fortunately, if used effectively, technology can be a great facilitator of these new demands for self-service. Overreliance on technology—or inconsistent application—can make customized interactions even more challenging and undermine the efforts of even the most diligent career services professional. So, what's the best approach? We're big believers in the idea that "one size fits none", and that the more you can customize your actions to meet expectations, the more you will actually exceed them. We understand that offering tailored solutions to a diversity of clients is not necessarily easy, and often requires more resources, but it often yields the best results and fosters intense loyalty. No one remembers the waitress who treated them like every other customer; they remember the one who went to the deli next door to get the brand of beverage they wanted because she knew how much it meant to them. Did it take extra time and effort? Yes. But the reward, both monetary and otherwise, made it well worth it.

Perhaps the most pressing need that employers have today is to narrow the top end of the recruiting funnel. As the web and social media became ubiquitous tools in the job search, the potential number of applicants for any individual job posting has grown exponentially. Sifting through candidates to find those that are actually *qualified* has become one of the most time-consuming activities in the life of a recruiter. As employers feel the squeeze to hire more students who fit their desired profile, there will be an increasingly smaller appetite to attend—or invest in—activities that are "one size fits all." Career services offices that can offer a more targeted approach to sourcing will enjoy a distinct advantage with employers of all sizes. One obvious place to start is with career fairs. In virtually every survey, focus group, and analysis, career fairs continue to be noted as a useful component of the campus recruiting process, by students and employers alike. When asked, however, to identify the most beneficial aspects of the fairs, employers invariably point to the opportunity to brand and connect with students who have the potential to be viable applicants for their companies. Similarly, students give the highest ratings to career fairs that afford them the chance to interact with companies that they could actually join in the future.

There are several strategies for customizing career fairs, and it need not be a complicated undertaking. Arranging the room by industry or discipline is an easy first step that career services professionals can take toward making the fairs more focused and "user-friendly." Assigning specific times or days for students to attend based on major, location preference, class year, and so forth is also a good tactic, particularly at large institutions. If resources and logistics permit, one of the best approaches we've seen is offering several smaller career fairs, each of which is focused on a particular group of employers. A "banking fair" or "journalism day" will go a long way in providing the most tailored opportunities for both students and employers. Further qualifying student attendees by requiring that they have either declared their major in the targeted discipline or have taken a minimum number of courses will further enhance the effectiveness of the event.

Most career services professionals already take an active role in coaching and guiding students toward appropriate employment opportunities. While employers understand that career services organizations have a duty to advocate for and promote *all* their students, any efforts made to proactively find a good match for both the employer *and* the student is viewed as real value-added effort. Some of the best practices that we've seen in this area include the following:

- Holding annual meetings to discuss changes in hiring needs and necessary qualifications, skills, and so forth.

- Collaborating with and introducing faculty to help establish connections that might not exist between the employer and targeted academic departments.

- Performing an initial review or quality check to ensure that student applicants meet the minimum qualifications of a job posting.

- Recommending to employers student clubs, activities, events, and so forth that might help recruiters identify targeted candidates.

- Seeking out associations or consortia that provide employers with access to students with desired majors and backgrounds from multiple colleges or universities. This is particularly helpful to smaller institutions.

There is no shortage of ideas on how career services can customize services to all their clients, including employers. If you're not sure where to begin, ask your employer partners for suggestions or ideas. We're certainly aware that some of the ideas offered may not be feasible. Your willingness, however, to treat each employer as an individual entity——similar to the way you successfully treat students as individuals—will help you to build strong employer relationships that will serve you, your students, and your institution well.

Faculty Partnerships:
Critical Enablers and Key Alliances

Rick Hearin

One of the unique and special aspects of our work in career services is the opportunity it provides for us to forge mutually beneficial relationships with our faculty counterparts within the academy. Indeed, for most of us, there is a strong desire to work as *part* of the academic enterprise, *not apart from it*. The more fully career services are integrated into the fabric of institutional culture and academic life, the greater the likelihood that students' career aspirations and potential will be fulfilled.

The question sometimes arises: "Couldn't career services work more efficiently if it did not have to work with faculty?" Perhaps, but think of the implications. First, is our focus to be efficient—or effective? If we are striving for effectiveness, the more allies we have in reaching out to students and engaging them in their own unique and individual career journeys, the better. In many ways no one can help us with this challenge better than the faculty. While many of us are experts in student development, in many ways no one knows their own students better than the faculty. This is knowledge we can use to tailor our programs, services, and resources to students' individual needs. It is through these relationships that we go beyond "one size fits all" approach to career services. This is a paradigm that never worked in the first place, and that now is totally discredited given the high expectations of students and their families and the tools now at our disposal to assist them with tailoring their own plans.

Second, it is the faculty who are best able to help us understand the key tenets of their respective disciplines, and, in turn, the key skills, insights, and perspectives their students develop through the study of these disciplines. This is important to us not only because it gives us valuable context for assisting students in identifying allied career opportunities, but also because it helps us to translate to employers the skills, insights, and perspectives students bring with them to the workplace.

Third, it is though working with the faculty that career services can best establish itself within the fabric of the academic enterprise. Effective work with our faculty colleagues confers its own brand of legitimacy within the academy—not just among the students with whom we work, but, politically within an arena where there is constant competition for limited institutional resources. If, indeed, we are to be effective in our work, the powerful advocacy of our faculty colleagues within the political and financial landscape that characterizes contemporary higher education will be key. Of course, there are many more answers to the question of why working with faculty is important, but there is no denying their role in ensuring meaningful ties with students and gaining a clear understanding of the benefits students bring with them to the marketplace, as well as reinforcing the true legitimacy of the career services function within the academy.

As strong a case as we might make for the benefits of working closely with faculty, there are contrarians who may question the return on the investment of our time and energy in fostering these ties. Certainly, it does take time and energy to build these relationships, and one might surmise that we need the faculty more than they need us. To be sure, there will be some faculty members—and, perhaps, many on some campuses—who view career services staff as interlopers in the academic enterprise, part of the institution's overhead, and a drain on scarce resources that can be better allocated elsewhere—including their own academic departments.

Admittedly, career services is not universally welcomed with open arms. Not all faculty will be receptive to our role and function. There is almost always, however, a core of faculty members in most departments who share our interest in the development of the whole student and the success of each student in his or her academic—and career—journey.

This brings to mind an often quoted reflection of the legendary major league baseball manager Casey Stengel, who used to say, "The secret of successful managing is to keep the five players who hate you away from the four guys who haven't made up their minds." And so it is in the realm of faculty relations and career services.

Anecdotal as it may be, there appears to be a nascent trend among many younger faculty members across the broad spectrum of academia. Unlike their senior counterparts, they have come of age at a time when the economic landscape for new college graduates has been mercilessly competitive. They have seen their own friends and contemporaries struggle to gain a foothold in an extremely tough job market, despite their talents and credentials. Many younger faculty are also more likely to have used career services offices as undergraduates and consequently more familiar with the resources and services we have available. In short, many of our younger faculty members "get it." Thus, they are more inclined to support and endorse the work of career services.

Nonetheless, given that many young faculty members face tremendous pressures as they make their journey along the tenure track, they are frequently limited in the amount of time they can give to career services initiatives. If properly acknowledged and embraced by career services leaders, however, they can become valuable allies, and often lifelong ones at that. Thus, the challenge is to seize the initiative to reach out to faculty to engage them in conversations about how student success is defined and how the resources available to them as faculty members, and to us as career services professionals, can be best focused and intentionally concentrated on ensuring that students get the types of academic and experiential opportunities that will assure success.

It is this shared interest in student success that provides the foundation for our work with faculty colleagues, and while providing career counsel to students is not normally the pathway to tenure, there is no shortage of faculty members who do what they do because they, too, are committed to student success. What sometimes derails the process for career services leaders, especially those coming up through the ranks, is that some of the more senior and established faculty members may not appear to be especially tuned in to our definition of "student success." Indeed, some are so completely focused on their own agendas that they seem not to be particularly approachable on or receptive to students' career development challenges and diverse opportunities.

If, however, you are willing to accept the premise that the one common denominator for most who work in the academy is student success, many of the perceived barriers to partnership-building fall by the wayside. By way of example, some years ago, a senior faculty member in the philosophy department, a full professor at that, told me, pointedly that his job was not "to help these students get jobs" but rather "to get them into graduate school." Owing to my youth and a tendency to be easily intimidated at the time, I took the dismissal to heart, but I also used it as an important lesson: Over the years it became clear to me that, in his own way, Dr. Philosophy was as committed to students' success as I was. He just defined it a little differently than I. Couldn't we have talked about that? Also, couldn't I have asked him about the students who were prepared for graduate school but who might decide against it? What about the skills, insights, and perspectives they would bring to the workplace? What about the value of the liberal arts? How does all this translate—in real terms—for students who ultimately must make their way in a brutally competitive labor market?

So what was actually a brief, and painful, conversation could have been transformed into a mutually beneficial exchange. Opportunity lost? Yes. Lesson learned? Definitely. As an aside, this is also when I learned that while the meek may inherit the earth, they are likely to have a real challenge on their hands in higher education!

The really good news in all of this is that most who work in academia do, indeed, share a common interest in students' success—even if we might all define it a little differently. The other good news is that, at most colleges and universities, there is a built-in organizational infrastructure that facilitates the process for career services leaders to reach out to our academic counterparts and to engage them in what we are all trying to accomplish.

There is a fairly standard organizational taxonomy at most institutions where colleges and schools define the major subdivisions, with each comprised of multiple academic departments. Within colleges, schools, and academic departments, there are positional leaders, most often deans in the former and chairs in the latter. These individuals are responsible for assuring the success of their individual portions of the overall academic enterprise. In this day of hyper-accountability, student success is a key component of the rubric. Now, does this translate into an open-armed reception for career services leaders? Perhaps yes, and perhaps no—keep in mind that these leaders have exceptionally challenging jobs, because not only are they "managing up," but they are also "managing down." As they manage down, they are attempting to manage a cohort that defies management. Nonetheless, these academic leaders are important partners in ensuring that the career development of students is incorporated into the institutional segments they represent. Regular, even periodic, discussions are encouraged, not only to remain abreast of curriculum changes and initiatives, but also to share student outcomes data and job market trends.

Most deans and chairs will not be reluctant to share their views on services their students want and what they, as academic administrators, need from the career center, be it graduation survey data, internship opportunities for their students, and even possible employer-support of some academic initiative. The key is that there is likely significant common ground, and given this, plenty of opportunity for collaboration and mutual benefit. And the real beauty of this is that students will be the beneficiaries of that collaboration.

While the work of academic deans and department chairs may be more focused on administrative matters, many schools and departments employ professional academic advisors and/or designate key faculty to serve in a student-advising role. Clearly, there is a natural linkage between academic-advising and career-advising staff, and the work of both is enriched and extended by the affinity advisors in both realms frequently enjoy. This can be extended even further by ensuring an ongoing dialogue with faculty members who serve as "Directors of Undergraduate Studies" or "Chief Departmental Advisors." It is often these colleagues who are most attuned to the needs of their particular students, and it is not uncommon that the career center will be best positioned to address these concerns. Likewise, it is sometimes from these relationships that innovative programming takes wing. One such example is "Bridging Academic & Professional Development," a collaboration at the University of Maryland between the Department of Psychology and the University Career Center, that integrated basic career development and experiential education fundamentals into a semester-long introductory course in psychology. This was a classical win-win-win innovation that benefited the Department of Psychology, the University Career Center, and, most of all, the students themselves. One of the side benefits is that this collaboration now serves as a model for other academic departments—at the University of Maryland and elsewhere—to emulate. Minimally, it serves as an example of what is possible when mutual ties are forged between career services and academic departments.

With the renewed attention being focused on internships and other experiential education opportunities, faculty have become increasingly attuned to how students' academic lives and career lives are integrated. Indeed, most enlightened faculty members view this growing trend as mutually reinforcing. For many, there is no better venue in which to apply classroom theory than the world outside the campus. Rich as this external environment may be, however, growing numbers of colleges and universities are capitalizing on the various opportunities for practical training that exist within their own institutions—in research laboratories, athletics marketing offices, centers for entrepreneurship, and any number of other sites, including the career center itself. The faculty members who oversee the experiential education programs of their respective departments are usually receptive to the willingness of the career center to support their efforts and to assist their students in preparing for the internship search and selection process. In turn, these faculty coordinators often become powerful allies for the career center and facilitators of even deeper engagement in the academic enterprise.

As students have become increasingly career-oriented, there has been a proliferation of academic/career clubs and organizations on campus. Many of these organizations host members of the career center on a regular basis, and virtually all of these student-run clubs have a faculty sponsor or advisor. Given their willingness to serve in this sponsorship role, they are already committed, at least to some degree, to students' career development, and they, too, can become key partners in supporting the work of the career center.

Of course, it is one thing to establish a relationship with an ally, but another to nurture it over time. Thus, it is imperative that career center leaders find ways to maintain meaningful contact with their faculty partners. Fortunately, most of this comes down to good old-fashioned human relations, buttressed now perhaps through any number of social media tools at our disposal. Periodic, formal touch-base efforts can be easily supplemented with an occasional e-mail to pass along an article of interest. Some career centers publish a periodic e-newsletter for faculty members just to keep the communication lines open and to share information of broad appeal. Even a clipping from a print publication would likely be welcome from time to time. An occasional three-way luncheon with a key employer can also be part of the career center's faculty relations strategy. In addition, more formal recognition ceremonies, banquets, athletic events, receptions, or other events to recognize faculty partners can also be very effective. The important thing is to ensure that faculty partners know that the career center appreciates and places great value on the relationships it has with its academic partners. "Thank you" is easy to say, but so often overlooked. A faculty relations strategy that builds in the "thank you" for these important allies is sure to be effective.

Those involved in the difficult work of diplomacy have an inherent understanding of the value of strategic alliances and, in many ways, so too do career services leaders. Left exclusively to our own regularly allocated resources, we would get the job done, if for no other reason than because we are so individually committed to students' success. How much better the outcome for students, however, when both faculty members and career center staff work with synergistic purpose and a shared commitment to student success? There is no better way to ensure that career centers work as part of the academic enterprise rather than apart from it.

Working Effectively With Legal Counsel

Joseph du Pont, Esq.

"The first thing we do, let's kill all the lawyers."

Shakespeare,
William, *Henry VI, Part 2*

Introduction

That famous Shakespeare quote has been repeated for centuries. But why? What is it about lawyers that inspires such venom and dread? The answer is pretty simple, actually – most people associate attorneys with negative experiences, such as being sued, or having to wrangle with the IRS, or even simply going through the hassle of buying a house, with all of the mundane legal hurdles involved. So it is somewhat understandable, although in perhaps a visceral, misguided sort of way, that many individuals, including career directors, are uncomfortable working with attorneys.

Read the play again. The reality is that Shakespeare wasn't blasting lawyers – in fact, he was speaking in favor of lawyers. Shakespeare, a brilliant writer and playwright, was well aware of the myriad benefits that a close, solid relationship with an attorney can bring. At its best, a strong relationship between a career director and legal counsel can help directors avoid looming pitfalls, take advantage of opportunities, and prevent bad decisions that are detrimental to students, the university, or even the director's own career.

Background

Although we as career directors might not spend much of our time thinking about it, legal issues have always had a significant impact on how we do our jobs. In the 1980s, FERPA (Family Educational Rights and Privacy Act, 20 U.S.C. § 1232) seemed to be the hot issue. In the 90s and early part of the millennium, FERPA took somewhat of a back seat to employer engagement – what interview questions were permissible; how students were selected for interviews; and whether the career office had any legal obligations to vet job postings made available to students.[1] What the next decade will bring in terms of legal issues that universities and career offices will have to confront is anyone's guess.

What is the lesson here? What is a smart, savvy career director to do? The answer is simple: Don't try to navigate these waters on your own. It is dangerous and there are plenty of rip tides waiting to pull you out to the sea. Moreover, given the constant shifting of the law, staying abreast of these changes is a full-time job best left to our legal partners with whom we need to collaborate closely.

By now, it should be clear that this essay is not an overview of all the relevant laws and issues affecting career services. An article addressing that topic would be several hundred pages and become outdated quickly. Instead, this essay is a synopsis of three basic, but often unheeded, lessons about how to work with legal counsel effectively: (1) building rapport with legal counsel; (2) keeping abreast of legal issues that impact your office; and (3) identifying resources to help you be better prepared to address the legal issues that will arise in our work.

Advice from our colleagues and peers: Building rapport

Let's consider the following situation. A student who is participating in an internship has just contacted the Dean of Students; she claims her supervisor is creating an extremely uncomfortable work environment. Moreover, the internship is not meeting the objectives set out in the learning agreement the employer agreed to. The employer happens to be an alumnus. The Dean has gotten in touch with you, since she was advised that your office had recommended this internship. You are anxious about this situation and how it might negatively impact the reputation of your office, as well as any legal repercussions that might arise. Frankly, you would like to brush the entire thing under the rug. What should you do? To whom can you turn?

In the increasingly complex university ecosystem where career directors work, you cannot be as effective on your campus as you need to be unless you have a strong working relationship with legal counsel. This might be a good time to ask: "When is the last time I scheduled an appointment with

---

[1] The climate today is no different. HIPPA (Health Information Portability and Accountability Act, 42 U.S.C. § 1320), paid vs. unpaid internships, questions around how colleges calculate placement rates in first destination

legal counsel?" If the answer is, "Gosh, I have no idea", then it's probably time for you to make one.

As you might imagine, I received a wide range of answers from career directors when I asked about how they work with their legal counsel. I was surprised that many didn't work with their legal counsel at all. "I don't" was a common response from many. More than one somewhat sheepishly admitted, "I don't even know who my legal counsel is." "We are so busy in our daily work here that I just tackle legal issues as they come up" was the most common response. It appears that many career directors have not contacted their college's legal counsel because they don't know what to ask them, or what to ask for.

Still, the majority of directors categorized legal counsel as one of the most important stakeholders on campus and went out of their way to ensure that this relationship was strong.

A recurring theme among this group was one of trust; these directors emphasized building a strong working relationship before potential legal issues arise. Tamara King is the Director of Judicial Programs for Washington University in St. Louis and a national leader in the field of student judicial affairs. In that capacity she has worked directly with the career office on many projects and succinctly captured the sentiments of many career directors who have a strong working relationship with their counsel. "You will have better outcomes in addressing legal issues if you have a pre-established relationship with general counsel. I can't emphasize enough how important it is to develop trust between your offices." And she added, "It is also extremely difficult to establish trust in the middle of a crisis, which is why it is important to build that relationship before a situation arises where you need to work with your legal team."

Steven Locke, deputy general counsel of Brandeis University, echoed the same sentiment:

> "You are really asking me how to be a good client," he remarked. "I want you to approach me about a potential issue before it becomes a real problem. Be frank with me about what the issue is. I need to know that you have told me everything so I can advise accordingly."

The role of the university counsel is to keep you within the confines and boundaries of the law. That can't be done if you're not honest and open with counsel about your office and its practices.

Because trust is such an integral part of any strong attorney-client relationship, you should know that anything you tell university counsel will be covered by attorney-client privilege[2]. So don't be afraid of sharing with legal counsel your concerns, doubts, and mistakes. You have to be willing to share everything openly so legal counsel can provide the proper advice to prevent problems from arising, or to ameliorate the situation.

Part of creating a trusting relationship and good rapport with your legal counsel is a comprehensive record-keeping system. Be sure to document everything (e.g., conversations with employers, meetings with alumni, inter-office, and intra-office memoranda) – you never know when it might be needed, and it will help your legal counsel help you.

Know your stuff

Let's consider the following scenario. A major employer agrees to be a corporate partner and provides a substantial donation to your office. Some of the benefits of the program include early access to sign up for interview schedules and recommendations from the career office about which students might be best fits for its program. The employer wants you to provide names of specific students who might be good candidates. You feel like this might raise problems, but since you're not sure and you don't want to alienate the employer, you decide to go ahead with the program. A student who wasn't selected finds out that you provided specific names and complains to the Office of the President about your actions.[3]

Your relationship with legal counsel will be that much stronger if you come to the conversation with at least a general understanding of the issues that can arise. While your university's legal counsel is expert in the field of law, you as the career director are expert in the field of career services, and your legal counsel will be looking to you to help identify the unique matters and concerns that arise in the arena of career services. University counsel has a multitude of clients with a wide variety of needs and issues, across all of the various campus offices, according to Nora Field, associate counsel for Boston College, and a well-prepared and knowledgeable career director will make her job that much easier. As she stated, legal counsel "can't help unless you can help identify the issues." Steven Locke concurred, noting that, as legal counsel, he wants to know "that you have done your

---

[2] There are exceptions to the attorney client privilege – and who would know those best – legal counsel of course. Make an appointment and ask about them.

[3] If you thought this scenario might potentially raise legal issues for the career office, you are right. See the Legal Issues section of the NACE website for details.

homework and are knowledgeable about your field so I can best advise you on next steps. In other words, know your stuff so I can help you."

Nora also notes the importance of understanding the institutional culture in which you work and how legal issues are addressed. "Each school is unique and has its own way of dealing with legal issues. You need to be aware of what those issues are keep an eye on them so you can be more effective in your job."

Mary Raymond, Director of Career Development and Associate Dean of Students at Pomona College, agrees. She opined that that trust is critical but emphasized that it is equally important for a career director to know what the relevant issues are that need to be addressed. In the past year, Mary served as part of the risk assessment team of her division. Many issues were discussed, and she was particularly concerned about matters such as protecting the university and students with respect to service learning agreements, unpaid internships, and employer site visits. She explains:

> "Too often, we career directors don't put our legal counsel in the best position to help us. It is our job to know where there may be legal risks in the context of our work. Just as legal counsel can't expect us to know everything about the law, we can't expect them to know the major issues impacting our work - not only isn't it practical, our legal team is just too busy to do this kind of legwork. We need to bring our knowledge to the table and provide insights and a perspective that are going to help provide them with the context to provide us with the necessary insight to do our jobs well."

In other words, you and legal counsel are partners, on equal footing. You bring certain knowledge to bear, and she does also; by working together, you will make your office stronger. You can't expect your legal counsel to know all of the issues that can arise in the area of career services, and if you wait too long to learn, it will be too late.

You shouldn't look for legal counsel to provide you with all the answers. Instead, think of legal counsel as a critical ally in helping you decide your options and provide some boundaries for you to do your job properly.

Identifying relevant resources

There are many legal resources available to help you navigate the legal implications of our work. Rather than produce a daunting laundry list of options, I think it would be more helpful to highlight a few that have a long track record of being helpful.

1. NACE - If I had to recommend one resource, it would be the NACE website. NACE devotes an entire section to legal issues since they have become so prominent in our field. As a NACE member, you have access to hundreds of timely articles that will inform your thinking and make your meetings with legal counsel that much more effective. The Legal Issues section of the website has been a great resource to help me identify topics our legal counsel should be aware of. In addition to deepening my knowledge of the pertinent issues in our field, it has also helped me gain credibility with the office.

2. Legal Conferences - There are many legal conferences that can help you identify what legal issues and resources you should be thinking about and leveraging. Unless you have a legal background or a keen desire to learn more about legal issues in higher education, it probably makes more sense for your legal counsel to attend these. Two of the best conferences out there are the conference hosted by the National Association of Colleges and University Attorneys and Legal Issues in Higher Education Conference hosted by The University of Vermont. These annual conferences provide substantive overviews of the diverse legal issues impacting the student affairs profession, including career services. If you have a good relationship with your legal counsel, she should return from the conference with information that can really help you do your job more effectively. NACUA has a great website with resources as well.

3. Your Peers - As career professionals we often tout the benefits of peer-to-peer learning to the students who frequent our offices. We should take that advice to heart - one of the best ways to stay abreast of legal issues is through your own peer network. I often find myself reading an article on the Legal Issues section of the NACE site and contacting colleagues to see how they are addressing similar issues. Too often we assume that the challenges facing our campus are ours alone, when that is really not the case. Almost all of us are members of consortia or benchmarking groups and have colleagues we can turn to in confidence to help us work through challenges we may be having.

4. LinkedIn and Social Media - I conducted a quick search in LinkedIn of "law and higher education" and found over 50 groups that fit these criteria. Think of groups like this and other forums via social media as an extension of your peer group. There are lots of individuals out there who can help us with our work.

We've had it wrong all these years. Shakespeare didn't want us to kill all the lawyers. If he were with us today, he'd probably tell us to embrace your legal counsel and create a relationship that will benefit you in the long run. Start by taking them to lunch.

Reality checklist

Take a moment to reflect on the following items to see if you are creating a climate that will help you work effectively with legal counsel and stay abreast of legal issues.

Build rapport

The best clients understand the value of an ongoing relationship with legal counsel built on trust, mutual respect and appreciation. If these attributes are present, you are more likely to have a productive relationship.

Tip from the Field: If you don't know who your legal counsel is or they don't know you, it is time to do something about it.

Schedule periodic check-ins

The time frame will differ dramatically based on your institution and your needs. You schedule periodic maintenance for your cars, so why wouldn't you do something similar with an important asset on your campus who can help make your job easier? This is the time to share information, provide updates and address questions about minor issues before they become major ones.

Tip from the Field: Schedule check-ins every six months if you haven't met in the interim. Don't think that just because nothing of concern has arisen that you don't need to have the meeting. Instead, think of these check-ins as prophylactic, proactive measures that will help prevent problems from arising in the future.

Provide enough time to do the work

There are moments when you absolutely need a quick answer to a question, but those are few and far between. Give your counsel enough notice about projects so they can do a thorough job and avoid mistakes. Quality takes time.

Tip from the Field: Most university counsel offices are small, two or three attorneys maximum. Some schools don't have anyone on staff at all and hire outside counsel for all their work. Given the small staffing and the amount of legal work a college campus can generate, it is important to give your attorneys enough time to produce a quality product.

Check your ego at the door

We all screw up, especially if you do your job long enough. Don't be afraid to swallow your pride and let your attorney know when you think something might become a bigger issue. Your attorney will respect you for being pro-active about raising issues because it makes his/her job easier in the long run.

Tip from the Field: Disclose all relevant information to your attorney. When you do have that meeting, don't hold anything back, even details that you think might be insignificant. Let your attorney decide what is significant or insignificant.

Create a culture of continuous learning for yourself

You shouldn't look for general counsel for the all answers, but instead to help you navigate the boundaries of the law. General counsel can help keep you from going out of bounds, but it is up to you to become knowledgeable about the major issues impacting career services.

Tip from the Field: As noted above, there are plenty of resources at your disposal to help hone your craft on legal issues. The biggest mistake is usually the failure to create a consistent feedback loop between you and legal counsel about what you are learning respectively. Establish some loose protocols to ensure that flow of communication exists.

Train your staff on issues with legal implications

Your staff is an extension of you and interacts with many more students, employers and members of the college community than you do. Make sure they are kept abreast of relevant legal information that could impact how they do their jobs (e.g., your latest meeting about service learning hold harmless agreements). We often forget that much of this information needs to be shared to have the maximum value.

Tip from the Field: There are many ways to implement this. Someone in your legal counsel's office may want to work with you on staff trainings. It might suffice to devote some of your professional development time as a staff to legal issues (e.g., there is always some new update with FERPA that is relevant to a career office). Each office will approach this differently. The important thing is that you find a way to do it.

The Role of Ethics in Career Services Leadership

Trudy Steinfeld and Emanuel Contomanolis

What it takes to be an effective leader in career services has changed greatly over the last decade and will no doubt continue to change, offering new challenges and new opportunities. One dimension of our leadership role that remains critically important and challenging is to ensure our organizations are committed to the ethical practices of our profession.

In the broadest sense, ethics are the accepted principles and rules of conduct that guide our professional behaviors and practices. In the field of career services, the National Association of Colleges and Employers (NACE) advances these guiding ethical principles through a series of documents and advisory opinions.

The NACE Principles for Professional Practice are focused on serving our clients and stakeholders in fair and equitable ways, ensuring a free and open recruiting and selection process, and providing for informed and responsible candidate decision-making. As leaders in career services, we must understand these principles and their application, and, most importantly, model ethical behavior for our office staff, clients, stakeholders, and professional community.

The ethics dimensions of our work is particularly important today. Growing public demands for accountability, demonstrable outcomes, and transparency have combined with rapidly changing technology, the ongoing war for talent, and global economic pressures to create a volatile, and at times contentious, business and professional landscape. The requests made of career services organizations by employers today, for example, are different than in the past and so too are the responses career services can provide. To be sure, the shifting legal and regulatory landscape influences our work as state and federal employment and equal opportunity laws, the growing concern with managing risk and compliance, and changing higher education regulations further complicate our operating environment. While ethics and the law represent separate areas of concern, they often combine and overlap in challenging ways for career services organizational leaders.

There is a dizzying array of ethical issues confronting today's career services organizations. Here are several examples of situations in which the profession's ethical principles can provide valuable guidance and direction:

- An employer asks the career services office to prescreen candidates and only forward the resumes of the "best" students who are diverse and U.S. citizens. The employer is a major financial contributor to your office and your institution.

- A student verbally accepts a job offer and then reneges, claiming the "unbinding nature" of a verbal acceptance. The student's parents and faculty advisor agree and advocate on the student's behalf.

- A student accepts a job offer in writing, and completes the onboarding paperwork, but fails to show up for the first day of work. In response to the employer's inquiry, the career services office discovers that the student has begun work at another employer.

- A student accepts a job offer, but does not inform the career services office and continues to interview for other jobs.

- An employer withdraws a job offer after the student has accepted the offer and cancelled other interviews.

- An employer extends an offer of employment with a specific compensation package and the student accepts. After further review, the employer realizes a mistake was made and lowers the value of the package. When you call the employer, you are told effectively that it's none of your business.

- A student informs your office that he is aware of another student who has accepted not only one job but two, and is still interviewing for other opportunities.

- An employer discovers that a competing firm is scheduling final interviews on your campus on a specific date. In response, the employer changes its on-campus recruiting schedule for the same date. As a result, many students find themselves now double-booked and want your help in resolving the conflicts.

- A parent calls and asks for a status update on the son/daughter's job search.

- A student comes into the office for a career counseling appointment accompanied by a parent, who insists on sitting in on the appointment.

- A parent contacts your office and asks that you help influence the son/daughter's choice of academic concentration or job choice in a field that to the parent seems more stable and lucrative.

- An employer wants to list a position as an "internship." After reviewing the description, you believe this position is more of a part-time job without compensation.

- The career services office has been informed that it will now be required to raise funds to make up for institutional operating budget cuts. The office has been instructed to raise these funds by creating new service fees and developing more highly priced employer partnership programs. Students and employers express unhappiness with this development and question the implications of access to services if they cannot, or will not, pay.

- A third-party recruiting organization has requested closer ties so that it can target alumni talent from the institution. The organization has access to some experienced-level jobs that would be of interest to your graduates. In return for closer ties with your office, the organization offers to give to your office a small portion of the fee it collects from the employer at the conclusion of the search.

- A commercial website that deals in job listings offers to compensate the career services office for access to the student data base so it can message students directly and make them aware of job opportunities.

- An organization that has given a small naming gift to the career services office is now requesting special access to services and use of space for meetings and events not related to the career center or student recruitment.

Although this is a long list, it is intended to be representative of the ethical dilemmas we face. In an age of increased government oversight, extensive and intrusive social media communications, increasing demands from internal stakeholders, and heightened expectations of external constituencies, highly complex ethical considerations are almost a daily consideration. Career services offices serve diverse constituents: prospective students, enrolled students and their family members, employers, faculty, partner and consortium institutions, public media, and community members to name but a few. Cultural as well as economic circumstances have influenced the ways in which these groups think about a plethora of relevant issues and ethical practices and what they expect from other entities, including career services, in terms of ethical behaviors.

As a leader in career services in this complicated working environment, there are a number of strategies for you to consider in ensuring your sensitivity to ethical practices.

Understand the resources available to you

NACE has developed a robust collection of resources to help you in navigating the waters of ethical practice. The Principles for Professional Practice includes three important sections—one for career services professionals, one for employment professionals, and one for third-party recruiters. All of these are necessary and extremely useful when dealing with complicated ethical issues that have implications for one or more of these constituencies. This document also outlines the process for requesting advisory opinions concerning specific topics that may not clearly be addressed in the Principles document as well as a suggested set of problem-solving procedures to help resolve potential conflicts between parties concerning matters of ethical practice.

Additionally, NACE has authored more than a dozen advisory opinions, position papers, and formal guidelines that help all professionals better understand certain pressing and timely ethical issues as well as provide useful steps to address ethical concerns. Further, NACE provides more than 20 specific case studies concerning typical ethical dilemmas, including topics such as confidentiality, candidate disclosures, questionable recruiting practices, candidate referrals, and reneging on job offers. Each case study provides a set of questions to consider, relates the facts of the case study to relevant provisions of the Principles for Professional Practice, and offers a set of possible solutions to the dilemma.

NACE provides on-going support for members in this area through the Principles for Professional Practice Committee. Comprised of member volunteers, the committee is responsible for identifying issues related to ethical standards and best practices and works with the NACE Board to address issues and communicate appropriate information and guidance to the membership and the profession.

Along similar lines, the Society for Human Resource Management (SHRM) provides useful resources for its members in the areas of ethical practices in recruiting, human resources work, and creating ethical business environments. SHRM also sponsors a Special Expertise Panel in Ethics/Corporate Social Responsibility and Sustainability, which is also comprised of volunteer members who report emerging trends, provide expert advice, and given guidance on policy matters. It serves the career services leader well to join SHRM and become familiar with how ethical issues are addressed from the recruiting and human resources perspectives.

Finally, the leader's professional network of colleagues can prove very effective in obtaining guidance and insight regarding ethical challenges. Often, other leaders have experienced similar situations and, having resolved them, are in an excellent position to share what they have learned and would advise others to consider.

Commit to being an ethical leader

As career services professionals, we are all faced with ethical situations, which can be complicated, time sensitive, and exhaustive. In some cases, depending on who is involved and the specific situation, the resulting decisions and actions may be politically charged and professionally tenuous. In other cases, we may simply be "too close" to a situation to see it clearly or to accurately evaluate all of the factors involved. Though senior staff may meet directly with students less frequently than counseling staff, much of the work in fielding opinions and weighing pressures from outside parties and constituencies undoubtedly falls to them. And, to no great surprise, the decisions they make have the broadest on-campus and external impact. It is vital that as a leader you are committed to these principles and model ethical behavior for your staff, clients and stakeholders.

It is the responsibility of the career services leader to be familiar with the Principles for Professional Practice in its entirety. Understanding the issues and principles from the viewpoint of the employment professional and third-party recruiters is potentially just as important to the office leader as understanding those issues and principles from the perspective of the career services professional. The NACE materials also contain guidelines for faculty as well as colleagues who are primarily concerned with internships and related experiential education programs. It is important to be familiar with those issues, principles, and guidelines as well and to stay abreast of any new developments that can be shared with staff, clients, and stakeholders as appropriate. The principles, guidelines, and case studies will enable you to have a framework for a decision-making processes, which will provide a helpful degree of clarity to help reach sound resolutions to ethical dilemmas.

Do not underestimate the importance of your leadership role in educating and advising your senior institutional leaders, faculty, administrators, and other key stakeholders concerning ethical issues in the areas of career services and recruiting. Sharing the NACE principles and guideline statements selectively with relevant individuals and groups serves the interests of your office well. This sharing puts the power of informed decision-making in the hands of others and provides valuable insight and perspective for the informed ethical decisions made by you and your office. Your ethical thought leadership has the potential to be highly valued by your institution.

Create an ethical culture in your office

If you can foster an office culture that has clear expectations and processes for dealing with ethical issues, then it is much easier for you and your team members to communicate to students and employers appropriately and consistently. The extensive array of resources NACE provides should be used strategically in training new staff and in the continuing education and professional development of seasoned staff members.

These professional standards and guiding principles will not only be important in guiding your work and protecting your operation and institution, but will also serve as an important example to your staff after which they can model their own work with students and employers. Tone-setting and establishing expectations on ethical behavior for your office team is always important, but it is also critical that you engage your staff in meaningful discussions that can demonstrate how this actually applies to our work. The case study is one excellent tool to identify and bring these issues to life and, more importantly, to establish a framework to come up with appropriate strategies and solutions to common ethical considerations in guiding your team in career services work.

College and university relationships and institutional cultures, as well as the experiences of career services leadership and staff, will influence how ethical dilemmas are addressed and resolved. Central to career services work is the fundamental commitment to connecting students and employers, and to providing various opportunities for engagement in meaningful and ethical ways. Understanding and maintaining a commitment to these professional standards of practice is the best way to lead career services offices ethically in these complex and challenging times.

Recommended Reading and Resources

National Association of Colleges and Employers (2012). *Principles for Professional Practice*. Available at: www.naceweb.org/principles/

National Association of Colleges and Employers (2012). Ethical Issues Index. Available at:
www.naceweb.org/Knowledge/Legal/Ethical_Issues_Index.aspx

Society for Human Resources Management. Membership information available at: www.shrm.org

Making the Value Proposition

Jeff Garis

It seems like everyone wants to become involved in delivering career services in higher education. Academic advising increasingly offers "developmental advising" and career coaching. Many academic departments control internship programs. Often, academic colleges create decentralized career services and recruiting programs including career days and on-campus interviewing without involving career centers. This essay will discuss how college and university career centers can offer value-added services to the institution in forging partnerships with a range of departments and colleges including academic advising, academic programs, alumni associations, and student affairs departments.

Career services offices should be recognized and respected by their institution as *the leader* in creating college/university-wide career programs and systems. Value-added career services must address the decentralization-centralization continuum and how career services offices can "friend raise" in creating innovative dynamic services such as: a) recruiting software systems led by career services while offered to other departments, b) institution-wide internship services coordinated by career services, c) academic advising/career services partnerships, d) career days and on-campus interview programs jointly sponsored by academic programs and career services, e) alumni career services f) career development courses for credit and g) college/university-wide systems led by career services such as ePortfolios and coordination of student engagement programs including service learning, leadership, global experience, research, and internship programs.

To be regarded as adding value to the institution, career services offices must begin with a solid internal infrastructure, including a clear mission, supporting comprehensive programs, and a commitment to customer service. A well-defined mission with comprehensive programs can, in turn, be clearly communicated to the respective college/university community. This essay begins with a review of four models or continua associated with the mission for the delivery of career services in college or university settings as well as a brief outline of core programs commonly associated with comprehensive career services.

The mission for the delivery of career services in college or university settings can be categorized in four continua (Vernick, Garis & Reardon, 2000) as outlined in Figure 1.

Figure 1
Career Center Continua

Involvement in Career Development

Low   High

Employment Advising Only   Comprehensive Career
With Career Counseling In   Counseling, Programming
The Counseling Center Or   And Assessment
Academic Advising

Involvement in Experiential Education

Low   High

De-Centralized   Mission for Cooperative
Experiential Education   Education, Internships And
Services   Part-Time Employment

Locus of Employer Relations

Decentralized   Centralized

Locus of Funding

Self-Supported Through   State / Institutional
Client and Employer Fees   Appropriated

The first continua reflects the degree to which the career center holds the mission for providing career development services with supporting career advising, counseling, assessment, and information. At many institutions, the mission for career counseling and assessment resides in the student counseling center rather than the career center. In such instances, the career center may provide assistance with employability skills, but does not offer programs for academic/career choice or career indecision. Career centers with this mission would fall to the left of the continua. At other institutions, the mission for counseling and assessment for career choice may be shared with a variety of offices, including the student counseling center, academic advising, and the career center, placing such offices in the middle of the continuum. In order to be regarded as comprehensive, the career services office should shoulder a strong mission for advising, counseling, assessment, and information supporting career decision-making, placing them to the right of the dimension.

The second dimension addresses the degree to which the career center holds the mission for providing experiential education services such as externships, internship, and cooperative education programs. Part-time, work-study, volunteer, or summer job programs could also be included in the continua. Many institutions have internship or cooperative education programs residing in academic units rather than career centers, placing them to the left of the dimension. Commonly, the institutional mission for delivering experiential education is blended with colleges, academic departments, financial aid, and career centers all involved in these programs, placing them in the middle of the dimension. Fewer schools located to the right of the model have career centers shouldering the complete mission for experiential education programs. However, experiential programs including internships have always been regarded as among the most important, powerful career programs contributing to student professional success. As a result, to be regarded as comprehensive, it is important for career services to include, at least to some extent, experiential programs in their mission.

Employer relations services shown in the third continua range from decentralized to centralized. Many institutions have decentralized career offices residing in academic colleges, placing them to the left of the dimension. Other institutions have primarily centralized career centers charged with the college or university-wide mission for employer relations and recruitment programs. Schools may fall toward the middle of this dimension through a hybrid model, with the university-wide career services office providing campus career and recruiting services in partnership with specialized academic college or department-based career programs.

Finally, the degree to which the career center is funded by the institution can be plotted on a dimension. At some colleges and universities, the salaries and operating budget for career services are not funded by the institution, causing career centers to generate their funding base completely through charges and fees to students, alumni, and employers and fund-raising efforts. At other institutions, career centers enjoy the full support of the institution for their operating budget, and any fees or contributions are used only as enhancement funds. Of course, many career centers will fall on the middle of the dimension, receiving institutional funding for staff salaries and some measure of central funding for operations, but covering additional operating expenses through auxiliary-fee based programs.

College and university career services falling at least near the middle and to the right side of the four continua reviewed above would generally be considered to be comprehensive career services adding value to the institution.

Additionally, core "basic indicator" programs associated with comprehensive career services offices would commonly include:

- Intake or drop-in advising or counseling,
- Individual career counseling by appointment,
- Assessment and computer-assisted guidance,
- Career information,
- Career planning classes for credit,
- Career education outreach programming,
- Experiential education and internships,
- Career days,
- On-campus interviewing, and
- Job listings and resume referral services.

It is imperative that career services offices hold the above missions and provide supporting comprehensive programs as a foundation to offering value to the institution. However, this foundation can be regarded as *necessary but not sufficient* to be considered a value-added career services office. Also, the commitment to customer service demonstrated by the career services office in offering programs and services will contribute significantly to the office's identity and value throughout the institution. Career offices regarded as value added are recognized for their energy, creativity, technological applications, and welcoming environments that include drop-in services. The next level of value that the career services office can offer lies in our ability to assume an institutional leadership role in creating college/university-wide career systems. Just a few examples of college/university-wide systems that can be lead by career services offices follow:

Resume writing systems

The career services office must be viewed as the leader within the institution for expertise in resume writing. Indeed, if the career services office cannot help with resume writing, it may as well board up the windows and close down! Traditionally, career professionals strongly discourage students from creating resumes based on simple fill-in-the-blank templates. However, relatively new sophisticated resume building software systems are available. Many academic programs believe that students should design resumes tailored to their particular profession. The career services office can purchase or create a resume writing system, then offer academic programs the opportunity to provide feedback and examples of resumes tailored to respective professions. In doing so, the career services office is viewed as the leader in offering an institutional-wide resume writing system that is available to all of the academic colleges and departments. Also, students can create resumes that are compatible with internship and job recruiting software programs in support of a seamless institutional software system.

All of us understand the limitations and validity of many very visible and published media rankings of university career services offices. However, it is always good to be among the leaders in any published ranking. Not long ago, a career center ranked number one nationally through student surveys attributed the ranking to the positive student response to a resume writing system that could be designed for a range of academic programs and professional fields. The career services office should lead a college/university-wide resume writing system.

Internship and job systems

Many departmentally or college-based career programs begin with the mission to offer internship opportunities. Obviously, this is due to the academic linkages with internship programs. As a result, internship programs can easily become highly decentralized with minimal involvement with a central career services office. However, many internship opportunities are available to multiple majors and many do not involve credit. Additionally, many academic department-based internship offices may use separate software systems, requiring students and employers to post positions and/or resumes at multiple sites within the same institution.

Acquiring institutional-wide internship activity data can also present challenges in such colleges and universities. Even in highly decentralized internship programs, the career services office can take the lead in creating a website that serves as a portal for students and employers that includes all of the existing available internship programs. Such web-based applications are frequently referred to as *internship central or internship headquarters sites.* While politically far more challenging, the career services office can recommend one college/university software system to support all internship programs. Such software systems can be designed to allow for departmentally specific identity and control but offer the following advantage: a) a single institutional software license rather than costly and confusing multiple licenses, b) employers need to interact with only one software system when choosing to post internships, c) students can post the same resume and need not register for multiple systems, and d) collection of institutionally wide internship data are available through a single software system.

Of course, the same decentralization dynamics often apply to full-time employment programs. As many universities become more decentralized, it is common for schools to have multiple career days sponsored by departments, student organizations, colleges, and career services. In addition to career days, the mission of specialized college-based career offices may include career counseling, resume reviews, mock interviewing, and/or on-campus interviewing. Also, college/departmentally based career programs may also use different software systems or hold individual licenses with the same software provided. Such decentralized practices can create a "silo model" for career services that is confusing to students and employers. In such institutions, the career services office can lead in creating a *landing page website.* The website does not change any departmental practices or control, but offers a portal for students and employers to view the range of existing career and recruiting programs available at the institution.

Also, as noted above, through the career services office leadership, an institution can choose to adopt a hybrid recruiting model that includes the advantages of academic department/college-based career programs coupled with a strong institutional-wide career services office. Such a model can be supported through a single recruiting system license that also allows for department/college-based identity and control. Regardless of the actual design, the career services office will add value to the institution by leading in proactively creating a career programs and recruiting system model that is endorsed university-wide and is understood by students and employers.

Career day systems

Career days are among the most visible recruiting programs at most schools. Here again, the organization and sponsorship of career days falls on the decentralization/centralization continuum. Increasingly, many career day events are outside of career services' control and sponsorship. However, the career services office may recommend an institutional system of career days that may include a range of sponsorship options: a) career services sponsored, b) joint sponsorship with career services and departments/colleges, c) departmental/college sponsored with career services' administrative/software support, and d) department/college sponsored, with follow-up interviewing conducted/scheduled through career services. The career services office can add value through proactively supporting the planning of career days without necessarily sponsoring and controlling all of the events.

Career information resource systems

There are many online systems available that support student career development, including occupational information, employer databases, career planning assessment and guidance, international career and employment information, and interview preparation/practice. Even in decentralized institutions, the career services office can take the lead in purchasing selected products and making them available to all majors college/university-wide. In some cases, highly visible online career resources can be included in the secure login page for the institutions' academic support software application.

Career development credit course systems

Many career services offices offer credit career planning courses. However, these courses can become more visible and systematic within the institution. For example, the career services office can take the lead in organizing a course and creating the syllabus, yet include other professionals from academic departments as instructors. Additionally, credit career planning courses represent a wonderful opportunity for instructional partnerships between career services and academic advising. In short, rather than controlling and teaching very limited sections of a career development course each year, the career services office can lead in creating multiple career-related courses and sections taught in various academic programs and involving varied instructors.

Alumni career program systems

Over the past several years, schools have increasingly been concerned with continued career support of their alumni. Accordingly, several models for alumni career services have evolved with varying degrees of involvement with the institution's career services office. Some examples of alumni career service delivery models include: a) entirely sponsored and delivered through the career service office, b) entirely sponsored and delivered by staff reporting to the alumni association, and c) joint sponsorship involving staff and programs from the alumni association and career services office. A value-career services office should be involved in the creation of the institutional system to address the career needs of its alumni.

Emerging institutional wide systems and programs

In recent years, new programs have been created that offer additional opportunities for career services offices to add value in supporting and/or coordinating highly visible institutional wide programs. Examples include: ePortfolios, leadership, and student engagement programs. Clearly, all of these programs hold the potential to support student career development. At some schools, career services offices have lead in the creation of ePortfolios that enjoyed the support of academic programs and became part of the institutional culture. ePortfolio systems often include skills matrixes where students can include evidence of professionally relevant skills acquired though a range of experiences. The skills are typically customizable for the student and their respective academic programs. However, examples of core skills available to students in creating ePortfolios include: communication, creativity, critical thinking, leadership, life experience, research, social responsibility, teamwork, and technical/scientific writing. Experiences supporting skill development may include academic course work, jobs/internships and related forms of work-based experiential learning, service/volunteerism, activities/memberships, personal interests, and life experiences.

Also, in some cases through the support of an ePortfolio system, career services offices have supported or led other university-wide initiatives such as student success, leadership, and/or student engagement programs. For example, student engagement programs can be created and led through career services that promote and recognize student involvement and accomplishment in the following areas: leadership. Internships, service, international experience, and research

Career services offices will not shoulder responsibility for all of the above engagement areas, but can assume administrative leadership for the overall program while partnering with academic affairs and other university offices associated with specific engagement areas. In doing so, the career services office clearly adds to its value-added identification throughout the institution.

Concluding thoughts

A thorough review of all of the opportunities for career services offices to create institutional-wide programs and systems is beyond the scope of this chapter. Examples of additional systems that can benefit from career services leadership include a) graduate follow-up surveys, b) pre-professional advising programs, and c) part-time job and/or civic engagement programs. However, with the advancing involvement of other agencies, staff, and faculty in the delivery of core career services, including career counseling, internship, and employment recruiting programs, career services offices must be proactive in creating institutionally wide systems. In offering value to our respective schools, career services will be viewed as the expert and leader in creating systems without necessarily controlling all of the resulting programs. Showing annual report activity, including number of students counseled, workshops delivered, career days held, and on-campus interviews conducted, will always be beneficial. However, showing career services' leadership roles in creating institutional-wide systems supporting student career development and employment will be even more important and valued in the 21st century.

References:

Vernick, S., Garis, J. and Reardon, R. (2000). Integrating service teaching and research in a comprehensive university career center. Career Planning and Adult Development Journal, 16(1), 7-24.

The Role of Internships

Deb Chereck

The importance of internships for students, employers, and higher education institutions has never been greater, and the role of career centers in effectively managing internship programs and relationships never more vital. I created a credit-based internship program at the University of Oregon in the mid-80s and have led that effort for many years This experience has taught me many valuable lessons and led to many student successes over time.

The term "internship" means different things to different people so let me begin by providing a standard definition of internships that the National Association of Colleges and Employers (NACE) advocated beginning in 2011:

> An internship is a form of experiential learning that integrates knowledge and theory learned in the classroom with practical application and skill development in a professional setting. Internships give students the opportunity to gain valuable applied experience and make connections in professional fields they are considering for career paths; and give employers the opportunity to guide and evaluate talent.

Internship opportunities differ significantly in whether they are paid or unpaid, but they are all ideally defined as well supervised with required orientation, training, and evaluation as well as the clarity of assigned goals and responsibilities. It is important, as well, in discussing internships that you are familiar with the definitional criteria established by the U.S. Department of Labor consistent with the Fair Labor Standards Act http://naceweb.org/connections/advocacy/internship_position_paper/ The criteria, as they relate differently to "for profit" and "not for profit" employers, are very helpful when discussing potential internship partnerships with employing organizations.

Students increasingly arrive on our campuses knowing that internships are an essential component of their education and their longer-term career success. This importance is well placed since employers reported in a recent NACE Internship & Co-op Survey that they converted over 58 percent of their interns to full-time hires. I believe the best ambassadors for our institutions are our student interns. They demonstrate to the employer first-hand the quality of our institution and academic programs. In return, students gain valuable related work experience, develop critical workplace skills, and establish a potentially powerful network of professional contacts to be leveraged for over the course of their careers. Students benefit, and so do the host employer organization and the institution.

From the employer perspective, internship programs are a very effective engagement strategy. They have the advantage of identifying talent—increasingly earlier in a student's academic career—and evaluating that talent over the course of the internship with an eye toward converting the best interns into full-time hires. Typically, successful interns earn a higher starting salary than "non-interns" and often will return to the same department or division where they can hit the ground running as full-time employees.

The outcomes for career centers are valuable in that we are often at the center of brokering these opportunities, serving the needs of our students, institutional stakeholders, parents, and employers. We are seen as a partner in retention efforts as well as admission-related recruiting when we can share the positive outcomes resulting from internship program participation. Managing successful internship programs also strengthens our ties with our academic colleagues and potentially enhances the educational outcomes of the institution.

Finally, successful internship programs also extend the institution's brand in the hiring community. With local employers, this strengthens the "town and gown" relationship, but, with hiring organizations as a whole, it creates potential new partnership opportunities for the institution in the areas of sponsored research, faculty consulting, continuing education and customized training participation, alumni engagement, and fundraising.

Let me share some of what I have learned about managing internship programs:

The focus of internships should be on student learning

I believe that the internship should serve as a lab for evaluating a particular employer or field as a potential career choice. It should also account for some appropriate form of academic credit. It all starts with a learning agreement that clearly identifies student goals, projects and assignments, hours expected, and specifics about when and how feedback and evaluation will be provided. Ideally, the work site supervisor will have experience in working with interns and a commitment to the program's experiential learning focus.

When communicating with potential site supervisors, I always let them know that this generation of interns is capable of working very fast and efficiently. Often employers over estimate how long and how much work is needed by an intern to complete a project. I advise employers to load the intern's plate with potential projects. The quality of the supervision is important in creating a sense of "fit" with an organization and in providing a challenging yet supportive work environment for the intern. Great intern supervisors are worth their weight in gold.

Some of the best internships are rotational in nature; allowing the student to be introduced to a variety of functions in the organization. Students' knowledge is often fairly narrowly defined, so this type of internship broadens their perspective and exposes them to diverse settings and situations. It also allows interns to make an even more informed decision about the work they are interested in doing and the organizations where they can best make that happen.

It does take time to cultivate these relationships, but a supportive academic partner is central to the long-term success of any internship program

It is vitally important that career services and academic departments work collaboratively. There are many different models for doing so, but every effective internship program is characterized by a strong partnership. For example, my office functioned as the employer, and I partnered with the doctoral level Counseling Psychology Program in the College of Education in creating a for-credit Career Development Internship Program. The Counseling Psychology program had a faculty research interest in career development and resources, which allowed it to fund graduate students. The arrangement benefited both our areas and, of course, provided valuable experience to the participating students.

Setting student and employer intern expectations is key

Students, for the most part, do not need to be convinced about the value of internships. The importance of experiential learning has grown significantly and is increasingly common even at the high school level. Students should, however, be encouraged to start early and intern, or participate in some other experiential learning activity, as often as feasible. Furthermore, it's important that students understand that while on the internship demonstrating initiative, doing their best work every day (even if it is a little boring on occasion) and receiving feedback gracefully (while making recommended changes) are keys to their success. Any internship is more valuable when the participating students have realistic expectations and a full awareness of their roles and responsibilities.

I realize that employers believe finding student interns early in their academic careers and inviting them back for subsequent work assignments is attractive. I believe, however, it is important for students to explore a variety of organizations in order to gain the broadest experiences and the insights necessary to make the best career decisions. Employers may have differing expectations regarding the outcome of their programs and, again, the varying models may all be effective. The key, of course, is to form partnerships where the expectations of the institutional program and the employer are most in sync.

If we are truly focused on student learning outcomes during an internship, then we must be flexible and willing to adapt the experience where possible to maximize the individual opportunities that maybe available at a site. By working closely with a student intern, and the employer, the student experience can be appropriately personalized while ensuring academic integrity and meeting the needs of the employing organization.

Interns should be compensated in some way for their efforts

Clearly there is a great deal of public scrutiny—and spirited debate—concerning the appropriateness of unpaid internships. It's vital as leaders in career services to stay abreast of developments in this area as the federal government offers new interpretations and guidelines with implications for higher education institutions and employing organizations. These important issues aside, given the rising costs of higher education, employers should compensate their interns whenever possible. If an appropriate salary cannot be provided, then alternatives should be considered. Creative alternatives include, for example, a stipend based on performance, reimbursement for the cost of academic credit, or compensation for meals and housing.

To help address circumstances in which employers are unable or unwilling to provide compensation, an increasing number of higher education institutions are soliciting funds from donors and creating "internship scholarship" accounts. The funds from these accounts are used to provide financial support to students who would not otherwise be paid on their internship assignments.

Internship programs offer great staff development opportunities

Career services staff involvement with internship programs is an excellent professional development opportunity. Staff advising of potential student interns, arranging work site assignments with employing organizations, and collaborating with the work site supervisor provides staff with industry knowledge and insights, enhances their interactions with students, and provides a direct and positive support to the academic enterprise. Additionally, it sends a strong and positive message to the employer when you assign a staff member to manage the partnership and grow it over time. It is important, of course, that assigned staff be strong ambassadors for the internship program.

In closing, the Education Advisory Board (2012) suggested that the career center of 2025 will need to be the nexus for networking opportunities and will "broker connections among student, alumni, faculty, and employers." Internship programs provide for us to assume the leadership and responsibility for providing high-quality internship opportunities to our students. It is a place where we can remain relevant and essential to our constituencies and administration while enhancing the student learning and professional development experience.

References

Education Advisory Board (2012). Developing next generation career services. August 3. Available at:
http://www.eab.com/Research-and-Insights/Student-Affairs-Forum/Studies/2012/Developing-Next-Generation-Career-Services

Fundamentals of Career Services Budgeting and Finance

Emanuel Contomanolis

Mention budgeting, finance, accounting, revenue, and many a career services professional gets a queasy stomach. The core values and interests that draw so many to career services work in higher education don't necessarily coincide with the world of budgeting and finance. For so many in the field, they never need worry or understand the in's and out's of the financial workings of their office or institution. This is a missed opportunity, however, since understanding these aspects of institutional and career services operations provides an important context for understanding the financial implications of office budget decisions and fiscal practices. For those that aspire to leadership roles, understanding the fundamentals of budgeting and finance are essential to the effective leadership of any successful office.

The shifting financial landscape of higher education

Every career services office has a budget, but the nature of that funding and its source can vary widely. Key to understanding this is being knowledgeable about the broader higher education fiscal landscape and its implications for your institution. There are powerful forces at work—economic, social, technological, and public policy—exerting significant pressures on higher education institutions. These circumstances, in turn, have implications for the financial support of career services organizations. These forces are attempting to slow down the rate of growth in the cost of higher education, create greater efficiencies in delivering programs and services, and demanding more substantive and measurable outcomes resulting from participation in higher education at both the sector and individual institution level.

Operating revenues for not-for-profit higher education institutions come from a variety of sources influenced primarily by institution type—public or private. In the public sector, the public policy effort to keep tuition costs relatively low, primarily for in-state residents, means that operating revenues come from tuition supplemented to differing degrees by state appropriations. Tuition revenues and appropriations may be provided directly to a public institution or through a state public higher education system that, in turn, distributes funds to its individual institutional members on some formulaic basis. In the public sector, additional student fees for service are common since they are used to generate additional operating revenues. Those fees may be specific to career services, or may include a portion of a broader fee (e.g., an institutional student activity fee) earmarked for career services. Increasingly, public institutions also rely on independent foundation entities that may generate revenues that in turn may be applied to certain institutional expenses or as cost offsets.

In the nonprofit private sector, institutions are more tuition-dependent since there are no state appropriations to help offset the real costs, but returns from institutional endowments are often used to fund annual operating budgets. Fees are not unusual, but tend to be less common in this sector. The size of the endowment and the extent of tuition dependency are the most influential factors in a nonprofit private institution's financial resources. For-profit private institutions are almost entirely dependent on tuition revenues and the resources provided by their investors.

Institutional revenues in both sectors are also influenced by external research funding, primarily through administrative overhead allowances for funded projects, as well as financial contributions and gifts-in-kind from alumni and others that may be restricted or unrestricted in their use.

Moody's Investor Service (2013) has determined that the fiscal outlook for the entire U.S. higher education sector is negative. Among the reasons for the negative outlook, Moody's cites increasing price sensitivity due to a continued weak economy; the rising burden of student loans and growing student default rates; strained non-tuition revenue streams, including declining state appropriations and shrinking federal research funding; and a volatile investment environment likely to result in weaker endowment returns.

There are two important lessons in these circumstances. The first is that it is essential to understand the particular financial circumstances of your institution since those circumstances will influence the financing and fiscal operations of your career services organization. The second is that all institutions must be increasingly mindful of their financial investments in services and programs since all revenue streams are increasingly constricted, and the competition for those limited resources is fiercer than ever. This is a trend likely to continue well into the future.

The career services budget—deconstructed

Fortunately, the elements of a typical career services budget are not difficult to take apart and examine. There are essentially three major components: 1) salary and benefits expenditures; 2) all other non-salary expenditures; and 3) fees and revenues. Budget expenditure categories and descriptors are determined by the financial practices of individual institutions or, in the public sector, by governing systems on behalf of their member institutions. In some instances, a particular office budget may only reflect lines for which funds are actually allocated and available but in most instances a budget will include expenditure lines that are common across all units of the institution whether those lines are funded or not. Except for unique circumstances, as a general rule budgets should be balanced at the end of the year. In other words, unless you have been specifically authorized to expend more or directed to cut expenses and return resources to the institution or division, your budget should reflect a "zero balance" at the end of the fiscal year. In most instances, institutions are concerned with the office budget "bottom line" balancing. In this case, as long as you have not overspent your overall allocations, the institution is not generally concerned that you overspent in a particular expense line, as long as you underspent in another, allowing you to achieve that overall balanced bottom line.

Typically, the total office budget is based on the institution's fiscal year and must be spent during that given fiscal year. There are exceptions, however, to the ability to "carry over" funds from one fiscal year to the next. These exceptions occur most often with clearly defined fee and revenue fund accounts. Fiscal years vary among institutions—with public institutions most often influenced by the state's fiscal year—but benchmark data suggest the most common fiscal year runs from July 1 to June 30.

In certain instances, your office may be the recipient of an externally funded grant. In these instances, to allow for appropriate accounting practices, you should expect to manage a completely separate "grant budget" with specific expenditure guidelines, accounting standards, and even a potential different fiscal year in accordance with the requirements of the granting organization.

Salaries and benefits

Benchmarks provided by the National Association of Colleges and Employers (NACE) consistently affirm that the average office will have from 75 percent to 80 percent of its total expenditures tied up in staffing and benefits. Clearly staff salaries are based on a number of factors, the most important of which tend to be position responsibilities; initial hiring market ranges established by the institution; and length of service in the role, office, and institution. Increases to initial salaries are most often attributable to variable merit pool allocations, typically provided annually, or cost-of-living adjustments, typically provided at fixed levels across the board to all staff. These amounts, in almost all cases, are provided centrally by the institution to individual offices for allocation as appropriate. From time to time, institutions conduct market reviews of existing position compensation levels and this too may result in adjustments to existing or new staff salary levels, depending on the results of the benchmarking efforts. Increasingly, offices that wish to promote an existing staff member or provide an increased salary for additional responsibilities are faced with the prospect of funding that increased salary by reallocating their existing department resources rather than receiving those incremental funds centrally.

At most institutions, the salaries component of a career services budget will also likely include student work–study allocations (federal and non-federal), temporary hire budget lines, graduate assistant stipend lines, and so forth. Benefits are typically not associated with these particular salary lines.

Benefits costs are directly tied to salary dollars and are based on a wide variety of factors influenced by the specific package of benefits offered by the institution and on any employee and institutional cost share arrangements, such as on health care costs, for example. The rising costs of health care certainly influence all hiring organizations, including higher education, and are often the most significant factor in benefit costs that now range from 30 percent to 40 percent of total eligible full-time staff salaries. Benefit rates for part-time staff members may sometimes be lower.

Non-salary expenditures

The non-salary portion of the career services budget tends to be the smallest and, relatively speaking, the most flexible portion of the office budget. This portion typically includes day-to-day operating expenses including, for example, office supplies, phone charges, travel, software lease and equipment rental charges, copying and mailing costs, and so forth. Typically, there are specific institutional guidelines, and often accepted practices determined at the office and division levels, concerning how these funds may be spent and in what ways expenditures must be documented and accounted for. Typical, for example, may be expenditure approval limits and allowable and unallowable expenses that, of course, vary by expense category.

Capital equipment lines (e.g. monies to fund computer equipment or other physical plant projects above a certain cost point) may constitute a separate section of the budget or be included among the non-salary and benefit expenditures.

Fees and revenues

Offices by design, or by necessity, may be expected to generate revenues by charging fees for services or soliciting donations, typically from employer recruiting partners. While not unique, this opportunity to solicit funding support from employers is distinctive to career services, and the process demands that care be given to the nature of the funding effort in order to avoid potential ethical conflicts. Employer fees and solicitations should always comply with the Principles of Professional Practice established by NACE.

Some offices may establish fees independently—for alumni access to services or employer career fair attendance, for example—or, as is more common in the public sector, may receive a portion of a more general institutional student services fee. Many offices receive a base budget allocation that they can supplement through fees and other revenue generation, using the incremental monies to further extend programs and services. In some instances the office may keep a portion of what they generate, sharing the rest with the institution to be used for other purposes. Other offices actually receive smaller base allocations with the expectation that they will generate additional operating funds, through fees and revenues, to offer the necessary range of programs and services.

Office fees and revenues, for accounting purposes, are often handled differently than other elements of your office operating budget. Depending on their purpose and how the payments are made, fees and revenues may be deposited directly into a specific line in your operating budget or be deposited into another budget altogether—apart from your normal operating budget but which you can access for approved transfers or other expenditure payments. Again, depending on their purpose and institutional practices, fees and revenues may be "carried over" from one budget year to the next in what are commonly referred to as "revolving" accounts. This is often the case with donations solicited from corporate recruiting partners— or, in some cases, alumni donors—through formal partner programs, or specific fundraising initiatives (e.g., scholarship programs to fund stipends for otherwise unpaid student internships).

Working with your budget

At the beginning of the fiscal year, the office budget statement provides a clean financial slate and a simple starting point to the year. Funds are neatly allocated to expense categories in amounts thought to be necessary to conduct the business of the office and expended in regular disbursements and payments easily tracked over the course of the fiscal year. The reality, of course, is quite different. Once the budget year begins and spending gets underway, thing can quickly get very messy and very confusing. Despite the complexities, and to be expected apprehensions, if you can manage and balance your checkbook, you can manage and balance your office budget. Managing the process requires some basic skills and good planning. The effective leader will learn quickly that there are various strategies that can be enormously helpful to the process.

Leverage the right people

Unless you are already knowledgeable in the areas of bookkeeping, accounting, and finance, seek out assistance and counsel from the budget and finance people at your institution. They are likely not only more knowledgeable, but also more familiar and conversant with the institutional protocols and systems you will depend on for your budget work. Along similar lines, if your office leadership responsibilities in other areas are more demanding, and your budgeting skills still evolving, you may want to consider using another staff member in your office for purposes of support and additional oversight. Some offices may already assign certain bookkeeping and accounting support responsibilities to a staff member. If so, leverage those skills and interests. If not, you may want to identify and cultivate other office staff that have the potential to support your efforts. These opportunities can be enormously helpful to staff members who themselves aspire to office leadership roles at some point.

Do not lose sight, however, of the overarching responsibility that will always remain with you as the leader of the office. No matter who else is involved, or their assigned responsibilities, you are ultimately responsible and accountable for the financial actions and decisions made by your office.

Learn the system

A critical budget tool, of course, is the system you will be using to monitor and approve office expenditures. Institutions generally use a variety of enterprise system applications that track expenditures and provide the full range of financial management capabilities. You will need to familiarize yourself with how those particular systems function and what information and reporting capabilities are available for your office planning purposes. In many instances, you may find the use of "shadow systems"—most often in the form of Excel spreadsheets—helpful in extracting and tracking fiscal data that may be more cumbersome to undertake in the institution's enterprise system. Most institutions offer orientations to their financial systems—especially for new office leaders—or periodic system training courses. Don't be afraid to take advantage of these opportunities to familiarize yourself with these systems and tools.

Along similar lines, many institutions also employ internal audit reviews to ensure offices are complying with institutional guidelines and policies—many of them focused on financial practices. Get to know how and when these audits are conducted and take initiative to reach out to the individuals conducting them to gain further insight into best fiscal practices at your institution. Audits can be intimidating, but ultimately they can significantly enhance your efforts by identifying and helping you address areas of potential risk.

Use the past to shine a light on the present

If you are new to an office or new to managing a budget, the best place to start is by determining what was spent in prior years and in support of what activities. Prior year budgets are easily obtainable through the institution's enterprise financial accounting systems and can be very instructive. Start by assessing whether budget lines were overspent or underspent and focus on the specific activities, services, or items those funds were expended on. You want to get the big picture sense of how your office funds have been spent and what items and activities take up the lion's share of those resources. It's also helpful to know at what point certain expenditures occur in the fiscal year so you can plan accordingly and not over-commit funds prematurely. You also want to know to what extent are expenditures "fixed", i.e., are committed to certain expenses (e.g., equipment or software leasing contracts; institutional chargebacks or service charges; set allocations for federal work-study student employment) or are "flexible", i.e., you have control over their use and you can reallocate among different expense lines if you so choose.

This process is especially important if your office relies on fees or revenues from employer partnership programs to offset on-going office operations. It's critical you understand the role these particular resources play and to what extent the office would be impacted by any change in those revenue streams.

Follow the leader

Your office will be part of a bigger division and quite likely you will be reporting to a vice president, dean, or an associate or assistant administrator in that larger entity. Although the institution will have many formal policies and guidelines for you to follow, many senior administrators may add their own financial management expectations and protocols—formal and informal—to the already established institutional ones. Make sure you are aware of the specific expectations of your supervisor concerning how you manage your office budget and, perhaps more importantly, how your supervisor likes to be updated concerning your budget expenditures and financial situation over the course of the year.

In the same way that most offices are expected to ensure that the overall budget bottom line is balanced, division or larger unit organizations are often expected to ensure a "division bottom line." This may mean that over the course of a fiscal year, one office in the division may be allowed to overspend while another underspends as long as the overall budget is balanced. Understanding how this dynamic works in your broader organizational unit is important to your own planning efforts and in understanding what, if any flexibility, you may have to deal with emergencies or new initiatives.

Monitor and track

While it may seem obvious, central to effectively working with your budget is monitoring and tracking expenditures so you can get an accurate feel for the ebb and flow of your activities over the course of the fiscal year and make wise fiscal decisions. If your office relies on fees and other revenues, it's important to understand the timing and flow of those funds into your actual working budget. Additionally, many systems will encumber funds in your budget to allow for on-going payments (e.g., equipment leases). The encumbrance is essentially a "set aside" of the funds required to pay the contractual arrangement. Consequently, you want to make sure you understand how payments and encumbrances are reflected in your budget so you have an accurate picture of funds that are actually available both short- and long-term.

Get into the habit of reviewing your budget and detailed budget expenditures—at least in major expense categories—at least once a month. Build this review into your schedule and keep notes about what you are observing and what you want to track more closely in future budget reports.

Assess the impact of your financial commitments

While there has been appropriate renewed emphasis in career services work on evaluation and assessment, there are still gaps when it comes to applying these principles and practices to budget analysis. It's critically important to assess the impact of your financial commitments. Focus on not just what a program, service, or activity costs, but on how effective that initiative was in accomplishing your goals and what role your financial investment played in its success. Could you be just as successful with a reduced investment? If you increase your investment, how much more success could you actually account for? Effective budget work demands that you try to assess the "opportunity cost" of your investments. In other words, if you were to free up funds by not doing something, could those funds be used to undertake something else potentially more impactful or useful to your clients?

Be clear about who can commit office funds

As the office director, you will be ultimately responsible for the budget whether you authorize others in your office to make and approve expenditures or not. It's important you are always clear in those cases as to who may approve expenditures, under what specific circumstances (e.g., for specific projects and activities such as career fair expenses), and with what specific controls (e.g., when you need to be consulted or informed). As the office budget authority, there will be certain types of expenditures or certain levels of expenditures you will need to formally approve despite the fact that someone else in your office may have already committed funds to an activity or purchase. Always be thoughtful about how you assign this responsibility, if you choose to do so, and spend time making your expectations and requirements clear with any staff involved in the process.

Always be prepared to make adjustments

Despite your best budget planning efforts, you will inevitably be required to make adjustments to your budget on the fly. Unanticipated expenditures, increased costs, new programming, or service opportunities and demands, among countless other changing circumstances, will all potentially demand that you make decisions to fund new efforts or choose among competing priorities. Often this will need to be done by reallocating your existing resources, by funding other activities at a lower level, or by cutting other expenses entirely to accommodate new initiatives. Don't be surprised or frustrated by this. It's a normal and expected part of your "fiscal life" and, if handled well, presents you with the opportunity to take initiative and potentially enhance the value of your office to your clients and stakeholders.

Keeping a close eye on where your resources are going and what they are actually contributing to is vital to making the best decisions regarding these ongoing adjustments. Always keep your office mission, goals, values, and service priorities foremost in your mind as you work your way through these decisions. One of the best times to make more formal adjustments to your next year's budget is toward the end of the current budget year when many offices have the opportunity to review and make final adjustments to their budgets for the next fiscal year. At this point, you can reallocate funds from one budget line to another in such a way as to both better reflect your actual expenditures and more effectively plan for the next fiscal year's anticipated activities.

Be open with relevant budget information and trends

There is often some reluctance on the part of office directors to share budget information and trends with office team members. Raising the overall understanding of your team concerning the budget and financial circumstance of your office can be a powerful tool in engaging staff and better managing office resources. Too often staff members don't understand the implications of the budget on their actions and activities and view the financial management of the office as "someone else's responsibility." Don't be afraid to review with the office team the annual operation budget in conjunction with strategic planning discussions and provide periodic updates throughout the year. Take the time to explain the major cost drivers and expenditure trends. A useful technique is to encourage staff members who are requesting or planning projects to outline budgets for their initiatives and share them as part of the planning and implementation process.

Strategic changes to your office budget

There are two budget-related initiatives that nearly all career services leaders are likely to experience at some point in their careers: cutting a budget and requesting and/or incorporating incremental resources into an existing budget. There are some helpful principles and practices to guide your efforts in both these areas.

Cutting your budget

Difficult institutional financial circumstances are increasingly common, and many career services offices are faced with the need to reduce their budgets. The extent of the requested reductions can range widely. In many instances, they may be modest enough to manage with minimal effort. At times, they can be extensive (e.g., including both staffing and non-salary and benefit line reductions). In managing these circumstances, keep in mind the following concepts.

Reducing your budget is a much easier process when your office goals and priorities are clear and your ongoing evaluation and assessment efforts have been effective in helping you understand what is central to your efforts and · what may be eliminated with less negative impact. A useful technique is to incorporate into your annual office strategic planning an exercise in which you and the office team brainstorm ideas in response to budget cutting scenarios of 1, 5, 10, or 20 percent. While you may not encounter the extreme of those scenarios, this is a very useful way to push you and your team to think creatively about the process and offers excellent preparation should you be faced with a real budget cut directive.

Be thoughtful yet appropriately transparent with office team members about required budget cuts. The rumors concerning anticipated budget cuts can be far more damaging than the cuts themselves. Be clear about the nature of the required cuts but thoughtful about providing a context for the circumstances and the strategies for implementing any reductions. This is especially vital if staff cuts may be required. Often, in those circumstances, the institution will establish protocols and extend advice and counsel to you regarding how staff reductions can best be approached and implemented. There are many ways to be creative in reducing budget resources, and office team members can often provide helpful insights and suggestions if they understand the circumstances and priorities. Staff reductions, for example, can often be addressed by not filling open positions or when current staff members use the circumstances as a trigger to adjust or reduce work schedules or consider retirement options.

Fight the urge to blame budget cuts for reduced services. As difficult at this will be, it's important to be positive—for your office team, clients, and stakeholders—and focus instead on what your office can do effectively under challenging circumstances. Ultimately your office will gain greater respect for taking the high road and keeping the focus on doing the best you can regardless of circumstances.

Managing incremental resources

You will likely have the opportunity to lobby for incremental resources for your office. At many institutions, this may be part of a regular process where your immediate supervisor is proposing a budget for the coming fiscal year and solicits your opinions about what support is needed in your particular area. Depending on the circumstances, your proposal may be included along with others in your division (or broader organizational unit) as part of an overall request and assigned relative importance by your divisional leader and/or institution. In other instances, your office may be assigned new tasks and responsibilities and your supervisor may make a request for you to assess what additional resources are needed for you to take on those incremental responsibilities. Occasionally, a donor may have interest in providing fiscal support for a particular program or initiative that would logically include your office (e.g., funds to provide student stipends for unpaid internship assignments) and you'll need to provide information about how these donated funds can best be used and managed by your office. Many offices have employer partnership programs or other fee-for-service programs and periodically you will want to consider raising those fees or partnership level commitments in order to generate additional revenues to fund your efforts. All of these efforts require some careful planning and strategic consideration.

Any request for incremental resources or increasing fees should be well-grounded and supported wherever possible by relevant data and information. Incremental resource requests should clearly support the office mission, strategic goals, and operating priorities. Don't assume this connection is always clear to those individuals and entities that make the final decision about the allocation of those funds.

When making the case for incremental resources or revenues, it's important to focus on outcomes. What will the investment of X amount of dollars actually accomplish? Too often, the stated result is too general, e.g., "We can do a better job helping students find jobs" or the impact unclear, e.g., "We can increase the number of student programs." Instead focus on the outcomes, e.g., "Currently we can only reach 35 percent of first-year students, but these incremental resources will allow us to double that to 70 percent, providing a greater number of students with the vital initial orientation to our services and a jump start on beginning their internship job search earlier."

Whenever possible and appropriate, use benchmarks to support your resource requests. Use NACE data reports and ad hoc surveys involving colleagues from benchmark offices and institutions to provide a broader context for your requests. Making the case for incremental staff positions, for example, can be made far more compelling and meaningful by sharing the student-to-career services staff ratios at competitor or benchmark institutions. Raising fees, by the same token, is easier when you can compare the fees you charge to those at other institutions.

As an office leader, it is always important to have a resources "elevator speech" in your mind. If a senior administrator were to ask you what was needed to help you provide more meaningful results, you should always have a brief and compelling storyline you can share. This is valuable both in a practical and strategic sense since you should always be revisiting that question as the answer may change over time, circumstance, or opportunity.

Some concluding thoughts

There is no simple way to capture the full range of budget and financial circumstances, scenarios, and conditions you may encounter in a career services leadership role. If you can keep in in mind some of the principles and techniques shared here, supplement them with your own good judgment, and maintain focus on what is important for your office at your institution, you will be as well prepared as anyone can be to carry out your fiscal responsibilities and challenges. Your confidence in your abilities will go a long way in demonstrating the effectiveness of your office and the added value you bring as a leader.

References

Moody's Investors Service (2013). US Higher Education Outlook Negative in 2013. Accessed at: http://www.moodys.com/researchdocumentcontentpage.aspx?docid=PBM_PBM148880

Show Me the Money:
Capital Fundraising for the Career Center

Jack R. Rayman

Increasingly career centers have become dependent on external funding to assure that adequate career services are provided to college and university students and their graduates. Most large career centers rely on career fair revenue and "corporate partners programs" (annual corporate sponsorships) to supplement their dwindling institutional budgets. It is not unusual for a center to rely on career fair revenue and corporate contributions to cover a substantial portion of its operating budget and some centers even use these funding sources to support staff positions and salaries. This chapter does not address these vital ongoing sources of revenue. Rather, its purpose is to provide a step-by-step process for raising substantial resources for major capital projects, facility renovations, or new construction. In the situation with which I have direct experience at Penn State, we raised 9.5 million dollars to build a new 40,000 square foot, stand-alone career center. The conduct of a major fundraising initiative is not for the faint of heart. It takes energy, initiative, and, most of all, persistence. I have outlined a proven step-by-step fundraising process below. The amount of time necessary to successfully complete this process will vary, but it is reasonable to assume it can be accomplished in 12 to 18 months, depending on prevailing conditions and circumstances.

Step One: Develop a vision—identify and define the project you wish to fund

The first and perhaps most important step in successfully funding a major project is to identify and carefully define the scope of the project that you wish to fund. In our case, we were seeking financial support to build a stand-alone career center of sufficient size to serve the career development and placement needs of a major university with an enrollment of 45,000 students. This first step of the process should have a basis in past annual reports describing historic activity levels and should incorporate projections

122

and visions of where you want your center to be in the future based on five- and 10-year strategic plans. The process of developing a vision should incorporate input from the entire career services staff, student affairs administration, the university office of physical plant, the development office, student representatives, central administration, and employers. Typically such a 20- to 30-page plan is called a "program statement," and it becomes the basis upon which architectural firms will ultimately bid on your project. Program statements contain general guidelines for the architects but avoid details. An example of typical program statement phrases might be:

> The new career center should contain a counseling suite, an interview center with eight interview rooms, a career library, seminar rooms, and a reception area. The interview center area should have a formal "corporate" feeling, while the library and counseling suite should be informal and inviting to students. Oh yes, and there should be convenient parking for employers!

The point here is that the program statement specifies the functionality, look, and feel you wish to create but leaves recommendations and plans about how to create that look, feel, functionality, and efficiency to the architects—that's what they do! The responsibility to assure that the program statement is ultimately carried out is typically vested in a building committee appointed by the vice president for student affairs. It is strongly recommended that the director of career services be a member of this committee (if not its chair), with representation from central administration, physical plant, key academic units, student affairs, student government, and at least one employer representative.

Step Two: Secure institutional support at the appropriate senior level

No capital project can be undertaken without the support of central administration. In the case of career centers, this usually means the vice president of student affairs. Often vice presidents of student affairs are conservative and careful when it comes to endorsing capital projects within their areas of responsibility. This might seem counterintuitive, but the reality is that vice presidents serve at the pleasure of presidents and boards of trustees, and they are often reluctant to propose capital projects within student affairs, especially if these projects are perceived as being in direct competition with other higher institutional priorities. It will be important for the vice president of student affairs to be fully committed to your project, because he or she will have to manage central administration support, making sure the president and trustees are on board as the project moves forward. In short, support from central administration is absolutely essential.

Step Three: Establish the ground rules with your development or fundraising office

Most colleges and universities have well-established development offices, and they will necessarily have some level of involvement in your project. Your institution may have a development officer whose sole role is to secure external resources for the division of student affairs. If so, count yourself as being among the privileged and take maximum advantage of this development officer. More likely, some member of the development staff may have responsibility for fundraising within student affairs, but does so out of his or her hip pocket, with most of his or her attention going toward the support of other university units. In whatever way your development office is configured, you will need to work with it to answer the following questions:

1. What will the role of the development office be in your fundraising initiative?

This could vary all the way from a very demanding and controlling relationship, where development office staff are micro-managing every aspect of your campaign, all the way to a totally "hands off" approach, where the development staff simply step back and let you run the campaign yourself. The reality is likely to be somewhere between these two extremes. Whatever the case, it will be important for you to establish a solid working relationship with someone representing your development office.

2. What are the development office donor access rules?

Most development offices have fairly strict rules regarding the solicitation of major gifts. It is not uncommon that key university administrators (e.g., deans, vice presidents) are assigned a formal and primary liaison role to major corporate donors, and all correspondence between the institution and that corporation must be channeled through that dean or vice president. In our case, this was true. Even though we had excellent relationships with a number of key individuals at a particular corporation, we were not allowed to discuss our fundraising initiative with anyone there without working through our dean of engineering who was the designated liaison between our university and that corporation. Other corporate relationships were similarly controlled by other key university administrators. While it is easy to understand the necessity of such rules to avoid "free for all" resource solicitation, it does erect barriers to productive fundraising dialogue between the career center and the corporation. In some cases, these barriers can be easily overcome, and in other cases they cannot. Be sure you understand the rules.

3. What are the institutional naming opportunity rules?

Most colleges and universities have rules that govern naming opportunities on the campus. The most common such rule is that a donor must cover at least half the cost of a building or space within a building if that organization's name is to be permanently associated with the space funded. The actual percentage is not important, but it is important to be aware that there will almost certainly be rules governing naming opportunities, and before you begin soliciting donors you will need to know what these rules are.

4. How does your project "fit into" the institution's overall development goals?

Most development offices work within a five- or 10-year institutional development plan, and projects that are not a part of that overall plan are not likely to be taken very seriously, let alone be funded. It therefore becomes paramount that your project be incorporated into the institutional plan. In our case, our career center plan had to fit within the student affairs-wide development plan that, in turn, had to fit within the university-wide development plan.

Step Four: Compile a master database of all corporate and individual contacts and prospects

Many of the potential donors to a capital project will be corporations and other employers with whom a great deal of political capital has been "banked" over the years because of strong and supportive relationships developed through the placement function within career services. An exhaustive list of these employer contacts should be generated for at least the past 10 years, including key individual contacts. These employer contacts, together with individual personal contacts who may be supportive of your project but with whom the office has had no official business, will comprise your master prospects database. This will be an ever-evolving database, with contacts being added and deleted as your campaign proceeds. In most cases, this database will be shared by the career center and the development office. A key component will be a meticulous record of past, current, and all future contacts.

Step Five: Do a longitudinal analysis of the prospects in your master database

Step five will be both a quantitative and qualitative analysis of all the prospects in your master database. In the case of employer prospects, the following will be critically important:

- Identify all past major donors. The best indication of future donor potential is past donor support.

- Identify the number of on-campus interviews conducted by this employer annually. If a prospective company conducts hundreds of interviews on your campus annually, there is little doubt that you will have a strong relationship with it, and the company is likely to benefit materially if you upgrade your career center facilities. Such a company is much more likely to participate in your fundraising campaign.

- Identify the number of alumni employed by each corporation/employer. If a prospective company employs hundreds or perhaps even thousands of your alumni, there will likely be a ground swell of support for your project among your loyal alumni within that company (we actually found that several large corporations employed more than 1,000 of our alumni!). Our experience suggests that even one alumnus "championing" your project within a large corporation can make all the difference. Do not underestimate the impact of one highly motivated alumnus champion on your chances of successfully garnering a large donation.

- Identify alumni who hold key positions within the corporation or other employing organization. It should be no surprise that highly placed alumni (e.g., CEOs, corporate presidents, and senior vice presidents) will have considerable clout both politically and financially and are, therefore, more likely to be effective champions of your funding campaign (if you can convince them of the importance of your project).

Step Six: Identify potential lead donors

As the aforementioned prospect analysis is being completed, it is not unusual that potential lead donors will emerge. It will become apparent that certain prospects have both the predisposition to support your project and the wherewithal to do so at a significant level. Depending on the scope of your project, lead donors may be classified as those capable of gifts of one million dollars or more. The identification of a small pool of potential lead donors will be a key to the success of your project. You and your development office staff will want to cultivate relationships with these folks and keep them regularly informed about every aspect of your fundraising initiative. Keeping them informed on a regular basis will give them the opportunity to become involved and will create the option for one of them to step forward and make a firm commitment as the lead donor.

Step Seven: Secure a lead donor

With luck and perseverance, one or more potential lead donors will finally commit a certain dollar amount to your project—the larger the commitment, the better. In the best of all possible worlds, your lead donor will commit 100 percent of the funds you need to implement your project.

Should that happen, your work will be done and you can build your project and tie a bow around it! It is more likely, however, that you will find a lead donor who is willing to commit only a portion of the funds necessary to implement your project. Then it will be necessary for you to secure a firm pledge (in writing) from this lead donor. The handling of this written pledge is what development offices do best. They will have a standardized form and will be sure that every "I" is dotted and every "T" is crossed so that you can move to the next phase of the funding process.

The establishment of a lead donor will set the tone for a successful campaign. Other potential donors will find it difficult to withhold support in the knowledge that a particular corporation has committed a lead gift of two million dollars. Often, key representatives from the corporation that makes the lead gift will publicly (and privately) "lean" on other potential donors in powerful ways. Your lead donor will be your best ally in the fundraising process.

Step Eight: Establish a building committee and complete your architectural plans, including artist renderings and floor plans

Secure in the knowledge that you have a substantial firm commitment from your lead donor, you can proceed to appoint a building committee and submit your "program statement" to area architects together with a "request for proposal." This process will vary from institution to institution, but usually this is an open bidding process where architects respond to your program statement by submitting a 10- to 15-page proposal to design your facility. This usually garners 20 to 30 architectural proposals that will be reviewed by a building committee appointed by the vice president of student affairs. The proposals will be winnowed down to some smaller number, say eight, and those eight firms will be asked to submit full-blown proposals. The building committee will then winnow the eight full-blown proposals down to three, and those three will be asked to make a formal proposal presentation before the building committee at which time the final architect will be chosen. Once the architect is chosen, you will have a source of preliminary architectural drawings that can be used to create concrete images of your project in the minds of potential donors. Meanwhile, the architects will be moving full speed ahead to design your project.

Step Nine: Prepare your promotional materials

In preparation for going public with your funding campaign, you will need to develop high-quality promotional publications that bring visual life to your project. Most potential donors need explicit descriptions (including artist's renderings, if possible) of a project before they are able to develop enthusiasm for financial support. The old phrase "A picture is worth a thousand words" comes to mind. Once the architects are selected, they can be "leaned upon" to develop "artist's conceptions" of your project for use in promotional publications, even if these "artist's conceptions" vary somewhat from the final architectural plans. At a bare minimum, you will need promotional brochures, poster-style architectural renderings of the proposed project, proposed floor plans, and proposed funding levels, all available in both hard copy and electronic format. These materials will be crucial to your success as you begin making contact with potential donors.

Step 10: Make initial contacts with potential donors based on your analysis

Armed with your edited database of potential donors and your promotional publications, you are now ready to begin making systematic contact. There is no one correct way to do this, but there is no substitute for individual personal contact either on campus or on the potential donor's premises. In our case, development office staff and key career center staff made initial contact in person, or by phone, offering to provide a project prospectus by mail or electronically. Then, development office staff followed up with each contact with an offer to make a personal call at the donor's headquarters. Nearly all potential donors agreed to sit down with a development office staff member for a personal discussion of the project. These initial visits were largely an effort to establish a firm personal relationship with the potential donor, explain the project fully, answer any questions they might have, and gauge the level of interest in participation.

Step 11: Establish donor "naming opportunities" and "benefits"

As you begin to generate interest in your project, you will need to establish naming opportunities and associated levels of sponsorship. In our case, we divided up our career center in much the way that athletic departments divide up their football and basketball stadiums with associated levels of sponsorship based on size and desirability of space. Thus, an interview room in the interview center could be sponsored for $25,000, a seminar room could be sponsored for $50,000, the career library could be sponsored for $100,000, the counseling suite could be sponsored for $500,000, and so forth. Keep in mind, these levels of sponsorship are based on the development office formula that requires that naming opportunities are available only if a sponsor contributes half the actual cost of construction of a given space. It is important to have this menu of opportunities so that potential donors have concrete examples of available sponsorships. The last thing donors want to do is contribute to a project feeling that their contribution may be combined with hundreds of others in an anonymous general fund. The goal is to develop a broad range of attractive funding opportunities at a similarly broad range of funding levels with associated donor recognition. In our case, the base funding level was $25,000 (to sponsor an interview room). This is a level of funding that most large corporations can manage from their annual campus relations budget without seeking funding from the corporate foundation—an important consideration. We also offered donors the opportunity to pay down their pledge over a five-year period—an installment plan that further reduced the impact on their annual budgets. Packaging is everything.

Step 12: Identify likely donors and create attractive events to cement the relationship

After initial contacts are made, it is desirable to create a series of attractive events to which potential corporate sponsors are invited. The most obvious of these for large universities will be athletic events—especially football and basketball games, where potential donors can be "wined and dined" in stadium skyboxes where they hobnob with university officials and are encouraged to become donors. The range of such events may vary depending on the interests of the potential donor groups. We created our events around football games, basketball games, professional baseball games, and NASCAR races, but musical and theatre performances, famous lecture series, and other interest areas are also possibilities. These events were jointly sponsored by our university development office and our lead donor. Once potential donors participate in such events, they are likely to feel obligated to move from potential to confirmed donor status.

Step 13: Secure written pledges from donors

The next step in the process is to secure written pledges from donors who have made verbal commitments. For the most part, this is merely a formality as nearly all verbal commitments are typically converted to firm written pledges. Your active participation in the fundraising process is now over. From this point forward, written pledges will be managed by the development office staff. They will maintain meticulous records, collect and deposit the donor checks as they are received, and issue polite reminders to donors if they fail to deliver on their pledges in timely fashion.

Step 14: Implement your project

The fundraising complete, you may relax and enjoy the construction phase of your project. While this phase has its own challenges, they are not the subject of this chapter. The final phase is described below.

Step 15: Dedicate your project

While it might seem that your project is complete, there is one final step in the fundraising process and it might be the most important of all— dedicating your project. This is the culminating event, and must be handled formally and tastefully while according appropriate recognition to donors, trustees, university administration, and career center staff. Most large institutions will have a development office staff member who specializes in coordinating these events to assure that your project dedication will be executed in keeping with university protocol. If it is done correctly, everyone will leave the dedication ceremony feeling good about their contributions to and participation in the project.

Lessons learned along the way

You cannot conduct a major fundraising campaign without learning a lot about yourself, your donors, and the fundraising process. Here are a few key lessons learned along the way:

Raising money for a project that you truly believe in is one of the most rewarding things you will ever do

Many people are reluctant to become involved in fundraising because they think it is a "dirty" business akin to selling patent medicine door to door. They have bad memories of having read "Death of a Salesman," and they shudder at the thought of asking for money. What we found is that if you truly believe that a project is for the greater good, the easiest thing in the world is to solicit support for that project from others who share in your belief and who stand to benefit from the successful implementation of the project.

Successfully raising money gives you serious leverage

You will be amazed at the clout that attends raising your own funds in support of capital projects. Everyone in the academic community will take you more seriously.

- You will be able to stand up to physical plant staff when they want to "value engineer" some of your most wanted features out of your plans.
- If there's one thing that administrators understand it's that "money talks." They're likely to be more appreciative than ever of your office.
- Faculty are very good at spending money but they are awe-inspired by staff who actually demonstrate the ability to raise money. You will find they are totally mystified and impressed that you have been able to control your destiny by raising your own funds for capital projects.
- Funding your own capital projects will give you newfound respect throughout the university community.

Stay in touch with your donors—they can help you in ways you'll never imagine

Once you have gained firm commitments from donors, it is important to keep them apprised of project progress. We mounted a web camera at our building site so that donors could "watch the construction progress." As issues develop (and they will) with members of central administration, the architect, or physical plant staff, donors can be powerful allies to assure that the project progresses as you wish. Corporate executives have access to university central administration that you as a university staff member simply do not have. Put simply, your university president will listen to your lead donor and provide him/her with access and project input that you simply won't have. Keep stroking the hand that feeds you!

Establish explicit stewardship parameters—stewardship issues will exist forever, so don't make promises you can't keep

No donation is ever made without some expectation on the part of the donor. The important thing is that you not promise anything to a donor that you are not prepared to deliver. Never promise anything in perpetuity—because nothing is forever. Be explicit with donors about the benefits they will receive in return for their contributions. In most cases, that will include recognition on a plaque in the lobby of the building. It may also include a naming opportunity of a particular room or space within the new building. Some other benefits may also be offered such as discounts on career fair fees, or preference on booking interview rooms. All such benefits may seem reasonable; just be sure not to over promise, because you will have to deliver and donors can be powerful enforcers!

Development officers can help, but in the end YOU must be actively involved

Many career center staff and university staff in general seem to think that the sole responsibility for securing donor support rests with development office staff and that they need not get involved in the development process. Nothing could be farther from the truth in our experience. The primary responsibility for the success of your capital campaign will rest squarely with the career center director. After all, you are the one who had the vision for the project, you are the one who stands to benefit most from securing the necessary funding support, and you will be responsible for stewardship once the donations have been received and your project is complete. No one cares more than you about this project, and if you can't bring energy and enthusiasm to the fundraising process, no one else is likely to do so.

Involve your staff early and often—that's how you secure their "buy-in" and support

During the fundraising process, everyone on your staff becomes a development officer. The more ownership members of your staff feel toward your project, the more willingly they will pitch in and do what needs to be done to raise the funds that will be necessary. You've often heard it said "Every success has many parents, every failure is an orphan." This aphorism is gospel when it comes to fundraising—get your staff to believe they are parents. There is no more powerful fundraising organization than a staff that has been deeply involved and committed to the planning and execution of your project from the very beginning. Involve them early and often.

Be prepared to compromise....because you will

No matter how much you raise, there will be pressure to keep the cost of your project down. No matter how modest your plan, efforts will be made to further reduce cost and compromise on size, quality, design, and so forth. The physical plant operatives will call it "value engineering"—a euphemism for doing it on the cheap. Don't compromise on the big things, but you will need to be ready and willing to make some compromises. Choose them wisely.

Finally, remember that once you demonstrate you can fund your own capital projects, it will become an expectation

Private fundraising can be one of the most demanding yet most rewarding processes in which a career center can engage. The risks are significant but so are the rewards. Go forth and "show them the money"!

Assessment in Career Services

Pat Carretta and Sam Ratcliffe

Introduction

Voices both inside and outside of higher education are demanding better evidence of students' learning and indicators of the value of their experiences. Keeling, et al. (2008) suggested they are seeking data in response to crucial yet difficult questions: 1) So what? 2) What difference does it all make? and 3) Was it worth it?

Consistent with the increased expectations for higher education institutions to demonstrate both accountability and value, the field of career services is at a crossroads. The more discerning scrutiny of stakeholders and audiences for career services has created expectations for success metrics, whether those metrics are developed by career services practitioners themselves, or by others.

A key metric prevalent today, one with significant external influences, has to do with graduate outcomes, specifically the employment, continuing education, and other plans of those students receiving degrees. While such outcomes are essentially institutional outcomes reflecting the multiple inputs and influencers of the institutional experience for students, career services is viewed by many as a major influencer of such outcomes. Consequently, the relevance and prominence of career services on many campuses is growing.

Evolving accountability expectations for career services

Just as career services units have evolved from placement offices into centers offering comprehensive services and programs, expectations for demonstrating accountability have become progressively more complex and important. The approach to accountability and assessment is becoming increasingly multi-faceted. During the last several years, there has been a migration from demonstrating productivity (e.g. activities and student contacts), to adding satisfaction measures for indicating effectiveness, to defining desired student learning outcomes, and documenting specific institutional or unit influences on the achievement of those outcomes.

On many campuses, the traditional focus has been on student-centered education where the emphasis has been on developing an educated citizen. Career services programs have added value to the academic experience and promoted well-rounded education for students. However, measurement of the actual influence of career services on student outcomes has often been inferential and indirect.

Meeting current accountability expectations means career services practitioners have to be mission-focused, politically savvy, and astute in demonstrating unit effectiveness. We need to be able to defend specific desired outcomes, assessment/evaluation strategies, and improvement-oriented decisions based on the results. Meeting accountability expectations has become a more strategic focus in recent years. Not only do career services professionals need to develop assessment and accountability expertise, but we also need to be more sophisticated, proactive, and self-directed in planning and implementing successful accountability strategies.

Evolution of assessment

As accountability expectations have changed, so have the types of assessment and related strategies. Previously, much of our assessment experience has focused on processes and operational outcomes. As career services professionals, we have traditionally collected and reported information about student utilization of services, programs, and resources. However, such data, when reported in aggregate numbers, do not lend themselves to discerning patterns and trends for utilization. For example, appointments are often reported in total numbers with little or no information indicating the number of unique clients, populations represented, who is participating and just as importantly who is not, the benefit of the appointment, and what intervention strategies might be appropriate.

We have also reported satisfaction data from clients using our services, programs, and resources, typically collecting data using Likert scales indicating the happiness or contentment of students engaged with our offices and the degree of helpfulness. Some have even migrated from student satisfaction to student reflection on the quality of their experiences, especially using student responses to indicate growth in areas such as learning and self-understanding.

Another assessment area familiar to most career services practitioners is that of needs assessment—ascertaining what services, programs, and resources are needed by students. Although such assessment is presumed by stakeholders, a question on a number of campuses is the frequency and substantive nature of needs assessment activities. Or, put another way, reflect on the last time you did a meaningful needs assessment to guide decisions about the portfolio of programs, services, and resources. What did you learn, and what decisions did you make? This may be the next big emphasis in assessment, as accrediting authorities and stakeholders have increasing interest in the evidence of need to support the types of programs, services, and resources offered.

Traditional assessment metrics, i.e., utilization, participation/attendance, satisfaction, outputs, efficiency and credits, do matter: Sound operations help create positive student experiences, which lead to student success. Without sound operations and processes, institutions and the experiences they provide to students will not be as effective. So we need to continue monitoring and documenting processes as part of an effective assessment strategy.

There has also been a migration from formative (process) methods to impact (outcome) methods—a move from satisfaction, counting, and efficiency measures to measuring changes in the learner. The practice of assessment has developed from being relatively non-invasive to being more invasive. Instead of simply asking whether the train gets there on time, we now ask whether the train gets to the right place (Keeling, 2009). Outcomes assessment is very complex, particularly student learning outcomes, which help indicate what impact our services, programs, and resources have on student learning. Producing evidence of student learning requires clear and measurable outcomes and expertise in developing appropriate and direct assessment strategies to show the progress toward such outcomes.

A business approach is increasingly being applied in higher education—one that requires practitioners to assess needs and deliver services with a demonstrated positive impact on institutional priorities, especially student learning. It can certainly be argued that student learning and development represent the product of higher education as a business. Both stakeholders and related audiences are asking whether the return on investment in higher education institutions is identifiable and acceptable.

Process, operational, and outcome assessment results are necessary for strategic planning, program evaluation, and continuous improvement, and to strengthen customer satisfaction. In addition, with data about process and operational efficiency and effectiveness, quality of service, and impact on learning, career services practitioners will be better able to define desired outcomes, inform policy and planning decisions, procure and reallocate resources, benchmark best practices, manage stakeholder expectations, and advance the mission and goals of the institution (Keeling, 2006b).

Professional challenges

Meeting expectations for accountability will require that we address a litany of related and key questions. Representative questions might include: Who do I serve? What do they want? What do they need? What can I offer? How can I reach them? To whom am I accountable and how? How well am I managing these expectations? How will I know when I am successful? How do I communicate those successes to stakeholders and audiences?

Because career services professionals play an important role in providing quality learning and development experiences for students, we must be strategic in producing evidence of the student learning taking place through involvement in career services activities. Four questions about the work of career services should be considered: What skills and attributes are necessary for success in the workplace? What will students learn through our programs and services? How do these student learning outcomes align with institutional and divisional goals? How can we document it?

Career services practitioners are now required to offer clear evidence regarding the learning and development we facilitate and the differences we make for students. The work we do must reflect an acceptable return on the investments made by key stakeholders. To do so requires that we develop the capacity to effectively use assessment to guide our planning and decision-making and to use the results to educate stakeholders on what we are doing and why. That is our professional responsibility and one of the criteria that distinguishes us as professional educators instead of merely service providers.

Current assessment issues

Calls for accountability and transparency, as well as pressures on institutions to address costs, access, and tangible results of students' educational experiences, will require frequent communication to stakeholders about the value and impact of career services and its contributions to the educational mission of the institution (Student Affairs Leadership Council, 2009). To do so successfully, we must understand what information stakeholder groups expect and value, and anticipate how to best present that data using context, language, and success metrics that are meaningful to both career services and the stakeholders.

Stakeholders

Given the variety of stakeholders and audiences seeking or expecting information about the work of career services (e.g., students' success in securing employment, outcome of recruiting activities of major employers, or impact of counseling on students' major/career decision-making), a single report or message is unlikely to suffice. For the purposes of demonstrating accountability and value the terms *stakeholder* and *audience* are synonymous and sometimes used interchangeably—they are all key influencers in the work we do. To effectively convey outcomes, value, and effectiveness to each audience, it is imperative that we take a proactive approach in identifying the audiences' expectations and in developing assessment strategies that produce data relevant to those expectations. As practitioners, we need to: 1) identify key stakeholders within and outside the institution, 2) understand their focus and priorities, 3) consider what career services operational success looks like from each stakeholder group's perspective and connect the work of career services to those expectations, 4) build alliances with those who can help produce informative data related to success criteria, and 5) use data to demonstrate explicitly the impact of career services in ways and with language that resonates with the stakeholders.

Internal stakeholders

Obvious key internal stakeholders for career services include the president's cabinet, senior leaders in student and academic affairs, academic deans and faculty members, and trustees. Career services should also consider its relationship to the following individuals or units and how to best inform and engage them: institutional research and assessment, student government, faculty senate, alumni relations, development, university and external relations, enrollment services (especially the dean of admissions), parent and family programs, office of budget/finance, and research and economic development. Why these particular individuals or units? They are included because they meet one or more of the criteria for identifying key stakeholders:

1. Shares a commitment to student learning and improving the quality of the student experience in and outside the classroom (e.g., faculty, student affairs)
2. Is in a position to help disseminate the information about the value and impact of career services to other key constituencies (e.g., faculty senate, student government, parent and family programs)
3. Can put to good use the body of knowledge, evidence, and outcome data from career services (e.g., admissions, university relations, development, academic deans)
4. Can assist in obtaining, understanding, and producing informative data (e.g., institutional research and assessment, alumni affairs, research and economic development, office of budget/finance)
5. Is in a senior leadership/decision-making role or position of influence within the institution (e.g., president's cabinet, academic deans, trustees)

External stakeholders

External stakeholders include parents and families, alumni, employers, accrediting organizations, and government agencies. Much of the push for accountability comes from escalating stakeholder expectations for institutional demonstration of the need, quality, efficiency, and effectiveness of specific programs and services. Accrediting agencies have played a key role in promulgating many of these outcomes measurement expectations (Ratcliffe, 2008).

Some of those expectations are driven by federal regulations. For example, the Southern Association of Colleges and Schools (SACS) accrediting agency requires evidence of student learning and development:

> "...the institution provides student support programs, services, and activities consistent with its mission that are intended to promote student learning and enhance the development of its students." (SACS, 2012, p. 20)

In response to federal statutes, SACS (2012, p. 39) requires documentation that the institution "evaluates success with respect to student achievement consistent with its mission," and includes job placement rates as an example of evidence that could demonstrate achievement.

As the accreditation example illustrates, career services practitioners are accountable to stakeholders for processes and outcomes by providing information that demonstrates both operational and mission effectiveness. Operational effectiveness considers such areas as utilization, quality, satisfaction, and efficiency, and answers this question: What happened? Mission effectiveness considers learning outcomes and addresses two questions: What changed? And, how are students different (Keeling, 2008)?

Alignment with institutional priorities

To be successful in demonstrating operational and mission effectiveness to stakeholders, career services should align its assessment practices with institutional and divisional priorities. This will require mapping its mission, goals and activities to those of the division and the institution in order to determine how it contributes to the body of evidence at the divisional and institutional level, and where the gaps exist. A good place to start is with strategic plans and the degree to which career services strategic priorities are aligned with them. The following questions will help guide career services through the alignment process:

- To which divisional and institutional goals and objectives is career services best linked?
- What career programs, services or activities contribute to division and institutional goals and objectives?
- To which goals and objectives would the impact or outcome of career programs, services and activities matter?
- What learning outcomes have the division and the institution identified, and to what extent does the work of career services contribute to those learning outcomes?
- How do data on utilization, success rates, or satisfaction by students or employers align with division or institutional priorities?

Key performance indicators

What should emerge are strategic areas of focus to guide the development of key performance indicators salient to division and institutional goals and an assessment plan to measure, track, and report. For example, an institutional goal might assure student access to an affordable college education; or enhance the teaching and learning opportunities, environments, and support for an increasingly talented student body (George Mason University, 2008). To align with this strategic goal, career services would map programs and activities that "enhance learning opportunities" and contribute to the development of a "talented student body." The assessment plan should define and describe expected outcomes, key performance indicators or metrics (quantitative and/or qualitative), and a success standard that can be measured annually and tracked over the duration of the strategic plan. Performance indicators are quantitative, practical measures that show direction and are used to inform planning efforts, support decision-making, and to effect change (Wikipedia, 2012). For example, a key performance indicator or metric for "talented student body" could be the employment of baccalaureate degree recipients as reported at time of graduation. The success standard could be defined as: new graduates of the institution reporting employment at time of graduation will exceed national average of institutions with enrollment over 20,000 (as reported by NACE) by 10 percent (George Mason University, 2012). This example uses data collected locally and nationally. Comparisons could also be made with peer institutions.

Other key performance indicators (KPI) common to career services include counselor to student ratio, number of programs and/or attendance at each, on-campus employment activities/opportunities, internships available, employer participation/contacts, career fair satisfaction for employers/students, number of employers/students at career fair, job placement/graduate placement rates, usage of facilities/services (in-person, phone, online), alumni involvement/usage of services, counseling/staff satisfaction (CampusLabs, 2011). If campus diversity is a strategic priority for the institution or division, career services should consider a KPI showing participation of underrepresented students and the establishment of targets for increased participation by these students. Many institutions are focusing on the sophomore student and persistence to junior level. To demonstrate the impact career services can have on retention of sophomores, career services could collect data on sophomores participating in programs such as major and career exploration, externships, internship readiness; follow up with the registrar the next academic year on who persisted; and then ask those students about the extent to which their participation in career services programs made a difference. Did a greater percentage of the sophomores participating in career services programs continue into their junior year than sophomores who did not participate?

Mining existing data

Career services practitioners have often been in a reactive mode to requests from stakeholders, responding on an ad hoc basis rather than anticipating questions, seeking help from experts, and gathering information in advance. Many at the institution can provide assistance in gathering and interpreting data: the registrar, institutional research, institutional assessment, alumni affairs, and office of development. Data may already exist from national or institutional surveys such as the NSSE. Career services should ask for help in mining data from existing surveys, and work collaboratively to collect and share data by requesting inclusion of key questions on surveys and combining survey efforts to increase response rates. As useful data and sources of information are identified, consider creating a data warehouse or repository comprised of data currently accessible through others and through career services' own databases. Additionally, consider questions internal and external stakeholders could ask. Being prepared to offer access to your data and knowing what data to seek will help in identifying and developing assessment and research partnerships with others. Career services should also consider the assistance faculty can provide, especially those whose teaching or research interests intersect with career services mission and outcomes. Faculty assistance could include collaboration or consultation on a project, referral to career services of graduate students engaged in a related thesis or dissertation, or access to courses enrolling student populations that are targets of your assessment plan.

In addition to closely monitoring students, employers, and key performance indicators, career services should closely follow local, regional, and national trends on work force, job hiring, and other key factors. Data and trend analysis resources might include faculty in economics, business, or policy at your institution; government agencies (e.g., economic development); business groups (e.g., chambers, trade associations); professional associations (e.g., NACE, NASPA, ACPA Commission VI); centers and institutes conducting annual studies (e.g., Collegiate Employment Research Institute at Michigan State University, Center on Education and Workforce at Georgetown University, Center for Cooperative Education Research and Innovation at the University of Cincinnati); and other career services and benchmark institutions.

Through purposeful assessment and analysis of student and programmatic outcomes and trends, career services positions itself to inform and educate students, faculty, parents, and campus administrators; to influence policy and decision-makers; and to guide continued quality improvement of programs and services.

The assessment process

A number of common words or themes are embedded in most definitions that may be used to describe assessment. Some of these key terms are process, systematic, information, evidence, improvement, outcomes, programs, and student learning and development.

Effective assessment reveals a number of salient qualities as noted by Bresciani (2006):

- Understood by practitioners and stakeholders
- Inclusive—involves as many as possible
- Practitioner, specialist, or expert driven
- Manageable in that it considers varying resources
- Flexible in that it factors in assessment learning curves
- Truth-seeking, objective, and ethical
- Providing evidence of proof and informing decisions for continuous improvement
- Promoting a culture of accountability, learning, and improvement

Assessment needs to be embedded in the work we do, and it requires reflection on what we believe our programs and services are to accomplish—it is the establishment of a systematic process that will answer certain questions on a continuous basis. Bresciani, et al. (2004) posited such questions are also reflective of the assessment cycle and might include the following:

- What are we trying to do and why?
- What is our program supposed to accomplish?
- What do we want students to be able to do and/or know as a result of our course/workshop/program/service?
- How well are we doing it?
- How do we know?
- How do we use that information to improve or celebrate successes?

- Do the improvements we make contribute to our intended end results?

These questions also cause practitioners to ask why programs exist and even if they should continue. Responding to such questions is the essence of the iterative or repetitive nature of the assessment process and indicative of the transparency, evidence-based decision making, continuous improvement, and closing the assessment loop on assessment initiatives as required by key stakeholders.

Outcomes based assessment

Components of an outcomes-based assessment plan

What are the typical components of an outcomes-based assessment plan, and how do the pieces fit together? Representative template elements for an assessment plan might include the following (Bresciani, 2006):

- Program Name and Description
- Program Mission or Purpose: These terms can be the same as each is intended to communicate the essence of your organization to stakeholders and to provide a framework for developing goals and outcomes
- Goals: Program goals should align with your strategic plan, institutional goals, division goals, and even department goals. Note: Goals and objectives may be synonymous in that both generally describe what the program is to accomplish. Objectives are essentially the detailed aspects of broader goals.
- Outcomes: Program outcomes and student learning outcomes
- Planning for Delivery of Outcomes: Includes concept mapping within the context of your strategic plan objectives
- Evaluation Methods: Include criteria for each outcome and include any necessary limitations
- Implementation of the Assessment Process
  - ✓ Identify who is responsible for completing each step of the evaluation process.
  - ✓ Outline implementation timetable.

✓ Identify who will be evaluated.
✓ Identify who will be assisting in the evaluation.
✓ Identify who will participate in data analysis and making recommendations or decisions.

There will likely be some differences in definitions of these items among different campuses. This illustrates the need to define these terms on our own campuses so there is a common language across units, programs, and even divisions.

Goals

Goals and objectives both generally describe what the program intends to accomplish. They are broad general statements of 1) what the program intends students will be able to know or do, and 2) what the program will do to ensure students will be able to do and know. They are evaluated by measuring specific outcomes related to each. Goals are also related to the mission and objectives of the institution and division.

A series of questions should be considered for each goal that has been created (Bresciani, 2006):

- Is it meaningful?
- Is it important?
- Is it a broad general statement of what the program wants or will do to ensure students will be able to do and know?
- Is it related to my department or program mission and objectives?
- Is there an accompanying outcome to measure this goal?

Outcomes

Outcomes are more specific, detailed, and measurable statements derived from goals (and objectives) and describe desired performance. Each outcome is linked to a goal (and objective), and enables you to operationalize that goal by describing what you want the end results of your efforts to be. Outcomes may be linked to and supportive of more than one goal, and there may be more than one outcome for each goal or objective.

Career services practitioners might consider a 3-M approach to outcome assessment, a tactic that emphasizes outcomes be meaningful, measurable, and manageable (Bresciani, et al, 2004). For each outcome, the following questions should be considered:

Is it meaningful?

- What is significant about what the outcome addresses?
- Will stakeholders likely understand and value what is being measured and how specific knowledge and skills will be demonstrated?
- Will stakeholders know who the target audience is?
- What does the outcome mean to internal and external stakeholders?
- Is the outcome linked to an espoused institutional or divisional value, priority, or concern?
- Will it provide you with the evidence that will help to make decisions related to continuous improvement?
- Will stakeholders know when the outcome is met and how it is linked to continuous improvement?

Is it measureable?

- Beyond counting the results, can you identify or observe the point when the outcome is met? Is the outcome observable or identifiable?
- What does meeting this outcome look like?
- Will the measurement strategies be understood by and of value to stakeholders?
- How well does the outcome lend itself to measurement? Does it need to be refined?
- Which measurement strategies will be robust enough to be accepted by stakeholders as valid?

Is it manageable?

- Can it be incorporated into the department routine and into the assessment cycle?

- Is staff capacity sufficient to effectively conduct assessment of specific outcomes? If not, how would you build it?
- Do you have the means and resources to deliver and evaluate the intended outcomes?
- Can you incorporate assessment of outcomes into the daily business of the career services operation?
- Can you create habits of assessment by embedding assessment of outcomes into programs and services?
- Can you build an outcomes assessment program incrementally over a period of years?

Your plan will most likely include assessment of program outcomes as well as student learning outcomes.

Program outcomes

Program outcomes describe functions and operations and address process, operational, or procedural initiatives such as need, satisfaction, utilization, efficiency, adequacy, and quality. Program outcomes include efficiency and effectiveness measures, comparisons to others, and compliance with standards for the profession. They essentially illustrate what you intend for your program to accomplish.

- Who uses our services? User assessment provides information about students, alumni, employers, and other constituency groups. Examples of assessment data might include individual appointments, internship/co-op participation, workshop/program participation, job fairs, website visits, resume database registrants, on-campus interviews, and graduation surveys. Just as importantly, user assessment helps identify those who are not using our services, programs, and facilities so intervention strategies can be developed.

- Are our services meeting their needs? Needs assessment provides data about the need for and current use of services, products, facilities, or information. It also provides client perceptions about key issues and indicates whether their needs are being met.

- How satisfied are our students and other clientele? Satisfaction assessment helps determine whether student/other client experience are of high quality and consistent with mission, and it is linked to needs assessment. Example of surveys might include graduating students, individual appointments/advising, programs and workshops, job fairs (students and employers), and recruiting programs (students and employers).

- How cost effective are our programs and services? An analysis of costs helps determine whether programs and services be delivered more efficiently and effectively and whether some should be continued.

- How do our programs and services compare to those at similar institutions? Examples of comparative data include services and programs, populations served, staffing, budget, facilities, sources of funding, fee structures, technology resources and applications, policies and processes. Benchmark assessment helps practitioners learn how others achieve their results and to identify best practices.

- How well do our programs, resources, leadership, mission, technology, and other criteria meet nationally accepted professional standards such as CAS (2010) or NACE (2009)? A structured framework of standards and prescribed self-study process helps identify areas to improve and develop related strategies for enhancement.

Student outcomes

The terms *student outcomes* and *student learning outcomes* are often used interchangeably. Student learning outcomes are cognitive, as well as affective dimensions you desire your program to instill or enhance (Bresciani, et al., 2004). Komives, et al. (2006) suggested these outcomes usually identify growth in some dimension of knowing, being, or doing, and such dimensions include knowledge (cognitive), attitude (affective), and skill (psychomotor). In essence, a student learning outcome is what any student should be able to do, know, or value as a result of engaging in the learning experience (Keeling, 2007).

Assessment of student satisfaction, needs, and service utilization is important. These indicators can help illustrate the helpfulness of a program or service. However, assessing satisfaction does not tell you how your program contributes to student development and learning, and the findings seldom help you make decisions for continuous improvement. But there has been a shift away from reliance on satisfaction indicators as the primary way to set priorities and plan allocation of resources. The premise for this shift is that outcomes matter more than immediate indicators of satisfaction. Certainly, practitioners should account for satisfaction and effectiveness, but emphasize outcomes. If outcomes are the priority and the outcomes are achieved, constituents will have abundant reasons to be satisfied (Keeling, 2006b).

Telling the accountability story and demonstrating value

Communicate and educate

Traditionally, career services practitioners have focused on providing information that stakeholders require—an emphasis on communication. But what happens if stakeholders, left to their own devices, fail to adequately "connect the dots" of the career services success story, fully understanding what was done, why, and the impact it had on those served?

A major challenge for career services practitioners is how to document excellence in our contributions to student learning; how to show the value of our programs and services; and how to be accountable to our diverse stakeholders. What matters or makes a difference in the work we do? Five key areas include quality of service, satisfaction of our customers, efficiency and effectiveness, outcomes or what difference our work makes in the long term, and goals that advance the mission and purposes of the university (Keeling, et al., 2008).

To tell the career services success story well, practitioners need to provide context for the career services story—describing the goals, objectives, intended outcomes, results of activities, and impact of specific programs and services. Such context will educate stakeholders and position them to better understand and use the information that will follow. This is a critical first step that is often overlooked in reporting to that group.

Reframing the story to improve accountability

Accountability links professional practice and effectiveness. As practitioners, our ongoing professional development should include attention to the value of documenting and enhancing the work we do. In telling the career services story to stakeholders, we should consider three key factors: transparency, evidence-based practice, and continuous improvement emphasis.

Transparency

Some career services practitioners fear assessment and view it as a pass/fail exercise, and, not wanting to appear lacking, approach reporting with some trepidation. Assessment is a strategic initiative and fundamentally a situational snapshot from which decisions will be made leading to longitudinal improvement.

Telling our career services success story connotes explaining the work we do, and the specific differences it makes, in ways that constituents can understand and remember. How we tell that story is to describe, record, measure, and document our experiences—to show what we did and accomplished, and what we still need to do (Keeling, et al., 2008). Authentic data collection, analysis, and reporting are vital to the process.

Transparency is important in building stakeholder trust and confidence in our ability to make effective planning and evaluation decisions leading to continuous improvement. It is critical to develop a system of transparency where the processes of planning, data collection/ analysis, evaluation, and decision making are such that stakeholders understand what is happening and why; and building trust to a level where stakeholders trust career services professionals to evaluate as they would if the processes were not transparent (Bresciani, 2007). Within the institution, transparency is vital for career services to maintain autonomy in doing business as it determines to be the best, and also to report information in such a way that top administrators understand the unit's impact on overall student learning and development.

Evidence-based decision-making

There are two key questions to consider for meeting accountability expectations. *"How well are we doing our work?"* requires indicators of quality. *"How well can we demonstrate that to others?"* requires indicators of performance effectiveness, fiscal efficiency, and resource productivity. Addressing these questions helps deal with the emphasis of regional accrediting agencies on research-based planning and data-driven decision making, with appropriate supporting documentation.

The best information source for career services professionals is evidence—an intentional purposeful aggregation of data with which to support decision-making and policy. Evidence-based practice requires a systemic view, one linking multiple program elements to strategic directions. Sharing with stakeholders the evidence we use for making decisions is a powerful educational strategy that supersedes previous impressions they may have held about our work (Keeling, 2006).

Bresciani (2006) suggested that it is reasonable for stakeholders to ask career services practitioners the following questions:

- What decisions did you make about your program last year?
- What evidence did you use to inform that decision?
- What was it that you were trying to influence about your program when making that decision with the stated evidence?

Intentionality is critical to establish program goals/objectives, compile evidence, and make related decisions. There are clear stakeholder expectations for research-based planning and data-driven decision making.

Continuous improvement focus

Overarching everything we do in career services should be a commitment to continuous improvement; that should be evident in the story we tell stakeholders. For practitioners undergoing regional accreditation review, the terminology describing a process of "closing the assessment loop" will become familiar. In essence, it is a multi-year ongoing feedback process to support continuous improvement initiatives.

For example, your office offers a new program or service. At the end of the event (or semester/year), you review your research-based assessment data (systematically gathered evidence). From that evidence, you make specific observations and draw definitive conclusions. You then plan detailed actions for improvement, and, at the end of the next event or reporting cycle, collect assessment data and evaluate the impact or consequence of the improvement action taken. Was the desired improvement achieved and if so, what does it mean? If not, what alternative actions might be taken to gain the desired improvement?

The development of a multi-year ongoing assessment/feedback plan will help provide the data needed to understand the impact of specific improvement initiatives. And, it will provide evidence to stakeholders of your overarching commitment to continuous improvement—something they will certainly expect.

Developing an outcomes-based assessment report

A significant conundrum for career services professionals is how to take various, sometimes even disparate, types of assessment data and use that information to construct a story for stakeholders that will demonstrate accountability and value. When it comes to reporting strategies, it is critical to know your data and to know your audience. Then develop the story and identify meaningful indicators to shape the story—scrutinizing the indicators for patterns and trends. Bresciani (2006) recommended that practitioners begin the story with the end in mind and be sure to involve end users in the process.

Bresciani (2006) noted that some typical components of an outcome-based assessment report might include:

- Program Name
- Desired Outcomes
- Results: Summarize the results of each outcome, along with the process to validate and verify the results.
- Decisions and Recommendations
  - ✓ Summarize the decisions and recommendations made for each outcome.
  - ✓ Identify the groups involved in the evidence discussions leading to the decisions and recommendations.
  - ✓ Summarize suggestions for improving the assessment process.
  - ✓ If outcomes are to be retained in the next assessment cycle, identify when each will be evaluated again.
  - ✓ Identify parties responsible for implementing recommended changes.

Your presentation should be geared to the audience, so be careful with complexity and simplify language whenever possible. Provide interpretation, identify convergent findings, discuss discrepancies, and emphasize implications of results as you tell the story. Language can be a landmine—use clear, concise language. Minimize text and use graphics creatively to capture and maintain attention of the readers.

As much as possible, organize reports around issues, not solely around the data you have. Interpret data so that it informs program improvement, budgeting, planning, decision making, or policies. Collect and present data that will help you make decisions for ongoing improvement.

Building capacity for assessment

Building success in assessment requires motivation, commitment, and capacity for those involved in the process. Staff enthusiasm and dedication are not enough—without sufficient capacity, assessment initiatives will fail.

Capacity is not a simple quality, and building capacity is not an easy task.

Among the challenges for practitioners as noted by Keeling (2006b) are:

- Understanding the meaning, importance, and purpose of defining and assessing student outcomes.
- Translating the daily work and goals of the department into manageable elements of assessment and practice.
- Creating assessment plans with metrics and indicators that fit organically in the work and strategies of the functional unit.
- Developing competency for training other staff members.
- Demonstrating administrative resiliency in dealing with the inevitable problems and impediments.
- Generating comfort with the collection, analysis, and management of data.
- The requirement of new knowledge, skills, and attitudes associated with building a culture of evidence and outcome assessment.
- Professional development and training with abundant opportunities for practice are vital—manuals are helpful for this but not most effective.
- A curricular approach uniting concepts of learning outcomes, assessment/evaluation methods, data collection/analysis, and interpreting/reporting results is recommended.

Career services directors will need a strong understanding of assessment and capacity to engage their staff in assessing co-curricular learning. Directors can build staff understanding and capacity by offering professional training, holding staff accountable, including assessment work in each staff member's position description, encouraging staff to work collaboratively, rewarding staff members who develop expertise, and insisting that new hires have assessment experience.

A practical assessment model

Career services professionals are generally adept at benchmarking and identification of best practices—or, put another way, they usually grasp the *"what I need to do"* in assessment, but sometimes struggle with the *"how do I go about it?"* implementation question. Assessment planning is complex and intensive, with multiple phases and a dynamic set of interconnected activities. Keeling et al. (2008) offered a 10-step practical model for assessment, emphasizing planning in stages, which can serve as guide in developing a culture of assessment within career services:

Stage1 This may include steps 1-3 listed to the right. During this stage, a foundation is established that anchors and provides ballast to future assessment activities	1. Determine who within the institution, division, or department will take leadership of assessment activities; clearly communicate the dimensions of that person's leadership role and expectations. This role is often defined as that of an "assessment champion."
	2. Consider the talents, aptitudes, and areas of expertise present among colleagues and establish an assessment team to work closely with the leader and also with other faculty or staff.
	3. Develop an internal capacity-building strategy that provides staff and faculty with accurate information, introduces them to key concepts of student learning, student development, and assessment practice; decide what elements of this strategy will be addressed by formal, intentional professional development and training, and what components will require either hands-on practice within the structure of existing positions and roles or self-study.
Stage 2	4. Create a glossary of terms that bring clarity and common

During this stage, which includes steps 4 and 5, an infrastructure emerges. The creation of a glossary will result in a common language. But more importantly, the process of developing the glossary allows time and resources to be devoted to asking important questions, engaging in discourse that brings clarity and rationale to assessment activities. Step 5 brings common concerns to the table and should include candid conversation about perceptions and realities of who on campus "owns" assessment; how assessment differs from institutional research; the roles of faculty, staff, and administrators, and their respective strengths and weaknesses.

understanding to pertinent concepts; make that glossary easily accessible. It is more important to have consistency within the institution than to make the institution's terms exactly the same as those of some other institution or professional organization.

5. Consider and respond to potential barriers, impediments, and challenges, including power dynamics, internal departmental or institutional politics, and various manifestations of change resistance.

Stage 3

This stage includes steps 6 through 8, which are processes of inquiry and assessment with which to inform the assessment plan. Important questions to ask during this stage include: Where do students naturally learn on our campus and in our community? What are the sociographics of our students? What is important to them? How do they learn? Why did they choose our institution? How can we best serve and educate them? What programs, student organizations, professional

6. Map existing campus and community resources—an institutional topography of learning.

7. Determine learning and developmental needs of students in relation to the institution's overall desired student learning outcomes.

8. Determine program strengths and areas of improvement—that is, define what programs address what areas of student learning

honoraries, and services are already in place to promote student learning and development? What programs and services could be enhanced? With what members of the faculty and staff should we develop partnerships?	and developmental needs, and then study the effectiveness of each of those programs in addressing those needs.
Stage 4 This stage incorporates the final two steps, 9 and 10, which synthesize much of the information gathered in the previous steps. Data about program and personnel talent can be arranged in a matrix that illustrates program names, departmental objectives, leadership, and professional development needs. In some ways, this stage is the culmination of all the planning. And at this point, the stage is set for developing and assessing student learning outcomes.	9. Develop an assessment curriculum, including a scope and sequence that describes and illustrates who will lead what program, what the learning outcomes are for each program, when and how learning will be assessed, and when and how data will be gathered, analyzed, and disseminated.
	10. Based on sound assessment data, evaluate the quality, or effectiveness, of programs and institute processes of sustainability or improvement.

Future of assessment

As much as assessment has become a critical part of the career services practitioner's world, there is much more that lies ahead in terms of assessment sophistication, documentation, analysis, and reporting. Schuh (2009) offered several observations regarding the future of assessment in student affairs and, by extension, career services. These include:

- The demand for program evaluation and accountability will continue to grow as stakeholders want to know the impact of programs and services in relation to the resources expended.

- There will be growing emphasis on assessment strategies that provide hard data to support claims of success in contributing to institutional, division, and unit goals.
- There will be increased use of institutional databases to answer assessment questions.
- Data-driven decision making will continue to grow in emphasis.
- Stakeholders will demand more transparency in assessment and reporting.
- Assessment studies will become increasingly sophisticated as predictive and analytical techniques will become more prevalent to augment descriptive techniques.
- Because of their perceived value, mixed method studies (qualitative and quantitative) will become more common.
- Upgrading assessment skills for practitioners will become a growth industry.
- There will be more use of technology in collecting assessment data.
- Human subject scrutiny by institutional review boards will continue to increase.
- Students will suffer from survey overload—practitioners will have to come up with alternative data collection strategies to augment surveys.

In many cases, we are already seeing evidence of these trends. Career services practitioners will be expected to develop and continually refine assessment skills and seek to embed assessment in our everyday work.

Closing thoughts

As we develop assessment expertise, our respective assessment efforts will become more proactive, decisive, and purposeful. Indeed, as professional educators, we should be influencing assessment direction and expectations for our departments. As functional area experts on our individual campuses, it seems then that we have a professional obligation to develop the expertise required to effectively assess our work and tell our story. In essence, that is our professional responsibility.

Keeling (2008b) suggested that telling our story signifies explaining the work we do, and the specific differences it makes, in ways that people who aren't us, or our professional colleagues, can understand and remember. How we tell that story is to describe, record, measure, and document our experiences—to show what we did and accomplished...and what we still need to do.

Effective assessment strategies help us tell that story. The challenge (and opportunity) is to embrace assessment and become accomplished in fully understanding our career services story built on assessment documentation, and its implications, before sharing that story with stakeholders. That is our responsibility as professional educators and demonstrates our expertise as career services practitioners in offering compelling evidence of the impact of our critically important work.

References

Bresciani, M.J., Zelna, C. L. & Anderson, J. A. (2004). *Assessing student learning and development: A handbook for practitioners.* Washington, DC: NASPA.

Bresciani, M. J. (2006)Assessing and accountability in student affairs. Presentation at the NASPA IV-E Conference, Oakbrook IL.

Bresciani, M. J. Using outcomes-based assessment for the improvement of student learning. NetResults. Retrieved August 27, 2008 from http://www.naspa.org/membership/mem/nr/article.cfm?id=1600.

CampusLabs. Buffalo, NY, 2011. Departmental Key Performance Indicators.

George Mason University Strategic Goals for 2014. May 2008. Retrieved from www.provost.gmu.edu.

George Mason University 2014 Strategic Planning Metrics. January 2012. Retrieved from www.provost.gmu.edu.

Keeling, R. P. (2006). Accountability, assessment & student success lessons and future designs. Presentation at the CAS National Symposium on Standards, Self-Assessment, and Student Learning Outcomes in Higher Education. Crystal City, VA.

Keeling, R. P. Reconsidering: Learning, educational outcomes, and the work of student affairs. Presentation at the University of Wisconsin-Whitewater, 2006(b).

Keeling, R. P. "Building a community of learners: Learning, accountability, and assessment reconsidered." Presentation at the University of South Florida, St. Petersburg, Florida, 2007.

Keeling, R.P., Wall, A.F., Underhile, R., and Dungy, G.J. (2008). *Assessment reconsidered: Institutional effectiveness for student success.* United States: International Center for Student Success and Institutional Accountability.

Keeling, R. P. (2008). Assessment reconsidered: Institutional effectiveness for student success. Presentation at the International Assessment and Retention Conference. Scottsdale AZ.

Keeling, R. P. (2009). Reconsidering: Learning, educational outcomes, and the work of student affairs. Presentation at the University of Wisconsin-Whitewater.

Komives, S.R. and Schoper, S. (2006). "Developing learning outcomes." In R. Keeling (Ed.). Learning reconsidered 2: Implementing a campus-wide focus on the student experience (pp. 17-41). Washington, DC: NASPA and ACPA.

Ratcliffe, R. S. (2008). "Demonstrating career services success: rethinking how we tell the story." NACE Journal, October, p. 43.

Schuh, J. H. (2009). Assessment methods for student affairs. San Francisco: Jossey-Bass.

Southern Association of Colleges and Schools Commission on Colleges. (2012). Principles of Accreditation: Foundations for Quality Enhancement. Decatur, Georgia, p. 20.

Student Affairs Leadership Council. (2009). The Data-Driven Student

Affairs Enterprise: Strategies and Best Practices for Instilling a Culture of Accountability. Washington, D.C.: The Advisory Board Company.

Wikipedia Online Encyclopedia, Retrieved August 12, 2012 from http://en.wikipedia.org/wiki/Performance_indicator.

Managing Technology

Chris Timm

Nearly every day, many career center directors receive e-mails, webinar invitations, marketing materials, and unsolicited phone calls, all related to various technology tools, applications, and services. These marketing overtures are expanded upon by vendors at conferences and the recommendations of peers advocating a particular service, product, or vendor. No one wants to fall behind with technology, but there is also trepidation for being the first adopter. It can be difficult to determine what is the next step.

Career center leaders have an important role related to technology. They serve as the primary catalyst for change. Leaders should be consistently visionary, considering what is on the horizon and often beyond it. Being visionary means also being a bit of a risk taker with a willingness to try new things without being assured of success. That visionary role is balanced with regular environmental scanning, organizational value identification, and regular communication with others. The leader looks for strategic partnerships that align with financial and human resources. The leader should be a role model by participating in educational programs that increase awareness of technology. The best leaders don't relegate technology usage to the "tech people" or the "young staff" but instead have a familiarity with the basic functions and need of such technology and go beyond casual user to decision-maker.

The most important thing for the career services leader to consider with any new technology, is how does this fit into the overall goals of the organization?

Some good questions to ask yourself are:

1. Does this technology duplicate or replace some other technology currently in use? This is an important step as career services staff are often quick to add a laundry list of possible tools but are not

always good at helping evaluate and focus on the best tools. Our stakeholders look to us to help them navigate the maze of options and prioritize those best for their needs. This review may result in eliminating some tools in favor of those more effective. A good environmental scan also may be helpful to see if the technology is being used elsewhere in the community or campus. Libraries, for example, may already provide this resource, and a discussion of who is in the best position to be the primary provider of the resource may be needed.

2. Does this technology enhance operations? In other words, does it add value to something you are already doing? In some cases, the new technology may improve services for stakeholders such as students, employers, or faculty. But it may also enhance operations internally and improve the work environment for staff.

3. Is this technology needed? This one is difficult as career centers did quite well years ago armed with clipboards and notebooks. Again, this goes back to the strategic direction of the office. Does this technology fill a stated gap? Does it propel your office forward? There may be a tendency to select the "shiny object" without considering the need and purpose of the technology.

4. How much support will this technology need? Vendors may minimize the level of support needed for their product. Consider the support needed for the initial implementation of the tool but also take into account the ongoing training and support. For example, if the tool requires dissemination of a username and password, who in your office will be responsible for providing that? Who is the backup for that approval? What checks will be needed to ensure that access is granted appropriately? Support may also include conversations with campus information services. While the vendor may indicate that access to a tool is easily provided through linkages to campus information systems, there still needs to be discussions about how those linkages work in light of campus security policies.

5. Have you sought input from your target audience? As young-minded and technology savvy as career center staff may be, they

still might not be thinking of how the target audience would use the tool. What we may think is important or a great tool may be seen as irrelevant or unnecessary by those who will use the tool. Ask students, employers, or other stakeholders to demo the tool and offer their opinions.

In overall technology management, there are a few principles that have guided me well:

1. You don't always have to be first to adopt a new technology. This is especially hard when staff may be pushing to implement something. See if the technology has been adopted elsewhere in your institution or with peer institutions. Ask those other users the questions above to make sure you understand not only the use of the tool but also the maintenance.

2. Form a technology committee that includes students (student staff and graduate assistants work well also). Have committee members review proposed technology and provide input into specific settings. In addition, have the committee draft language for marketing and training materials. This way, they are more invested in the success of the technology and are not just passing responsibility onto the computer tech.

3. Recognize the psychological side of technology and change. People react very differently to change, with some ready to adopt the latest and greatest, and others resistant to any change. Even the smallest change can significantly impact how someone does his or her job. Some people may view technology additions as a means to eliminate their job or as a reflection of dissatisfaction with work performance. Others may just resist change and will try to continue to use the older, but more familiar, technology. Some may be hesitant to ask for help in learning the technology, so will try to hide their lack of skill and comfort. Give people plenty of notice about the proposed change (enlisting the support of the technology committee) and provide opportunities to ease into the technology, if possible. Once the technology is in place, continue to provide ongoing training, perhaps using a peer-to-peer approach. Use staff

meetings to discuss the technology, and allow staff to share their own tips. This creates a shared experience and encourages widespread adoption.

The career services profession is full of people who are innovative and willing to share both successes and challenges. At its strategic best, technology serves as a force of innovation with the power to energize people, improve process flows, and provide enhanced services. It also has the power to overwhelm, frustrate, and complicate lives. The effective leader always walks a fine line between caution and risk before adding a new technology and having the courage to "jump in with both feet" to try something new.

The Value of the Consortium

Pat Rose

All career center directors are trying to do more with less. One way individual directors can extend their reach and increase their value is through membership in a consortium.

A consortium is a group of individuals who share a common role or purpose, who join forces with others for one or more reasons. These can be one or more of the following:

- To provide a service to students or employers,
- To benefit from special pricing from vendors,
- To benchmark services and, occasionally,
- To determine policies that all members will adhere to.

In addition, some consortia are formed purely for networking and the sharing of information that will inform the work of all members. Here are some examples of the most common kinds of consortia:

- An internship consortium. Similar schools band together to share internships. Employers who post to the consortium can expect to hear from qualified students from all schools, thus saving them the time of posting at each. Individual career centers benefit if the other consortium members have a different geographic or curricular focus, or have strong relationships with particular employers. This is useful for schools who recruit students from throughout the country but tend to have more regional internship listings; additional listings add breadth and depth that could not be achieved through an individual office's own efforts.

- A consortium career fair. Offering a joint career fair with other, similar schools will allow the sponsors to attract more employers than any individual school could alone. Liberal arts colleges in a particular region or state frequently have career fair consortia, as do all the public institutions in a particular state or region. Even large schools participate in consortia, which are frequently held in a large city with many employers. For example, schools from the same athletic conference may offer, as a consortium, a career fair in New York. Or a consortium fair can focus on one type of employer such as, for example, not-for-profits or government agencies, technology companies, or start-ups. These fairs may also include recruitment interviews on the same day or the same week.

- A virtual career fair. Similar schools join together to offer a virtual fair, particularly around a career field or discipline they all share, such as biotechnology. Employers can access students at all the schools on one platform. No one needs to travel, and the fair can remain "open" for weeks if appropriate. Virtual fairs are particularly attractive to international employers, or others located at a distance from many of the consortium member schools.

- Group pricing discounts. A number of vendors agree to provide a group rate to schools in a consortium for annual subscriptions, especially for online content. This is of enormous benefit to small schools that have very limited budgets.

- Benchmarking consortium. Similar schools participate in an annual survey to gauge effectiveness and range of services, size of budget, or salary levels, among other metrics. These surveys are extremely valuable to directors who need to make a case for increased staffing, salary, or budget dollars.

- Consortium shared policies. Occasionally, schools will agree as a consortium to maintain similar policies. Just as admissions officers may all announce their acceptances on the same day, so too will career centers at peer institutions develop similar policies on when recruiting can begin or how long employers should keep offers open. They may also develop common reciprocity policies for consortium members, whereby members agree to provide similar services to each others' students or alumni who may move to their area.

In most of these cases, the consortium model allows each school to spread the work and responsibility around, which is extremely important for small offices with two and three person staffs. Staff at small centers wear many hats, and can leverage a consortium for the benefit of their students.

One of the most valuable reasons to join a consortium is to meet new colleagues, particularly other directors who are dealing with similar issues. Fellow directors are likely to share the same concerns and frustrations. They can be enormously helpful in providing advice or in brainstorming solutions. They can serve as a sounding board. These colleagues become valued members of your network, who may at some point recommend you for a committee assignment for NACE or a regional association. They might suggest collaborations on projects, articles, or other work. They could even recommend you for a position at another institution. Getting to know other directors is one of the most beneficial aspects of consortium membership.

If you are not currently in a consortium, consider starting one yourself. Start with a manageable idea or project. Approach directors at peer career centers with your idea. Offer to host the first meeting, or if distance is a factor, the first conference call. If you are new to your position, quickly determine if your office is already in a consortium, and contact the chair or convener to express your interest in participating.

If you are already a member of a consortium, participate actively. Share in the organizational responsibilities, or volunteer to head up a new activity if other members are interested. Be sure to take full advantage of the power of the group, and the wealth of expertise represented by other members. In a world of limited resources and new organizational models, the more you can learn from consortium colleagues, the better you will be able to advocate for your own office. Finally, joining with others enriches one's professional life in numerous ways. Anyone who works in career services today knows how gracious and helpful colleagues at other career centers can be. One of the best ways to draw on these resources is through a consortium approach.

The Small Career Center

Catherine Neiner

I believe I have taken every career assessment ever devised. Here are some things that never show up on mine: entrepreneur, teacher, market researcher, budget manager (especially that one), or events planner. Interestingly enough, I am each of those every day. Why? Because I am the director of a small career center.

When you are the director of a small career center, you are not a specialist. On the other hand, you are not a jack-of-all-trades. But you do function on both a strategic and tactical level at all times. I get to think critically while allowing my creativity to flourish, to respect the tried and true while flaunting the innovative, and to be a knowledge expert while thriving as a learner. Because I am just one professional in the career center staff, I have to pay attention to the details and the big picture.

The small career center plays a monumental role in a student's universe. As the only professional staff member in mine, I have the unique opportunity to make an immense, long-term impact on each individual student. I like to say that, in "my" career center, I educate for life.

I consider one of my most important roles on campus to be the person who most accurately models the presence of a professional that students will encounter in the real world outside of academia. I strive to do so in my appearance, my behavior, and even in how I manage my small office. There is no one to counterbalance me particularly in the student's eye. One of the things I do is quite simple and far from showy but, I am told, has an interesting effect. When I walk across campus, I walk slowly. I walk purposefully, mind you, but I never rush. I want students to see a professional getting where she needs to be but doing so in a manner that shows she is in control of her time. I always try to bear in mind that it's the small things that can make the difference, even when the big things are what people remember.

I have to admit that sometimes I do look at the larger career centers with envy: specialists for each aspect of the work of the center. But in my role, I get to do it all. Rather than thinking about limited capabilities or about doing more with less, I get to think in terms of what can be done and how. Rather than feeling at the relentless mercy of time and resources, I get the chance to figure out ways to make things happen. And yes, you'd better believe I pat myself on the back when it all comes together in a really great way.

In my small career center, I walk the same line a large office does. I have the same three constituencies: the students, external friends including recruiting entities, and the university community. Rather than seeing this as serving three masters, I consider myself to have three sets of allies that I leverage to meet the challenges of time and resources. Sure, each of those three has specific wants, and I understand the importance of meeting those. Doing so ensures the viability of my work in the career center. But in finding ways to make my constituencies wants intersect with the career center's needs, I get those teachable moments in which I can educate about the true mission of a comprehensive and vibrant career center—and get done what needs to be done.

Even more important, I get to know so many different people on so many different levels. Because I really have no choice but to expand the number of helping hands I use in the career center, it has been my good fortune to make many professional friends and get to know many talented students. I call in reinforcements all the time: alums, corporate friends, board members, and motivated students. I call on my colleagues in my state ACE and NACE as my sounding board and, sometimes, my support system.

Recruiters come and go, but they often consider me and the career center— or even my college—as one entity. A recruiter has told me more than once, "I'm not coming to recruit because of your college; I'm coming because of you." "That," I tell them, "Is exactly what my college pays me for." I particularly get a smile when a recruiter learns what college I am with and says, "Oh, you look like you come from there." I always wonder what that means exactly. But I hear it over and over, and I just go with the thought that it's a good thing!

Students, on the other hand, will give me that ego-boost I need every once in a while. Students that I was not so sure of when they graduated will come back and tell me one thing I said that they have remembered over the years. I believe that the high level of individual interaction with students that I am privileged to have because it is just me, allows me to make a true difference in individual lives.

And I get to know people across campus, too. I want to make sure that I have some influence on what admissions people are telling prospective students. I want to make sure that external relations people remember to propose internships to their pitch. I want to make sure that alums and college friends who volunteer feel valuable. For them, I keep an ongoing list of activities such volunteers can be put to work on right way.

I'm not going to lie: Sometimes it does feel as if I am running in every different direction. So how do I maintain my equilibrium? Trite but true, I keep organized and keep focused. My career center has a mission statement. Every time I consider a program or request, I run it through the mission test: Does taking this on advance the mission of the career center? If not, I let it go no matter how interesting it sounds. Based on the mission statement, I establish priorities, short term and long term. Does the program or request help me fulfill my priorities? If not, I let it go—again, no matter how interesting it sounds. And the mission statement and solid priorities give me a foundation on which to explain my decisions to stakeholders. That relieves me of the emotional pull that tempts me to take on something I know I really shouldn't. I consider my career center's mission statement and its related priorities to be one of the greatest gifts I have given myself in my role as director of a small career center.

I also make time versus money decisions all the time. If my budget allows for it, I automate. I resisted resume software for the longest time because of the cost, but after I finally bought it, I just wished I had done it sooner. If my budget allows for it, I hire it. An honorarium for an expert, or even for someone who can just present what needs to be presented, is worth it. And, as we all know, students will hear a guest speaker so much better than they hear me even if we say the exact same thing. If my budget allows for it, I splurge on giveaways. The giveaways always have my career center's name on them, and they are always something that is extremely visible when used. I think of it as free advertising even though, I suppose, it is really not free.

As much as I like thinking up great ways to do the work of the career center more effectively and more engagingly, I try never to reinvent the wheel. If I have an idea, I see if someone else has done something similar. Chances are they have. I can pick and choose and revise and modify to fit my college, and it feels new and fun.

The good news about my small career center: I am in control. The bad news about having no staff: I am in control of a lot. The good news about being in control of a lot: I can be creative and innovative. The bad news about being in control of a lot: While I get to be creative and innovative, I have to be really, really focused all the time.

But the thing I remember every day, the thing that makes my days worthwhile is that I educate for life. How great is that?

Life as an MBA Career Services Director

Jim Beirne

MBA career directors are never as good, or as bad, as placement results indicate. Understanding clearly the particular expectations and demands of this specialized career services leadership role is critical. Effectively managing and responding to the expectations of your dean, your office team members, students, recruiters, alumni, advancement staff, and faculty can make this a wonderful leadership role, or a public debacle.

An outstanding MBA career director will create a well-informed, transparent, and fundamentally fair marketplace at his or her school. Recent rankings, geography, your faculty's relative expertise, how updated and "new" a curriculum you inherit are all important factors you need to understand, from both internal and external perspectives.

Strong relationships with key recruiting organizations will go a long way to sorting out the thorny issues that both recruiters and students get themselves into every year. Cultivating personal connections with your key recruiting leaders will pay dividends when you have a crisis, and can get a recruiter to pick up your call on a moment's notice.

Not to be overlooked is your office team—very often overworked, underpaid, and underappreciated. Living vicariously through the lives of the students they encounter, your staff can make your life wonderful, or miserable. An MBA career director who clarifies expectations, builds in sufficient training, identifies and customizes low-cost perks for valued employees, and *always* publically supports the staff can overcome most obstacles during the year. Of all the constituencies a career director impacts, paying close attention to the staff will pay the highest rewards, and ameliorate most of the student and recruiter challenges that come your way. Interestingly enough, I've found that when students' leave for the summer is the time to pay most attention to staff needs—as their focus turns inward with a vengeance.

What should you expect when, as a new MBA career director, you encounter...

Rankings

They come with the territory. Get to understand quickly which ones are most important to your institutional leaders. They'll probably include *Bloomberg Business Week* and *US News & World Report*. Take time to understand what they are ranking, and how they compile their data. Life was easier before these publications realized they could create an entire industry out of these lists, but it has also brought greater sophistication into schools and their curricula. How are rankings calculated? When are they published? Develop your talking points to respond to the discussions that will surely ensue. The MBA CSC (Career Services Council) is an excellent source for all this information. Frankly, experienced recruiters really don't pay much attention to any one set of rankings. They are more concerned about your school's strengths in particular functions they hire into, and the quality and quantity of your student body.

Experienced MBAs

Recruiting organizations traditionally hired MBAs because they fit the traditional candidate profiles—prescreened for four to five years of solid work experience, along with a 30 percent female, and 10 percent underrepresented minority, talent pool. Today, most *Fortune* 1000 recruiters still think in those terms, but most MBA program student profiles, and curricula, vary dramatically—from fifth-year undergraduates with no real world experience to 31 year olds with a decade of one-year experiences attempting to re-launch their careers with their newly punched MBA ticket. As a credential, the degree has become quite ubiquitous, and can consist of a broad array of educational experiences—some of which fit the traditional profile and curricula. Experienced MBAs present additional challenges, and opportunities, if you can reconcile your orientation and educational programs with realistic expectations on their part. An MBA degree can come from a part-time, weekend, executive one-year, two-year, international, and joint-degree program. Depending on the industry, an MBA could be an asset, table stakes, or hindrance to a candidate reaching for that dream job. Two main consumers of MBAs—investment banking and management consulting, much to a candidate's chagrin, rarely value experienced MBAs.

Placement

While you don't want to use the "P" word, and it has disappeared from most offices, it is still a very important indicator of the success of your program. Quantifying success is important. How do internships translate into full-time roles by industry? How many entering students are career changers, career seekers, and career accelerators? How successful was last year's class toward their goals? What are the milestones and hurdles to overcome to meet their objectives? Partnering with your admissions officers and dean's offices to manage expectations, based on your curriculum and admissions requirements, go a long way to "placement" success, student satisfaction, and your well-being. Bring data to any and all discussions.

International MBAs—Not to be confused with Global MBAs

International students, not having the ability to work long term in another country, have created an industry in themselves. Bringing the benefits of their cultures, languages, and business methods, they also challenge career services offices around the world. Early attention, clear guidelines, significant skills training and practicing need to take place to increase your international MBAs' chance to succeed. Market conditions still are key determinants of how successful an international MBA can be. Specific profiles are even more important. A Brazilian engineer with a US MBA is much rarer than an American citizen with a UK MBA seeking a local finance role, and will find more opportunities. Partnering with your admissions officers on your messaging and capabilities can preempt some of your most challenging students issues.

Global MBAs

Understanding how global markets function is crucial to every MBA graduate. How they earn that understanding and communicate that to recruiters is even more important. Research has shown that being able to communicate the relevancy of the international experience and education to the particular position under discussion is the key component to a successful interview. While every CEO declares he or she is looking for global talent, the hiring manager and recruiting manager know they have a specific job to fill, and, in 95 percent of the cases, "being global" is a nice to have, not a requirement. Educate your students how to translate their courses, internship, overseas project, or junior year abroad to the specific requirements of a position.

Faculty challenges

It is important to understand who the faculty leaders are, along with who are strong student advocates, and where the land mines are located. It is impossible to obtain support from the entire faculty (the deans will be the first to tell you this), but it is important to build relationships with several leaders. Get to know what is important to them, read up on some of their work—it will also provide data for informative conversations with your recruiters and students. Developing strong relationships with a few key senior faculty will pay off when discussions behind closed doors turn to career services, and your champions will be there to support you.

Staff you inherit

Whether you parachute in, or are promoted from within, meet one-on-one with everyone. Find out what matters most to them, what they would like to see from management (more of, less of, start doing, stop doing), and take notes. These dialogues will be invaluable in your future leadership decisions. Not only will you get a sense for who is most interested in advancing and contributing, but also you will identify many great ideas and those who would like to champion them.

A lousy job market

Take heart, as students will pay more attention to career service advice!

Leading your organization, contributing directly to your school's success, and engaging on a daily basis with industry leaders—discussing business and talent challenges—can make for a very satisfying career. Reach out immediately to your peers—other career directors who have battle-hardened experience: Reach out regionally, and reach out nationally. The unique position you hold in your university can be lonely. By reaching out early in your career, you will find that there are very few situations that directors at other institutions haven't already encountered. They will be delighted to share with you what works, what doesn't, share some laughs, and remind you that we are all working to improve our institutions—not competing with each other in a zero sum game.

MBA talent acquisition still occurs in a very inefficient marketplace. Staying humble, learning from others' experiences, and being open to solutions from all levels of your organization will allow you to enjoy the amazing benefits of your new role. Stay focused on your key goals, stay flexible, keep learning, and enjoy the ride!

The Decentralization of Career Services

Marva Gumbs Jennings

With over 8,900 institutions of higher education in the United States and over 20 million college students, college administrators are challenged with a number of issues, the foremost of which is their ability to attract and retain a comprehensive and diverse student population. The service operation designed to deliver comprehensive career development and management services to students as well as alumni has become increasingly important to this bottom line.

At one point in its evolution, career services was considered a service for graduating students, but for many students and their parents, career services currently factors significantly into their decision about which college to attend. With this as a backdrop, as well as the ongoing struggle by institutions about where to expend finite dollars, adopting the model of a single career center designed to serve the needs of all students and alumni is currently undergoing transition.

Across the country, and depending on the culture and goals of the particular college or university, there exists career centers that are centralized, others that are school-based funded, and some that form a hybrid model where, as one example, career staffing is deployed to school-based settings, with active reporting and organizational lines to a central center. The extreme case on this continuum are those campuses where each school or department has its own well-established career center with no central center operation.

Decisions related to the maintenance of a centralized center or the growth of an independent career office are certainly complex and multi-faceted; and many folks in our profession have spent as much time discussing the reasons for the value of each model, as well as railing against the perceived or very real division the decentralized model brings. There is a natural tendency to become concerned, and, in some cases, alarmed around the establishment of an independent office(s) from the main career center on campus.

Why? Seasoned career practitioners are aware that if a career center becomes functional without the collaboration of or in partnership with the central operation, a variety of issues are likely to surface. These could include a concern about the natural competition that more than likely will arise out of the outreach efforts by multiple center staff, to the finite set of employers interested in the college-educated work force, or, certainly, the unfair comparison of the effectiveness and value of each career center.

Whatever your stance or position on this matter, it is clear that a variety of forces, many beyond our control, in higher education today will continue to have an interesting impact on decisions made regarding career services. Some of these factors include competition for resources, political positioning, branding, the need to provide customized services, accreditation, the school's ability to make students feel "special," and other related issues.

What defines centralized and decentralized career centers?

The National Association of Colleges and Employers (NACE) provides a comprehensive description from its career services benchmarking survey by defining a primarily centralized office/campus as a school having only one career services office or campus with more than one career services office, with most offices/functions reporting to one main career services office. A decentralized campus is a school having more than one career services office, with most offices reporting to different individuals.

These decentralized "centers" run the gamut from the one-person office to comprehensive offices with student- and employer-specific staff functions. Typically, decentralized career offices are supported by their schools or departments, which independently fund these operations. As a result, the finite resources identified are only available exclusively to their population of students.

Why do centralized and decentralized career center models exist?

The rationale for why institutions choose one model over another, or ultimately land on selecting a hybrid of both, is as complex as the institutions themselves. At the simplest, school-based level, the competition for donors, the need to provide customized services to support admissions efforts, an interest in cementing ties with alumni, the rankings race, and competition with other market basket or aspirational schools are some of the stronger reasons to seek a separate career center function.

While I believe strongly in a centralized model, there are distinct advantages to a decentralized model as well.

Advantages to decentralized career centers:

- Perception of an exclusive and targeted service for a particular group of students and employers.

- A greater connection with school-based faculty who embrace and "own" the service.

- Career services staff are able to focus services and support on a specialized and frequently smaller student population.

- Allows staff to develop expertise in particular subset industries and fields of interest.

- Provides employers with the opportunity to connect with and hire students as part of their target recruiting strategy exclusively from specific academic programs served by that center.

- Opportunity to brand a particular school or program with constituents.

Disadvantages of decentralized career centers:

- Unrealized cost efficiencies related to redundant services and programs.

- Expectation that employers who target students from different academic programs may have to work with multiple centers to connect with these students.

- Lack of access to specific employers by qualified candidates from academic programs not served by a particular center.

- Confusion among students about which center or centers are available to provide them with services and/or the perception by students that they would be served better by a center not available for them to access.

- Expenditure of precious time multiple centers must spend communicating with each other to coordinate services, programs, and messaging.

- Lack of a unified career services model ultimately hinders the building of campus unity.

- Frankly, the biggest issue with a decentralized campus is not in the area of career development services. The real issue and struggle is most frequently in the competition for employers.

- In particular at the undergraduate level, a significant number of employers are committed to recruiting "all majors" based on their recruiting needs. This is interpreted by those of us involved with a centralized model as a "call" to provide opportunities and access to a wide cross section of students with diverse majors and skills. Splitting out employers to recruit students across a number of centers seems inefficient.

So how or why does an institution choose to support a model where all students receive services equitably? Does it support the creation of multiple career centers created or designed to serve a target group of students? Is there clarity around which model best serves their evolving and competing institutional goals and interests?

Without clarity, decisions frequently lead to the creation of career entities separate from the traditional career center, and as such, create a climate that is simultaneously conducive for specific student groups, while creating confusion for all constituents. Overall, the appearance of multiple career centers seems to be one of disconnection on campus.

Can both models work together?

Yes they can! There are a number of campuses where both models work well. So what does it take?

- Recognition that multiple efforts to source the same employer reflects negatively on the entire institution.

- Consistent communication and sharing is key to eliminating confusion and connecting the right students (regardless of major) with a particular employer.

- Developing a structure and system for openly sharing information about relationships, contacts, and the changing needs of employers.

- A shared understanding that we have a responsibility to work on behalf of all students, not just the ones for whom we have direct responsibility.

- Leadership support that drives the goal of mutual cooperation.

What types of leadership skills are valuable in this framework?

As you can well imagine, it is beneficial for leaders who work in a decentralized environment to use a different—or I should say—an enhanced skill set to achieve success in this evolving environment. First and foremost, it is essential that leaders understand the issues or factors that influence the decisions and operating guidelines for their colleagues. Besides the three "p's" of patience, positivity and perseverance, other primary abilities include the following skills paired with a set of discrete questions it is important to consider:

Listening: Do you have a clear understanding of your colleagues' mandates from their deans or their reporting structure? How do they envision responding to and completing that mandate?

Consensus Building: Are you able to provide the type of ideas or incentives to bring about a win-win situation for all parties?

Negotiation: Do you subscribe to the philosophy that a mutual agreement may mean that you give up some tangible "thing" in an effort to achieve a larger goal?

Collaboration: Is there a singular mutual benefit that spurs cooperation and perhaps even an alliance? Can your collusion result in spurring some other entity or stakeholder within the university structure to work in concert with you (such as the IT department)?

Creativity: Are there new ways of doing business that rise out of the sharing of financial resources and talent that is brought to the table by mutual interest and partnership?

Most significantly, does the leader truly believe in supporting and serving all student and employer stakeholders (not just a target group) and have the ability to work openly and consistently with all colleagues to carry out the institutional priorities? In other words, can you get buy in that the "good of the many outweighs the good of the one/few"?

An effective leader must also stay alert to the changing tides that change positive relationships through periodic meetings and updates, support of each center's events/activities and programs, and consistent discussion of and realignment of mutual goals. This takes hard and sometimes thankless work!

At the heart/core of the effort to work collaboratively within a decentralized campus is the institutional value of and support for career services! The career center must be raised to the level of a high institutional priority and be funded appropriately to have an impact on attracting and retaining students.

Ideally an institution needs to engage in a process from which comes clarity about the strengths and weaknesses of career services offered across the entire university, and the best ways to enhance weaknesses and market the strengths. This should be coupled with a structure that assures the maximum level of coordination among centers, with clear accountability and outcomes designed to support the importance of cooperation and the minimization of problems.

Other ways to build trust may be advanced with the deliberate sharing of resources (could include CSM or CRM or other databases, online resources, staff expertise, space, events such as fairs), the crafting of a joint web page/site, and the development of comprehensive collateral materials that showcase our students and the collaboration of the multiple centers.

On my own campus, the leadership has actively driven a review of the current mix of central as well as decentralized models that has developed over time. The review has resulted in the establishment of a formal structure that brings all centers together under a unified council sharing several technical resources. The decision was also made to elevate the leadership role for career services to that of assistant provost.

As higher education evolves, the continued decentralization of career centers seems inevitable as institutions expand domestically and globally. It behooves us as practitioners to anticipate these changes by consistently seeking partnerships that advance multiple institutional goals (both internally and externally), saves dollars (or is creative about the use of funds), and sends a positive message to employers and other stakeholders that their business and professional relationship is a top priority.

Overall, is it not also about the distribution of fair and equitable services and outcomes that satisfies students, their parents, and alumni?

The Inspired Role of NACE and Professional Organizations

Andy T. Ceperley

To describe the importance of professional associations such as the National Association of Colleges and Employers (NACE), I'd like to take you to a place that inspires me. The summit of Cowles Mountain is the highest point in the city of San Diego, where I lived. Its height is 1,593 feet, and the ragged trail I hike to reach its summit consists of 1.5 miles of sand and rock switchbacks, level and meandering in some places and steep and rocky in others. Even the most aerobically fit climbers find themselves winded as they touch the monument atop Cowles with their hands, a gesture symbolizing they have reached the trail's peak. While catching my breath at the top, I can enjoy a most extraordinary view. To the south, the Mexico border and the city of Tijuana; to the east, the region's East County and the desert beyond; to the north, coastal towns including Pacific Beach and La Jolla; and to the west, the sprawling San Diego skyline with the bay and ocean just beyond. If you can picture that view from high above, or one like it from your own experience, you probably can relate to my feeling of inspiration as I marvel at the panorama before I carefully clamber back down Cowles Mountain, at twice the speed I climbed it. Throughout the ascent, rest, and descent, I feel energized, alert, and creative.

My involvement in NACE and other professional organizations has tapped a level of inspiration not unlike my Cowles Mountain climbs. I can remember my first national conference in 1992, when NACE was known by its original name the College Placement Council. It was held at the San Francisco Hilton at Union Square. I was new to the field and had made arrangements with my boss to split the cost of the trip. Conference travel was limited due to the financial challenges that swept through higher education at the time. I was determined to go, and I'm glad I did. I knew no one but managed to meet people as I navigated the keynote addresses, concurrent sessions, and networking meals. I couldn't get enough of all of this! I was energized in a way I never knew before when I returned to my position as a career librarian/publicity coordinator at the Office of Career Planning & Placement—OCPP as students called it—at the University of Virginia. I had made some contacts and learned some different approaches to our work. I started to experience a sense of pride for a profession in which I still had much to learn. I have not missed a conference since.

My career in higher education has taken me to four outstanding universities, each proud of their unique traditions and steadfast in overcoming their challenges. Through these professional campus tours, my involvement in regional associations (ACE's), NACE, and benchmarking groups continued to grow. These collaborative networks of professionals became my welcome committees of choice. Their members were who I first called when I was trying to get the lay of the land in a new city. Their events and conferences brought me up for air when the day-to-day had me feeling submerged, and their published content and member expertise boosted my confidence as I tried to position my office strategically in an unknown political landscape.

Now, a few decades later, I can't imagine a better supplement to my day job than involvement in professional organizations. Here's why...

Getting out of my head

The fresh ideas I receive from professional associations help me examine my center's challenges through a different lens. I become aware of how ultimately these challenges are shared, and I find myself humbled by the ingenuity and persistence through which my colleagues overcome them. They provide me with a fresh perspective and an array of best practices I can adapt.

Spotting the trends

In our college and university settings, we find ourselves named as the unofficial, or possibly official, voice of all things "career." Our professional associations, NACE in particular, stays out in front of us, conducting research on hiring trends, starting salaries, and new innovations. When called by the media, we not only have a perspective from our individual campus setting, we can frame it within a national backdrop.

Presenting positions I can endorse

The professional issues that keep us up at night have become increasingly complex. Try as we might to find the bright lines clarifying right from wrong, we struggle through the gray. We benefit from the ethical thought leaders in our professional networks. Many of them are volunteers, crafting position papers on issues as complex as unpaid internships and social media. By no means do these advocates tell us what to think. Rather, they consolidate many agendas within an issue and present a statement intended to guide our actions as professionals, not mandate them.

Bolstering relationships

How many transformative conversations have you had at a conference, the ones that weren't programmed? They happen on the fly in the vendor area and they happen on the shuttle to the airport. They surprise us in that they remind us how much we have to share and often how much listening we have to do. Up-and-comers pick up sage advice from those who have been there and done that. Tenured thought leaders learn a thing or two about new approaches from those newer to the profession who have eyes wide open to all that might be in the future of our combined work.

Stepping up

Research has demonstrated that students who become involved in college life outside the classroom perform better academically and are more engaged in their education. Perhaps the same is true for us when we step beyond our day-to-day and volunteer for a NACE committee, present at a conference or a webinar, or pursue a position of leadership on the NACE Board. The more involved we become, the more we realize that though we may be able to innovate on our own, we innovate with sure footing when we take full advantage of the connections, insight, and expertise of our professional networks.

There is one more helpful feature on the Cowles Mountain climb. There are several rest stops on the way up where wearied walkers can step off the path and take in the scenery as more zealous hikers pound past them, determined not to break stride. That's not unlike our connection to our professional networks. Every now and again, we plateau, take a bit of a break, and soak up the view. Soon we step back out into the path and climb alongside others, aware that the summit is just ahead. Energized. Alert. Creative. Our work as career services practitioners demands from us a high level of inspiration, a broad perspective, and a clear view from high above.

Managing Your Career:
Career Advice for the Career Advisor

Marcia B. Harris

We all have heard about the shoemaker's children, or the caregiver who takes care of everyone but herself. Sometimes those of us in the career services profession are really good at helping others maximize their career potential, but neglect doing the same for ourselves.

Here are two examples of career services colleagues' experiences:

Don started his career as a career counselor at a small private liberal arts college. Through careful planning, networking, and hard work, he advanced to associate director. He then was hired as director at a mid-size university. Eventually, because of an opportunity for his spouse, he moved within the state to take a position as associate director of a large state university. All along, Don periodically examined his career goals and continued to build his skills and to gain visibility in the profession. Because of his family, he did not intend to make another move that would require relocation. However, he continued to grow professionally. Don was a well-respected career services professional. He had been quite active in professional associations, having served as president of one of the regional "ACE" associations and on several state, regional, and national "ACE" committees. Don was well-known through this service as well as through the numerous presentations he gave at professional conferences and the articles he has written for the *NACE Journal*. After being in his associate director position for a number of years, Don was laid off due to budget cuts, in spite of his consistent superior performance reviews. Naturally, he was quite disappointed and fearful about finding another job, especially because of the tight job market at the time and his limited geographic mobility. Fortunately, Don had an extensive network of professional friends who were avid believers in his ability and who provided strong support to him. Through his research, strong qualifications, and network of contacts, within a few months he received several interviews that resulted in job offers. Ultimately, Don was offered a directorship at a nearby institution within the same state system. While the position entailed a fairly long commute, he was willing to pay this price. Don not only landed on his feet, but the turn of events that at first appeared so unfortunate, resulted in a far better position for him, with higher salary, status, job challenge, and improvement of his future state retirement earnings. Was this all a matter of luck? Unlikely. This is a great example of the quote, "I find that the harder I work, the luckier I get." Throughout his career, Don had been developing his "brand," progressing in terms of skills, contacts, and experience, and preparing for his next move, whether it be one that he initiated or was forced upon him.

The next example isn't quite as positive. Janet also began her career as a career counselor with aspirations to one day become a director. She moved to several different institutions as her career progressed to associate director. After a few years as associate director, she applied for several director positions at both large and mid-size schools, but never even got to the interview stage. Janet had been gaining experience and building some skills as she advanced to associate director, but she never deliberately considered what she would need to become a director. In her associate director role, she had no budgetary or assessment responsibilities, and she had not sought other means of acquiring this knowledge and experience. While she had served on several state committees and had held office in her state "ACE" association, she was not known outside of her state. She had not made the effort to publish or present at regional or national conferences. Janet never did achieve her goal of becoming a director. Several months before her retirement, which included a move to another region of the country, she began to consider her post-retirement career. She reached out to colleagues who had been successful in establishing "encore careers" in areas such as consulting/external reviews, private career counseling, and working with vendors. As she repeatedly heard comments such as, "These opportunities generally come from word of mouth," "I'm usually contacted by the school, (vendor, individual, and so forth) because of a previous association with them or with someone they know," Janet remarked that she wished that she had been far more active in a wider arena of the career services field and that she had been more deliberate about preparing for her next steps.

So how do these examples apply to *you*? Regardless of where you are in your career, whether you are just starting out or are an experienced professional, whether you have aspirations of becoming a career services director or not, the messages are 1) Consider where you want your career to be in the next few years as well as long term; 2) Develop a concrete plan of action to attain your goals; 3) Reflect on what you want your personal brand to be and how you are going to manage it, and 4) Take the necessary steps to enhance your career, while also enhancing value to your organization.

Where do you want your career to go both in the short and long term?

Even if you are in a great job right now and are not considering leaving for a while, you should be thinking about what the next desirable step for you would be (assistant or associate director, director, consultant, or perhaps a lateral move into a technical or communications area within career services (or possibly a position outside of college career services, related to higher education or human resources/recruiting or in an unrelated field). Similarly, prepare for a Plan B (just as we tell our students) in case of an unforeseen event that would force you to seek another position—perhaps a layoff or relocation of your spouse's job. Although your ultimate career goal may be a long way off, think about it as well, since the steps you take along your career path will be instrumental in determining whether or not you achieve it.

Keep in mind that in order to advance in the field of career services, it is often necessary to move to a different institution, which may require you to relocate to another geographical area. Only you can decide if this is a sacrifice that you are willing to make.

Develop a concrete plan of action to attain your goals.

Rarely are promotions or hiring decisions based on seniority. Rather, they typically are made on the basis of who is deemed to be the *best qualified* candidate in terms of skills, experience, attitude, and organizational fit. You need to review your qualifications objectively, and ask yourself if you have what it takes to progress to your next desired position. Seek out professionals in the field whom you respect and ask for their opinion of your credentials. Where do they think you need to build skills and experience in order to advance? As you probably have observed, moving up in career services requires far more than being a good career counselor. Skills that are an asset, and that certainly are a prerequisite for a director position, include comfort with technology, understanding of assessment and statistics, budget, management and supervisory experience, excellent written and oral communication skills, and knowledge of program development, public relations/marketing, fund raising, and social media. (No wonder there is a shortage of strong director-level candidates!)

Choose a yearly time period that is easy to remember -perhaps the week of your birthday or the first week in January - when career office traffic may be a bit lighter, to review and update your resume. Write down your career goals for the next few years as well as for the long term. These may change from year to year as the economy, the career services field, and your personal circumstances change. Next, write down two to five concrete steps that you will do in the next year to move toward each of your career goals. For example, if your short-term goal is to move from a counselor position to an assistant director position, you may need to begin to gain management experience as well as more responsibility for planning events. If this were the case, you could ask your director or manager if you could supervise the office work-study students or student ambassadors/career peers. You could also volunteer to take on responsibility for planning a small event, such as a niche career fair or all of the department networking nights. If your long-term goal is to be a career services director, you would want to gain knowledge and experience in some of the areas listed above that you lack. You might ask to attend a conference or training program on assessment and then volunteer to assume responsibility for some area of assessment in your office.

It is important to keep your resume current, review it at least once annually with a critical eye, and develop and follow through on a plan to overcome deficiencies that are obstacles to attaining your goals.

What do you want your personal brand to be and how you are going to manage it?

Much has been made recently of a "personal brand"—the overall impression that people have about you. While most of us have heard this term, and perhaps in the back of our mind understand that we should be consciously developing and managing our brand, few of us actually do this on a deliberate basis. Consider what your current brand is: Write down 10 words or phrases that you think professional colleagues would use to describe you. I'm assuming that most, if not all of these, will be positive attributes, such as "smart," "reliable," "punctual," and "well-spoken." Now stretch yourself a bit and write down five words or phrases that may not be quite so positive, such as "not ambitious," "weak with numbers," and "low professional visibility." Ask for feedback on both the positive and weaker aspects of your image, or brand from mentors, co-workers, your supervisor, and professionals in career services who know you. Once you have a fairly good idea of what your present brand is, decide which aspects you want to keep and which you want to discard or improve. Remember that your brand is composed of many different aspects, from your appearance, to your work habits, the personality you project, your professional contributions, your communication style, and even your social media presence. Think of yourself as CEO of the business of YOU. You want to position yourself and your brand to achieve the goals you have set for yourself.

Take steps to enhance your career while enhancing your value to your organization.

It's always a boon when you can "double-dip," or kill two birds with one stone. Often, when you are taking steps to further your career qualifications, you are also adding value to your department and institution. Here are some steps to consider as ways to enhance your present credentials:

- Work hard and well! It should be obvious, but the most critical component of advancing your career is to excel in your current job. You need to gain the respect and support of your supervisor, co-workers, and director in order to be tapped for consideration for greater responsibilities and to have strong references.

- Develop expertise in at least one mission-critical area such as transfer students, parent relations, social media, or assessment. Become your department guru and then branch out to share your expertise with others on and off campus.

- Speak up! Gain a comfort level in verbal communication, and force yourself to overcome any reticence you may have about contributing and asking questions at staff and division meetings and in larger forums like conferences. Record yourself giving presentations, and work on overcoming annoying habits such as using "speech fillers" ("um," "like," "you know," "I mean"), frequently clearing your throat, twisting your hair, or playing with objects (pens, paperclips, rubber bands).

- Expand your professional network of contacts and mentors through the use of LinkedIn and in-person connections. Most experienced career services directors are happy to mentor up-and-coming new talent, so don't be shy about reaching out and asking for advice.

- Create your professional look and consistently maintain it. As we tell our students, nonverbal impressions count. This includes much more than how you dress; consider your posture, stance (especially when presenting), walk, hairstyle, make-up (for females), male facial hair, and accessories. And no gum chewing, please! You want to project the image of a professional. It is difficult to be taken seriously if you dress like a student, have visible tattoos, and so forth.

- Beware of burn-out. Bring positive energy to the environment, whether you are in your career center, serving on a board or committee, or participating in an association workshop. If you feel your motivation flagging, take action—go on a vacation, volunteer for a new project, or embark on something in the career services field to re-ignite your professional spark, such as writing a journal article, developing a conference presentation, or seeking association work.

- Create your own personal board of advisors of two to three individuals who know you and are willing to meet with you occasionally to give you advice and feedback about your progress in moving toward your career goals. Your board should be comprised of someone in the career services field, someone higher up in your organization, and someone who understands what you want out of life.

- "Come to play!" Whether you are attending an association board or committee meeting, a department staff meeting, or just coming to work on a daily basis, consistently show up on time, prepared to engage in discussion, ready with any assigned work, and with an enthusiastic attitude. All of this will be noted by others, as will it's lack.

- Challenge yourself to learn two new skills yearly. Examine your performance review to see where you might improve, and seek training in these and other areas of interest to you.

- Set yearly professional goals that will help you gain visibility in the career services field. Examples include conducting a survey and communicating the results, submitting an article for publication in NACE's *Journal* or in your state or regional publication, and submitting a proposal for a conference presentation.

- Continue to stay abreast of new developments in career services. Make it a priority to read relevant publications such as *The Chronicle of Higher Education*, *The Wall Street Journal*, *Business Week*, the *NACE Journal*, and NACE's Spotlight. Be an active member of NACE and your regional and state professional associations along with social media groups such as career-related LinkedIn groups. You can gain visibility by making regular insightful, relevant comments to these group discussions.

- Get your creative juices flowing! Either by yourself, or brainstorming with office colleagues, consider developing something innovative in career services—a new approach to programming, new technology, and so forth. If you are successful, submit your idea for a NACE, regional, or state award. Receiving an award, or even being selected as a finalist, brings you and your office recognition.

- Invest in yourself. While it's a nice perk if your institution can provide funds for your professional development, if funding is not available don't be short-sighted and forego the continued training, networking, skill-building, and visibility that you need . Some career experts recommend that you take 5 to 10 percent of your annual salary to create your own career development fund.

- Don't be afraid to take risks! If you ask the movers and shakers in career services (and probably most other fields) if they felt *ready* to take on many of the major roles they engaged in, you will often hear that they were a bit worried about whether or not they had enough experience, skills, time, and such to do the job. We all feel that way at times. However, one of the significant differences between those who have noteworthy accomplishments and others is the willingness to have faith in themselves, overcome fear, and take the leap to try something challenging. Don't pass up exciting career opportunities such as writing a book, giving a conference presentation, taking on a leadership role, or accepting a higher level position, and seek out those that may not necessarily come your way. The recommendation is not to be foolhardy and accept a task that you are totally unprepared for, but rather to be willing to stretch yourself in order to grow professionally.

In conclusion, your career is ultimately in your own hands. Regardless of the job market, your personal circumstances, or the whims of fate, all of which can certainly have an impact on your career, you have a great deal of control over whether or not you will advance. As we often tell our students, it is up to you to determine what you want and to decide how hard you are willing to work to get it. Best wishes as you move forward in the exciting field of career services!

A Search Consultant's Guide to the Successful Career Services Job Search

Valerie B. Szymkowicz

Many career services professionals who spend their time offering sage advice to college students and recent graduates on the importance of crafting compelling job search materials and strengthening their interview skills too often do not heed their own advice when conducting their own job search. Sometimes they fail to discern critical differences between a job search at the entry level versus one at a more senior leadership level.

From the perspective of a higher education search consultants, we have seen this play out many times. There are notable exceptions of course; however, our intent is to help everyone who wishes to advance in the professional field of career services to put their proverbial best foot forward.

First steps...exploring new opportunities

Consider your strengths, talents, professional, and personal aspirations. In what environments have you done your best work? Think in terms of incremental as opposed to monumental growth. If you have served as a successful associate director and believe you are ready to move into a first directorship, consider applying for opportunities at institutions that share a similar mission to colleges or universities where you have already proven yourself and determined your values are congruent. If much of your work has been at small institutions, look for new positions at similarly sized institutions or those just slightly larger. In evaluating a new position, prior to submitting an application, take a close look at the staff size and budget to be managed. If your experience to date is limited in these key areas of responsibility, you would be encouraged to look at new opportunities that will place reasonable demands on you as you hone your staff and budget management skills. Jumping into a search for a position that has oversight of a staff in the double digits or budget in excess of a half million makes for very long, and probably unrealistic, odds for the candidate who has never directly supervised full-time professional staff or previously managed a sizeable budget. You will greatly improve the likelihood that your candidacy will receive serious attention if you move your career forward in incremental steps.

The truth is most search committees and hiring authorities are a little risk averse. Everyone wants their new hire to be very successful and well-equipped to ramp up quickly to move their career services organization forward. Most hiring authorities are looking for change agents—someone who can take an organization to the next level, raising its visibility and value. You will greatly improve your chances for advancing in a search if you put yourself in the shoes of the decision-makers and work to address and/or minimize their concerns. As a candidate, you really do need to articulate how your demonstrated skills, experience, and accomplishments at your current institution dovetail with the mission, values, and specific demands of a targeted institution and position. Showcasing experience that closely parallels an institution's needs and culture is the most effective means of immediately moving into the "yes, I want to interview this candidate" pile as search committee members sort through applicants.

Remember to think about your competition. Actual job titles for positions that you have held are likely less important than what you have accomplished. Not everyone who applies for a leadership position in career services will come out of higher education. Increasingly, individuals who have a good understanding of today's marketplace and what it takes to be a successful applicant for jobs in a wide range of employment sectors are being viewed as attractive candidates for higher education, career services positions. Do not assume because you have been working in a position closely allied to the next role to which you aspire that everyone will appreciate your capabilities—unless you specifically state them.

Leadership traits and talents

SJG—The Spelman & Johnson Group—is a higher education search firm that has partnered with hundreds of higher education institutions—large and small, public and private—to fill mission critical leadership positions. In just the last five years, SJG has facilitated over 30 career services searches for small elite private colleges, large public research universities, and regional and graduate institutions of just about every size and stripe imaginable. Based on in-depth discussions with key stakeholders and scrutiny of search outcomes, we have compiled the following list of competencies, management skills, and knowledge areas that repeatedly are sought in ideal candidates for senior career services leadership roles:

- Strategic planning and visionary orientation: experience that demonstrates an ability to think and act strategically, to craft unique approaches to address emerging career and work trends, and to differentiate one's career services organization from that of other similar institutions;

- Supervisory and team building skills: ability to bring out the best in individual staff and to build high performance and resilient teams;

- Budget management and fundraising capability: ability to creatively manage available resources to optimize results and to seek outside funding, where possible, to support innovative programs;

- Understanding of outcomes-based programming/services and the need for a return on investment on programming and services for students: the ability to use data to assess and make strategic decisions about allocating resources to provide value to students in their job-search process;

- Creativity in developing services for students and employers: balancing the need to educate students to be successful in the long-term management of their careers against the need to have students be employed post-graduation;

- Management style that is flexible, dynamic, and entrepreneurial: ability to react quickly and lead change, to respond to external forces impacting the institution, students, and the job market;

- A solid understanding of the economy, emerging trends and markets, and how this impacts work force development and employment of college graduates;

- Superior relationship-building and networking capability: proven ability to build successful working relationships with varied constituents, including local and professional communities, within specific corporations and industries, and to continuously expand network contacts;

- Professional, yet approachable image and persona: must be an excellent ambassador for the institution with external and corporate constituents and also able to relate well with college-aged students, faculty, parents, and staff;

- Understand and build on the interconnections that exist between the college admissions process, career services, and an institution's ability to build alumni affinity;

- Collaborative approach to accomplishing work-related objectives: must be comfortable building partnerships with a wide range of on- and off-campus constituents;

- Inspirational: able to motivate others to set and achieve high goals, as well as to cultivate buy-in of a shared vision;

- Enjoy learning: demonstrate, through a track record of personal and professional growth, a keen desire to continually expand and diversify one's base of knowledge, particularly with regard to emerging technologies, global work force development, and employment issues.

Interestingly, there is nothing in the list above that indicates candidates for career services leadership positions must have well-documented backgrounds that include extensive knowledge of either career development or student development theory. We are not discounting the value of this knowledge; however, increasingly key search stakeholders are telling us at SJG that theoretical knowledge is not a primary factor in determining whether or not a candidate is well-suited to a career services leadership position. While there is certainly a desire to attract candidates to leadership positions who can demonstrate familiarity with varied job markets, the emphasis is squarely on transferable skills that will equip a new director or assistant dean with the abilities to set a strategic course; build the relationships needed to execute a vision; and the tactical skill to spot trends, seize opportunities, and adjust programming and services to meet evolving needs that will serve a college audience. All this opens the door to competitors from many sectors of the economy (corporate, not-for-profit, government) and raises the stakes for individuals already working in career services to manage a flawless campaign to secure advancement positions.

Executing the search

As stated above, there is no room for error when it comes to managing your candidacy. To get things off on the right footing, you need to carefully research the position, institution, cultural milieu, and strategic priorities as articulated by stakeholders to determine if there is a good fit with your background, skills, and interests. A key resource early during this assessment period is the search consultant (if there is one) facilitating the search. A search consultant will have spent time on the ground meeting with key stakeholders and will be well-positioned to offer subtleties to the position that expand any printed description and also offer feedback regarding your experience and ability to be highly competitive in the search process. Do not be shy in engaging the search consultant before you apply!

While it may sound obvious, you also need to take a long and hard look at where the opportunity exists and consider whether you can realistically envision yourself relocating and thriving in that environment. If you want to be thorough (which usually translates into being "successful"), you will need to spend a good deal of social capital, time, and energy evaluating the opportunity from many angles before applying. There is no sense in applying for a position that you know is not right for you or your family members. Employing institutions and search consultants take a dim view of candidates who apply simply to leverage their position at their current institution and who have no serious interest in actually accepting a new position if offered.

All of your job-search materials—cover letter, resume, references, and ancillary materials that may be requested—must be presented in the best possible light. Here is where career services professionals (and others who wish to join these ranks) must practice what they preach. Craft your cover letter in a way that speaks to the specific position at the specific institution, demonstrate that you understand the key mandates of the role, and that your experience and accomplishments align with these strategic priorities. Employ an outside reader to help with final proofreading of all your job-search documents. Yes, you are likely a good proofreader of other's work, but seeing the simple errors in your own work is another thing entirely. Follow your own advice, prepare your materials in advance of stated deadlines, review all documents several times, and secure an outside reader to make certain you have not missed an otherwise embarrassing error (or worse yet, a fatal flaw that could knock you out of the running!).

Apply correctly. That is simple advice and yet so important! There is no need to provide information that is not requested. For example, if there is no mention in the application requirements for a list of references, do not supply one. Chances are the search consultant, search committee, or hiring authority has their own idea of what will constitute appropriate and valuable references. Do not try to second guess them; be confident that you will be asked to supply this information at the appropriate time and with sufficient instruction to meet their specific needs. Apply through the proper channel; if you are directed to an online application site, carefully follow instructions for submitting your application materials. This is no place to ad-lib the process.

As for letters of nomination, generally one strong letter that speaks to your background and unique ability to meet the needs and challenges of a specific position, written by an individual who is well-regarded and has direct knowledge of your professional capabilities, will suffice. Attempts to enlist the support of multiple individuals to submit letters of nomination on your behalf can backfire as search committees can easily become overwhelmed with too much information, too early in the search process. Ask the nominator to forward an electronic copy of the letter directly to the consultant managing the search, the chair of the search committee, or hiring authority. If you are unable to discern a person to whom the nomination letter should be sent, you might want to revise your plan and simply enlist the individual to serve as a reference as the search progresses. A well-written letter of nomination can be influential; however, is not imperative for an otherwise well-prepared candidate.

References requested for a particular search may vary from position to position. Some applications require you list a specific number of references at the time you announce your candidacy (e.g., at the time you submit your cover letter and resume). If such a request is explicitly stated, provide a list with the exact number of required references with full names, titles, employer affiliations, phone number, e-mail address, and the working relationship to you for each reference (e.g., indicate if the reference is a former supervisor, colleague, former employee, and so forth). Often, applications do not require a list of references, so read carefully. Submitting something that is not required may cast you in an unfavorable light. At a minimum for a career services leadership search expect, as the process unfolds and you advance to progressive interviews, to be asked to provide references from all supervisors who have overseen your work for at least the last 10 years. Generally, you will be able to withhold your current supervisor until a point in the search when you know you are on the "short list" of candidates being considered. That said, you should expect to be asked for this reference and, as with all references, it is important you take the time to personally inform your supervisor of your engagement in the search and bring him/her up to speed on what the position entails before s/he is contacted by someone facilitating the search process for a conversation. In addition to supervisory references, typically candidates will be asked to provide references from direct reports (individuals whose work has been supervised directly by the candidate), colleagues (from across the organization with whom they currently, or previously, have worked), employers, and collaborators (individuals with whom the candidate has partnered with to advance key initiatives).

Any and all interviews—whether conducted by phone, video, or in-person—are critical in supporting your quest to advance your career. Interviews provide tangible evidence of your ability to know how best to present your experience, engage your audience, demonstrate an understanding of the institution and its priorities, and express your genuine interest in the position. While you do not want to come across as "slick" or "pushy," the skill with which you interview will directly translate in the minds of search stakeholders into how well you will be able to support college students in their ability to present themselves effectively in the job market. Do not underestimate this; you are seeking a career services leadership role. You must present yourself as professional, personable, and proficient in key areas of responsibility. Keep in mind the three universal interview questions, and be prepared with answers and accomplishments that back them up: 1) Can you do the job? (Address the relevant strengths and abilities you bring to the job.); 2) Will you love the job? (Address your motivations for seeking the job and why you are excited about the position and the institution.); and, 3) Will others enjoy working with you? (Address the "fit" of the job—why you are the right person for this position at this institution at this time.)

Especially as you prepare for campus interviews, think through your vision for the position and department you wish to lead. Expect questions on this topic and be ready to articulate your thoughts. While it is understandable your vision and strategic priorities may evolve as you continue to learn more about the job and the context in which it is situated, stakeholders in the search want to know you have given serious consideration to the position and the institution and that you have a pretty good inkling of where and how you will need to focus your energy. Remember—at a senior leadership level, it is expected that you will answer a question about vision and strategy with a vision and strategy answer—not an operational answer.

Just as you would advise students, if you are a candidate for a position you will need to send a follow-up note after interviews have concluded to reaffirm your interest and offer some salient remarks based on the conversations in which you have been engaged. A timely, electronic note to the person primarily responsible for coordinating your interview(s) is sufficient, accompanied by a request that s/he express your ongoing interest and appreciation to others with whom you recently interviewed. That will spare you the effort of finding something unique to say to all 30 people with whom you spoke during an on-campus interview. Of course, if on reflection you determine the position is not as good a fit for you as you had originally hoped, or if you are offered and accept another position, informing the individual managing the search process of your decision to withdraw in a timely fashion is imperative. It is a small world out there and word travels fast. Campus finalists are in the public eye, so every effort should be made to remain highly professional, gracious, and respectful of the process—even if you decide you must step away.

Stepping into a new position

Now that you have successfully leveraged your skills and experience and find yourself in a new leadership role, how you manage during your first 100 days in the job will be critical. A good strategy is to first develop a core group of advisors. Often members of the search committee would be appropriate to cultivate in this manner as you already know they have a stake in your success. Round out your group of advisors by involving your staff and seeking their suggestions, as well as considering other constituents who may not have had an active role in the search process but nonetheless are important given the mission of your career services organization and institution. Gather input from advisors, create a participatory process through which staff can contribute ideas regarding strategic direction and priorities, consult with your supervisor and other senior officers of the institution, and conduct your own assessment of the organization you now lead, its mission, values, staffing, programs, and services. Look for early "wins"—changes you can implement quickly that signal new leadership, energy, and a spirit of collaboration with others in the campus community. Develop and deliver a draft strategic plan to your supervisor and be open to feedback that will help you refine your goals and methodology, as well as strengthen your success.

Building your reputation and impact

Once articulated, review your strategic plan at regular intervals to evaluate progress and refine priorities. Strategic plans need to be dynamic and cannot afford to be shelved only to be reviewed at times of accreditation review. Stay attuned to changes within the institution and in the local, regional, national, and global job markets. Strive to position yourself as a trusted expert on matters directly impacting student success while in school and upon graduation, as well as on issues pertaining to members of the Millennial generation and their employers, the job market, and labor trends in general. Keep building your network as you build the brand of your department and institution. Remember that service to students is at the core of your work; make time to interact with students, understand their perspective, appreciate their in-class and out-of-classroom experiences, and champion their dreams. It is rewarding work, serving as a career services leader, and every institution is looking for just the right person to balance the challenges and opportunities of the position with success.

Leading Innovation in Career Services

Gary Alan Miller and Katherine Nobles

Introduction

We are working in times of change and turbulence. From the "higher education bubble" and a difficult economy to third-party career services providers and the widespread availability of career development information on the web, career centers face many challenges and opportunities. Our future successes hinge upon how we merge the best of our current approaches with innovations to maintain relevance to our stakeholders.

But, how innovative are we? This was the core question we initially asked when we set out to study innovation in career services. However, as we discussed how innovation happens in organizations, we landed upon a different question that formed the basis of our 2012 study: Are career centers positioned for and capable of innovation? From the outset, we wanted to move beyond the misconception that innovation is synonymous with technology or creativity, and, for the purpose of our study, we defined innovation as the implementation of creative solutions.

It is important to recognize that there are many factors that can influence an organization's capacity for innovation. Certainly the people within the organization are a primary element. The skills and perspectives provided by the staff of a career center will undoubtedly influence the types of ideas that center can generate, as well as the approaches it takes to executing them. While our study did not lead us to ask questions or dig deeply into the literature surrounding this idea, the less scientific, but well-respected *Ten Faces of Innovation* (Kelley, 2005) has influenced our thinking. Our research instead focused on "three capabilities," derived from two studies by PricewaterhouseCoopers (1997, 2000). Their model establishes three primary factors that have an effect on how innovative an organization can be—climate, leadership, and process.

Our survey instrument was sent to approximately 1,200 institutions, with the goal of reaching both the director and one additional staff member, where possible, at each. Only institutions with baccalaureate, master's, and Research Carnegie Classifications were included. We received responses from 626 individuals, who represented 48 states plus the District of Columbia. The majority (63 percent) of the respondents indicated they were "director/leader" of their center. From the resulting data, we gleaned valuable lessons for those wishing to lead with an innovative mindset.

Overcoming obstacles

In addition to our questions on climate, leadership, and process, we explored a few other relevant data points. Specifically, we asked participants to indicate their biggest obstacles to innovation, to provide their most and least used sources of information and inspiration for their innovations, and to outline the volume of their new or significantly improved services, programs, and technologies. Respondents were also prompted to provide a self-evaluation of their center by indicating if they thought their center produced more innovation, about the same amount of innovation, or less innovation than other centers. For the remainder of this essay, we will refer to these as the "more group," "same group," and "less group."

While the "more group" made up only one-third of the total survey respondents, they accounted for a little more than half (51 percent) of the total innovative output during the two academic years prior to the study. The "same group" was nearly the exact inverse, having comprised half the respondents but providing one-third of the innovations. The "less group" made up 16 percent of the study and accounted for 17 percent of the innovations.

While there were many differences in these three groups, a striking commonality for all respondents was the barriers to innovation identified by each, with lack of budget and lack of time cited as the greatest obstacles. All higher education professionals know that budget and time are scarce resources. But, if these obstacles are the same for all, what additional factors allowed the "more group" to produce significantly more innovations? Our study supports the idea that the three capabilities of climate, leadership, and process have a positive impact. Career center leaders interested in innovating would be well served to engage with staff around each of these areas.

Climate

An organization cannot be an innovative one without obtaining buy-in and support from the group as a whole. Innovative organizations create a desire for growth among all of their members, looking beyond day-to-day change by establishing an enthusiasm for growth that pervades the organization (PricewaterhouseCoopers, 2000). The first question in our study related to climate had to do with welcoming change. We found that the majority of respondents (85 percent) agreed or strongly agreed that most members of the staff welcome change, and those that do tend to produce more innovation.

While this openness to change is generally positive for our field, to be best positioned for innovation, we must not only welcome change, but encourage it among one another to inspire growth and improvement. The most influential factor on people's perception of climate is the behavior of role models and leaders within an organization (PricewaterhouseCoopers, 1997). For this reason, it is imperative that leaders establish a shared responsibility of trust, openness, and idea generation.

We also asked if many different viewpoints are shared during discussion. Again, the majority of respondents agreed or strongly agreed with this statement. We found that centers that are more likely to consider diverse viewpoints are also more likely to include the generation of new ideas in their strategic plan. If staff members are aware that creating and implementing new ideas are a part of the organization's long-term goals, they may be more likely to not only chime in, but also listen to and be compelled by others. Most importantly, it is important for leaders to encourage all staff members to speak to avoid relying only on their own ideas or an outspoken few for idea generation or feedback. By bringing as many perspectives to the table as possible, a greater number of new ideas can be shared and better developed as appropriate.

The third question in the climate section asked if new ideas are encouraged from those higher in the organization. Eighty-eight percent of the "more group" reported this as true for their organization, whereas only 61 percent of the "less group" did. In practical terms, it is important for leaders to assess each staff member individually to best understand what will motivate and encourage them to generate ideas. Encouragement can come in many different forms, and our study did not attempt to document all of these. However, our study did reveal a connection between a sense of encouragement and the availability of budget and/or time. Intentionally budgeting time or money for innovation appears to send a message to staff that new ideas are valued and encouraged.

The last question we asked related to climate inquired if people felt they can take bold action, even if the outcome is unclear. Here, we found a striking difference between directors and staff members, with 72 percent of directors compared to 53 percent of staff members agreeing or strongly agreeing with this statement. This difference represents an opportunity for career center leaders. One key to unleashing innovation is for directors to better convey their comfort with this kind of uncertainty and work to develop a climate that is equally open. To do so, directors should minimize negative consequences for failure and instead celebrate and reward the implementation of new ideas, regardless of their initial success.

Many may assume that some organizations are simply innovative by nature, while others are not. We would be remiss if we 1) believe that some organizations inherently have "what it takes" to be innovative while others do not and 2) accept organizational climate as static. Yes, the climate of an organization is rooted in history, prior leadership, and relationships; however, a strong leader can drive climate change within an organization. Creating a climate conducive to innovation takes work, and leaders play a critical role in doing so.

Leadership

It could go without saying that effective leadership is required for innovating. Since you are reading a book focused on career center leadership, you no doubt already have an appreciation for the complexities of the topic. In some ways, leading for innovation involves the same approaches as leading in general, including providing support and open communication. But, leaders are generally more used to taking and encouraging actions that result in efficiencies, consistency, and productivity. Leading for innovation requires using different perspectives, expectations, and approaches. We believe this is true for individuals who are in formal leadership positions, as well as those who lead from within.

The first leadership question asked in our study focused on vision. We found that centers produce more innovation where the leader has a vision for the future of career services that is known to others in the organization. In fact, we found that a connection exists between leaders having a vision and many other innovation-supportive areas of our study. For example, respondents who identified their leaders as having a vision for the future of career services also felt they and their colleagues could take bold actions with unclear outcomes. While we are not suggesting causality, we are assuming from analyzing the data that leaders who have a vision for the future of career services are also proactive in creating a climate and processes that are supportive of innovation.

One example of intentional, proactive efforts is to include innovation as a formal part of a strategic plan. Sixty-nine percent of our respondents agreed or strongly agreed with the statement "new or novel approaches to our work are part of my office's strategic plan." However, for the "more group" this number rises to 85 percent, whereas the "less group" indicated this only 50 percent of the time. Thus, we can deduce that the effect of this action is to increase the potential for innovation. However, our data also revealed an interesting discrepancy that directors are more likely than staff members to agree that innovation is part of their strategic plan. To us, this discrepancy represents an easy opportunity for improvement, as it indicates a communication problem rather than a planning problem. It is a must to articulate the strategic plan to everyone on staff in a clear manner. Our study shows that there are identifiable results when the strategic plan refers specifically to innovation.

The greatest area for leadership improvement revealed by our study was in response to the statement, "leaders of my organization move quickly to adapt to changing circumstances." This was one of the few prompts in our survey that received more negative responses (55 percent) than positive (45 percent). When we view responses from staff members only, we see little improvement (53 percent negative versus 47 percent positive). Even more dramatic results are found when looking at this statement in relation to the volume of innovative output. Specifically, only 29 percent of the "less group" indicated their leaders were quick to adapt to change. While we are unsure if these responses are indicative of leaders not being *aware* of changing circumstances or simply choosing to not adapt to them, they clearly point to a gap in career center leadership.

As expected, our data show that centers led by those who do adapt quickly to changing circumstances, few though they may be, are more likely to produce innovations. Much like the "vision" statement in this section of the survey, this adaptability characteristic was also commonly correlated with other "innovation support" capabilities from climate to processes.

On the whole, our survey participants indicated that improvement is needed in the realm of leadership for innovation. Slightly fewer than half (48 percent) of even the "more group" responded affirmatively on all the questions in this segment of our study, and the "less group" responded affirmatively on all of these questions at an abysmal 17 percent. Our conclusion: Innovation does not simply occur, and our data indicate most leaders are not being proactive in this realm. Intentional and well-articulated actions from leaders are needed to demonstrate that innovation is valued, desired, and actively sought.

Process

Keeping in mind that innovation is the *implementation* of creative solutions, we have to actually act on our new ideas to move forward. Thus, we should not approach innovation haphazardly. Instead, organizations must be strategic, first by researching target markets, identifying goals and objectives, and capturing new ideas to meet these goals (PricewaterhouseCoopers, 1997).

We've addressed the fact that budget and time are the greatest obstacles to innovation, but in this section of our study we directly inquired if budget and time are made available for employees to explore their own ideas. It is no surprise that the majority (62 percent) of our survey respondents indicated that budget and time are not made available. Within that data, we found that a full 80 percent of respondents within the "less group" and a still-significant 42 percent of respondents from the "more group" responded that budget and time are not made available. From this, we can see that leaders associated with the "more group" are providing more support for innovation. But, we also deduce that since fewer than half of the "more group" have budget and/or time made available, the other factors we have explored here have a notable effect on the production of innovation.

Only 53 percent of survey respondents indicated that their office has a system for capturing ideas from staff members. When we asked for examples of such systems, the majority of survey participants responded with various types of meetings. Although meetings can sometimes be effective, we are all aware of many instances where this is not the case. According to PricewaterhouseCoopers (1997), an effective process to capture ideas is one that 1) provides opportunities for people to connect and share information; 2) gives people the tools and skills necessary to become aware of such connections and then take action based upon them; and 3) exists to make knowledge a shared resource, not a source of power. It's important for leaders to assess what systems are in place, if any, and how they match up to these criteria.

Ideas can come from anywhere, but too often we look to the most readily accessible sources around us for inspiration and information. Our choice of sources is influential, as "the quality and uniqueness of *stimulus in* has a direct impact on the quality and uniqueness of *ideas out*" (Allan, et al, p. 4). Our survey respondents indicated that they most frequently use students, employers, and career center staff for such guidance. On the other hand, our survey revealed that career services professionals are generally not looking to organizations outside of the profession, social media, or parents for information and inspiration. This presents a missed opportunity among our profession in which we could be learning from and using resources that would push us beyond our everyday thinking and often limited perspective within higher education.

As seen in the following chart, the process portion of the study was the section receiving the fewest "all affirmative" responses. In fact, this is the only section where even those in the "more group" fell below the 40 percent line in answering all questions affirmatively.

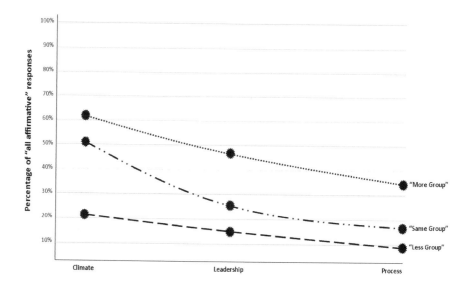

Clearly, there is work to be done in this area, as just over half of survey respondents have a system to capture ideas at all, and those that do rely primarily on meetings. The lack of systems to capture ideas combined with the fact that career services practitioners are seeking inspiration from limited sources of insight further exemplify that we need better processes in place to develop and implement creative solutions. It is simply not enough to have an innovative climate or leadership. Putting processes in place that drive innovation is vital to moving the field forward.

Conclusion

Our study asked respondents to document the number of new or significantly improved programs, services, and technologies implemented over the two years prior. Since the responses were given in ranges, an exact number cannot be produced. However, we can say that minimally our field implemented approximately 1,600 for students and 600 for employers during the 2010-2011 and 2011-2012 academic years.

We found that in reporting their innovative output, career centers have a tendency to focus heavily on technology-driven initiatives, while under-reporting new services and programs. Survey respondents reported examples such as dabbling in the realm of mobile apps and continuing to offer a host of web-based products. Use of social media is now commonplace, and centers are using technologies ranging from screen-capture software to tablet devices to interesting ends.

We were intrigued by novel projects like the center reporting to have computer kiosks across the campus that are locked to allow only for access to the job posting system, and the center that hosts a weekly radio show focused on career development. Several centers report they are beginning or have established programs to support student entrepreneurship, as well.

However, for all these examples, our study also revealed that the overwhelming majority of our new or significantly improved programs, services and technologies (96 percent of output for students; 94.5 percent of output for employers) were based on the work of other career centers. Only 67 total innovations for students and 33 total innovations for employers were reported as being new to the field of career services. While obtaining best practices is a proven way to offer services comparable to our colleagues, we feel relying predominantly on this approach to influence our offerings ultimately restricts the profession and limits the value we can provide to our stakeholders.

Comparatively, the new competitors we face that are providing career development knowledge/services and building connection points for employers are unbound by the history and traditions of our offices and institutions. Simultaneously, our students are not restricted in the resources from which they can seek the information they need. For many students, the career center is not viewed as "the" resource, but rather just "a" resource. They are perhaps more likely to complete a web search to find career advice than they are to use our services.

With these scenarios in mind, the question leaders must ask is whether we are content to simply replicate past successes, or if are we truly prepared to innovate our services to provide the most compelling, meaningful, and educational experiences possible. We have the capacity to do so, and we must enhance our climate, leadership and process capabilities to help us rise to the challenge of positioning our profession for the future.

References

Allan, D., Kingdon, M., Murrin, K., & Rudkin, D. (2002). Sticky wisdom: How to start a creative revolution at work. Oxford, United Kingdom: Capstone Publishing.

Kelley, T. (2005). The ten faces of innovation: IDEO's strategy for defeating the devil's advocate and driving creativity throughout your organization. New York, New York: Doubleday.

PricewaterhouseCoopers. (1997). *Innovation survey.* Archives of PricewaterhouseCoopers, London.

PricewaterhouseCoopers. (2000, January). *Innovation and growth: A global perspective.* Warwickshire, United Kingdom: Davis, T.

The Impact of Social Media on Career Services

Lindsey Pollak

Social media has profoundly changed the recruiting and hiring process. It is no longer an innovation, a novelty or a "nice to have" for employers to use sites like LinkedIn, Twitter, and Facebook to source candidates, vet talent, and market their opportunities. In just a few short years, social recruiting has become a fundamental human resources practice.

This means that social media must be a fundamental practice for student job seekers as well.

As the late New York City Mayor Ed Koch might have asked at this point: "How're they doing?"

So far, not that great.

According to a 2012 Jobvite survey, a massive 92 percent of U.S. companies used social media to find talent in 2012 (up from 78 percent five years earlier). NACE's 2012 Student Survey reveals that only 41 percent of 2012 recent college grads are using social media to help them land positions.

That's a pretty big gap—or, as I'd prefer to see it, a pretty big opportunity. Career services professionals (and external career advisors like me) are learning more and more every day about how to guide students through the new world of social media recruiting.

Just as we teach students to have resumes, we now must teach them to have professional social media profiles. Just as we teach students to review the websites of prospective employers, we now must teach them to follow those employers' social media communications. And just as we urge students to network at company information sessions and career fairs, we now must teach them how to network at Tweetups and Google+ hangouts.

How else is social media impacting career services? Here are three broad themes, along with some best practices for integrating them into the work of your career center:

Social media is now second nature

For the Millennial generation (those born approximately 1982 to 2000, i.e., today's college students), social media is the Internet and the Internet is social media. When a member of this generation is looking for information, advice, recommendations, ideas, or pretty much anything else, he or she is most likely to look on Facebook, Twitter, LinkedIn, Tumblr, Pinterest, YouTube, or another social site. With Facebook's new Social Graph search tool (which allows you to search based on what your Facebook friends are posting about or what fan pages they are liking), this tendency is liable to become even more pronounced.

This means that as a career center, you have to make sure that you are visible in the places your students and alums are searching for information and advice. Make sure your workshop schedule is posted on Facebook and tweeted on a regular basis. Post informational videos on a career center YouTube channel, and be sure to include detailed descriptions of each video so students can find them. Post resume and interview outfit examples on Pinterest. Announce scholarship opportunities in your LinkedIn group. If you're only relying on your website or e-mail blasts to market your services, you are not reaching the majority of today's students.

Referrals matter now more than ever

"Who you know" has always been important, but thanks to social media, finding and tapping one's connections is easier than ever. Companies are taking full advantage of this increased ability to network. Increasingly, employers are using their own employees' networks to bolster their recruiting success (and, of course, to lower their recruiting costs).

According to a January 2013 article in *The New York Times*, employee recommendations now account for 45 percent of non-entry-level placements at Ernst & Young, up from 28 percent in 2010. At Enterprise Rent-A-Car, the *Times* reports, the proportion of workers hired through employee referrals has risen from 33 percent to just under 40 percent in the last two years. And at Sodexo, referred employees are 10 times more likely to be hired than other applicants.

While this practice is not currently as prevalent at the entry level, companies like Ernst & Young, Enterprise, and Sodexo are known for their large campus recruiting programs, and I believe it's only a matter of time before this trend spreads to hiring at the entry level.

This means that now is the time to provide opportunities and guidance for students to connect in meaningful ways with alumni. Career centers can help facilitate these career-building interactions. For instance, Michigan State University has created a LinkedIn group called Spartan LINKS, designed exclusively for students, alumni, and recruiters to discuss career issues and opportunities together. And Brandeis University requires that students sign an Integrity and Social Responsibility Contract for Campus Recruiting and Alumni Networking, which includes specific guidelines for how to network with alumni in an appropriate manner.

At a time when high student loan debt is causing many people to ask, "Is college worth it?," career services professionals can help show that part of the value of a university education is the vast network of potential job connectors and career supporters that every graduate becomes part of. Social media can be that bridge connecting students and alumni for a lifetime.

When employers talk, we need to listen

Social media has also become an indispensable tool for employer relations. The majority of employers now want to communicate with students and career centers through social media, so careers professionals need to be there listening. If I worked in a college career center, I would follow every employer and potential employer on every social network. This would not only help me advise students about which companies or industries are active on which social networks, but it would also help strengthen my career center's relationships with our current roster of employers and companies we were trying to bring to campus.

For instance, if a student walked into my office and said, "My dream is to work for GE," I could reply, "Well, you absolutely must follow their Facebook page; it's a great resource for information on how the company is innovating and would give you excellent conversation topics to chat about when you visit their booth at next month's career fair." Or, if I were trying to entice Red Hat, an open source technology company, to recruit my students, I could say to the lead recruiter, "We've been following the unique ways you are communicating with students on Google+ and you may have noticed some comments on your recent posts from our top computer science students. Can I send you some information about our program?"

Is it time consuming to follow the activities of dozens or hundreds of employers on social media? Yes. Is it time consuming to teach students how to create professional social media profiles and how to interact appropriately in these forums? Yes. Is it time consuming to follow developments in social media to make sure career centers stay up-to-date with the methods employers are using to source, vet, and communicate with students? Yes.

But there is simply no choice.

Social media is the present and it is the future. It is quickly replacing many forms of marketing, phone calling, meeting, and event promotion. When used correctly, social media shouldn't add work to our days but give us a different way of spending our time to achieve the same goals that careers professionals have always achieved: helping employers find young talent, helping students begin their careers, and helping to shape our shared future. I suppose it just takes some getting used to the fact that we now have tools that can achieve all of this in 140 characters or less.

The Future of Career Services

Tom Devlin and Suzanne Helbig

Introduction

Career centers have come a long way since the job placement era of the 1950s and 60s. In the ensuing decades, we have made great breakthroughs, embracing career planning, experiential learning, and networking. Now, with an accelerating rate of technological innovation, the shifting landscape of higher education, and a new generation of career services professionals and students, our profession is poised to make an unprecedented transformation.

This essay presents six strategic themes that will converge to drive the advancement of career services through the next decade. Giving serious thought to these themes is essential for career services leaders who aspire to elevate their organizations from a position of simple relevance to an esteemed and essential need for stakeholders. Before presenting the themes specific to career services, let's acknowledge several major external drivers behind them:

The explosion of technology and social media. Students and career services professionals of the near future will be complete "digital natives," bringing with them expectations of access to instant, self-service, mobile technology. Lifelong social media enthusiasts, they will be highly connected and accustomed to being the media, not merely consuming it. Employers will become much more integrated into the student social space and will have a wealth of social media tools for increasing their brand awareness and targeting highly specific student segments for just-in-time hiring.

The next generation. While there is debate over what the post-Millennial Generation will be called (current contenders include Generation Z, Generation Wii, and the Homeland Generation, a nod to the desire to stay close to home in a post 9-11 world), there is no denying that it will add a unique flavor to college campuses and the workplace, bringing different sets of values, experiences, and learning styles. For example, social media will inform instructional methods and provide the ties that bind, not a unified set of media outlets, a majority population, or a dominant family structure. In addition to a new breed of connectivity, another defining characteristic of this generation will be its outlook on job duration. Graduates of the future will tend to have two-year-time horizons for a string of individual jobs that will make up their careers.

Expectations of practicality of a college education. With the confluence of college tuition sticker shock and the increasingly popular view that college is primarily a ticket to economic advancement, students and their financial aid providers like parents and federal and state governments are demanding to see more evidence of college and career outcomes. Whether students major in the liberal arts, business, or engineering, there will be more pressure and expectations for a demonstrable return on investment.

The value of higher education. While higher education will continue to be highly valued, its traditional funding sources can no longer be relied on. While widely acknowledged that a robust higher education system is necessary to be competitive in the global workplace, state and federal governments, often with the consent of voters and tax payers, will continue their divestment in their public institutions. This will have many implications for who can and cannot afford college, and ultimately for who is available and prepared for the careers of tomorrow. It will also drive campus units to shift more attention to entrepreneurial pursuits to innovate or to simply stay in business.

Recruitment processes of tomorrow. With the above factors in play, hiring at college campuses will evolve greatly in the coming years. For example, traditional resumes will almost completely give way to platforms like LinkedIn and its off-shoots, and today's three main distinct face-to-face forums—campus interviews, fairs, and information sessions—will no longer stand alone. Instead, they will blend into multi-faceted "employer showcases" enhanced by virtual forums that provide seamless integration of traditional employment documents, networking, and candidate demonstrations of workplace skills. Employers will use these showcases, other communication channels, and internship programs to ramp up early identification efforts to the point where many students will have full-time job offers before their senior year, especially in high demand fields.

Six strategic themes for the future

The major drivers above provide the underpinnings for the following six themes for career services that we will now explore in more detail. While no one can predict the future with 100 percent accuracy, depending on who you are and your level of experience, you may confidently consider these themes as either food for thought, a framework for strategic planning, or a highly prescriptive set of guiding principles as you position your organization and your professional trajectory for the future:

1. Reshaping the professional portfolio: Tomorrow's multi-dimensional leader
2. Rethinking communications: Influencing conversations across multiple channels
3. Redefining the scorecard: Metrics, outcomes, and accountability
4. Revolutionizing access: Embracing innovation and self-service delivery
5. Revitalizing our resources: Gaining strength from a national organization
6. Reinventing career services: The new organizational paradigm

Theme 1: Reshaping the professional portfolio: Tomorrow's multi-dimensional leader

With campus career services at the very visible intersection of employment and academics, and career outcomes under growing scrutiny by campus administrators, students, parents, and government officials, successful future career services leaders need to possess a broad range of skills and the ability to deftly employ them as new partners, challenges, and opportunities emerge. While core leadership competencies such as supervision, communication skills, strategic planning, and an understanding of career development theory and a curiosity about the world of work continue to lay a solid foundation, the multi-dimensional leaders of the future will also count the following skills and characteristics among their portfolio:

A champion of coaching: To remain relevant to students who can turn to multiple outlets for career advice, tomorrow's successful leaders will lead organizations that enable students to easily connect with the information they seek and their employers of interest. This marks an evolution from a reflective counseling approach to an in-the-moment coaching approach wherein career centers seek to add value based on individuals' immediate needs and preferred learning styles.

An advanced facility with technology: For credibility and fluency among the "digital native" students and employers of the near future, more than an enthusiastic embrace of technology will be critical. Along with the expectation that leaders will create their own digital and social media to connect with audiences, leaders need to be able to identify opportunities or gaps where technology can play a role and have the technical knowledge to create new systems, articulate a vision to project staff, and evaluate and customize vendors' products.

An enhanced capacity for collaboration: Already a cornerstone of a successful career services operation, the importance of collaboration skills will only grow in the future as campus belt tightening will result in new reporting structures and alignments, and student organizations and academic departments will want to offer their own versions of career services. Tomorrow's leaders will require acumen with negotiating, a willingness to do the hard work behind surfacing satisfying and sustainable group decisions, and a heightened sense of emotional intelligence allowing them to read social cues and act appropriately in both heady and heated moments. Effective leaders will go well beyond building collaborations built on personal relationships; they will establish strategic interdependencies within their institutions that transcend staffing changes.

A quest for data: As calls for accountability and expectations for instant, real-time data increase, leaders will need to be adept at developing qualitative and quantitative data collection mechanisms, interpreting statistical data and identifying trends, and translating data and trends into digestible indexes customized for both internal decision making and external messaging purposes.

A global perspective: As campuses and employers broaden their reach, career services leaders need to develop a global mindset to ensure their organizations are offering services and resources that meet the expectations of their diversifying clientele. Beyond satisfying student and employer needs and often advancing institutional objectives, embodying a global mindset and valuing diversity is a key driver of innovation.

An enthusiasm for entrepreneurship: Budget issues are not going away any time soon, and many career centers will need to initiate ways to generate more revenue to support their programs. Career services leaders of tomorrow not only need a thorough understanding of their budget sources; they also need to be able to articulate the fluidity of employer support to campus administrators to help their organizations stem the tides of the economy and campus budget cuts. Then they need to engage staff and collaboration partners in strategic planning around revenue generating activities such as enhancing employer visibility programs, entering into financial agreements with academic units to provide customized services for students, tapping into alumni supporters, and offering the right mix of large and small forums to bring students and employers together in ways that simultaneously add value and generate revenue.

Theme 2: Rethinking communications: Influencing conversations across multiple channels

When it comes to communication channels, what's old is new again: Content is king and the phone is back. Of course, for now and into the foreseeable future, we are referring to smart phones and the growing expectation that content is highly customized for customer segments, is fresh, and ideally, interactive.

Although social media and mobile technology is well on its way from infancy to adolescence, at press time e-mail marketing still reigns supreme for career services. While e-mail will have its place—essentially as an announcement platform—the proliferation of social media continues to erode traditional linear communication pathways, transforming one-way announcements into conversations across multiple channels and elevating social media "friends" into trusted brand ambassadors. As a result, a challenge for the future is to deliberately align our messaging and influence conversations across multiple channels. Part and parcel of that challenge is to gain an understanding of our audiences' needs and expectations, proactively share our organization's story in a way that resonates, and continuously scan the social media and mobile app environment to identify the channels our audiences frequent most.

Bearing in mind social media is but one communication channel category, we must continue to align our messaging across other channels as well, including traditional print pieces and e-mail, and we must offer easy and on-demand online collaboration tools, such as interfaces that allow our customers to participate in video conversations (a current example is Google Hangouts). Beyond social media, we will need to make our websites and portals (optimized for mobile, of course) highly customizable by allowing users to pick and choose content that is most applicable to them.

Finally, it is our responsibility to educate our audiences, especially students new to the college employment scene, about new communications trends and best practices. For example, with platforms like LinkedIn emerging as the resume of the future, career services professionals are obligated to help both students and employers make the most of the tool and avoid its common pitfalls, including potentially harmful disclosure issues.

Theme 3: Redefining the scorecard: Metrics, outcomes, and accountability

Get used to the spotlight! As more questions are raised about the return on investment of higher education, career services units will be under greater pressure to show the value we add for our students, institutions, and local and national work forces. While many career services units currently use annual placement figures, program evaluations, needs assessments, and office usage statistics to drive internal decision making, in the future our focus needs to turn outward as it will be our campus and external constituents who will compel us to reevaluate and expand how we use metrics.

While there will continue to be great value in annual graduate survey results, stakeholders of the future will expect access to year-round, real-time statistics that they can manipulate to answer specific questions germane to them. For example, campus academic advisors may want instant access to data they can sort to show how many of their seniors have started the job search in October so they can craft an appropriate call to action in November, well before graduation in May. Beyond access to raw data, external users will want to see content-rich and customized student profiles. For example, an employer may want to know how many internships business administration students held as undergraduates, their average salaries coming out of college, and how many job offers they received. Consequently, career services offices will need to offer intuitive self-service student profile creation tools.

Program evaluations and needs assessments to gauge awareness, interest, and satisfaction will continue to be essential for helping career services units make improvements and decisions about where to focus their energy. Forward-thinking career services units will augment these surveys with student learning outcomes to show how their offerings align with greater institutional objectives. In addition, career centers will form student advisory boards focusing on specific populations or career fields to provide highly illuminating context to quantitative measurements. Our stakeholders will also look to us to translate our metrics into accountability statements, and more career centers will engage in cost/benefit analyses to demonstrate that their resources are allocated to high demand or critical need areas.

To make the most impact with metrics, career services leaders will need to work closely with campus partners to integrate career center findings into institutional databases where they will be highly visible when campus budgeting and strategic planning take place. To further advance their interests, career centers should present dashboards that translate individual data points into simple and compelling stories (for example, it is much more powerful to present the aggregate of how many employer-student contacts were made rather than lists of fair participation and campus interview numbers) and use easy-to-understand infographics and data visualizations to make data come to life. Finally, career centers will need to leverage campus partnerships to coordinate survey dissemination in an effort to manage student survey fatigue and increase response rates.

Theme 4: Revolutionizing access: Embracing innovation and self-service delivery

Long gone are the days when students and employers had to visit career center offices during business hours to get what they needed. The integration of the Internet into career services continues to change expectations as it has evolved from a simple announcement platform offering easy access to information into what it is now: a place where students and employers interface with our offices to complete transactions. The next step in this evolution is to offer more customizable self-service options, an advancement that will free up staff to move from transactional to transformational work and deliver a more effective mix of high-touch and high-tech services that sync with the needs of the next generation of students and employers.

Technological and self-service options will be the preferred delivery methods for many career center functions in the future, for example:

- Students and employers will no longer accept our static homepages as an entrée to our services. Individuals will have great flexibility to create their own portal and apps featuring the services and information that resonate with them. They will be able to customize settings so that specific job postings and event updates are pushed to their mobile devices in real-time.

- Access to alumni will evolve and increase. Beyond better online conferencing tools for featuring alumni from across the globe on career panels, the future also promises the ability for students to highly customize their alumni access through online interactive alumni galleries. Using their mobile devices, students will be able to select alumni from the gallery on their mobile phone, view their video profiles, and instantly chat or set informational interview appointments.

- Career courses and workshops will be offered online and the content will be driven by students. For example, students will be able to customize content in real time by choosing the next module that makes sense for them in the moment, and they will be able to interact with facilitators and other remote viewers while simultaneously watching the workshop and sharing documents.

- Counseling will regularly be offered via robust online video interfaces, allowing for sessions to transcend geographic boundaries and traditional business hours. Advancements in handheld tablet devices will also open up possibilities for career center staff to take their services beyond traditional brick and mortar boundaries: Staff themselves will be "mobile" as they carry tablets throughout campus and interact with different constituents.

- When students and employers visit career centers in the future, instead of being greeted with the print libraries, reception desks, and waiting areas of today, they will encounter self-service kiosks as well as greeters equipped with tablet computers who can help them quickly find what they need and orient them to other services they can use at their convenience.

- A wealth of electronic resources will push aside the print collections found in many of today's career libraries. Career centers will rely heavily on career services professional organizations and other vendors to provide online information and tools that the patrons of the future will expect.

Theme 5: Revitalizing our resources: Gaining strength from a national organization

Great shifts in technology and society in the last 30 years have exponentially accelerated rates of change, and meeting the quickly evolving needs of a diverse set of stakeholders will put unprecedented demands on career services staffs, making the need for a robust, nimble, and comprehensive national professional organization more critical than ever. Our profession has the advantage of such an organization, the National Association of Colleges and Employers (NACE), which was founded in 1956 and has evolved over the decades to meet the changing needs of career services. This will continue to be an essential requirement for our profession as we look ahead to revitalizing our resources into the future.

While associations targeting geographic regions, quasi-formal network groups, and similarly structured institutions will continue to have an important role for their members, a national association such as NACE will be the essential support system that undergirds and aligns career centers across the country. In today and tomorrow's "do more with less" and outcomes-driven environments, a national association will free up administrative time in many ways, allowing career centers to increase productivity and devote more attention to serving customers. The expertise and creativity of its diverse membership will allow it to evolve into a compelling voice for career centers, becoming their strongest advocate as they face increased demands to demonstrate value in a future filled with calls for greater accountability from many corners.

For example, a national organization can greatly assist with timely and customized assessment design, distribution, and interpretation by saving time, greatly informing decisions about policy, and providing data for both accountability and messaging purposes. With its national reach, the organization will be best positioned to gather, vet, and present the field's very best practices as well as curate the information presented in numerous websites into a reliable and comprehensive knowledge base. The knowledge base will also feature of-the-moment position papers on the latest legal and ethical developments developed by the organization's cadre of legal experts—once again saving career center staff time and ensuring an interpretation based on specialized expertise. Finally, a national association will be best positioned to enable career centers to learn and adapt to global best practices and develop ties internationally with our colleagues around the world.

Our national professional association will have the best infrastructure to provide enhanced online and in-person forums for career centers to collaborate with campus and employer partners and thought leaders without geographic limitations. Its broad view will allow it to identify opportunities to develop and deploy tools career centers need most, including a consistent, national set of professional standards, professional development activities, and innovative in-person and online ways to serve and engage our students, employers, and campus partners.

Theme 6: Reinventing career services: The new organizational paradigm

A diversity of institutional missions and student bodies means there cannot be a one-size-fits-all approach to how career services offices of the future will be structured. While we may remain centralized, decentralized, or increasingly somewhere in between, for all of us moving from collaborating to actually integrating with campus, employer, and external vendor partners will be necessary, and it will fundamentally change our organizational models. How this challenge is handled will mark the difference between surviving and thriving in the future.

Those who will succeed will shed old identities, no longer seeing themselves as the sole career services provider and others as interlopers. Challenges facing us now and into the future will lead to recasting today's competitors as partners in innovation, entrepreneurialism, and customer service. Career centers will assume a new role as the sun in a solar system of orbiting service providers who will have different needs for sustaining life. Being the bright spot in the future will require extreme flexibility and continuous communication in order to present a united front of seamless service to students and employers. Nothing less than an aligned experience will be expected; anything else will be quickly dismissed.

Career services partners of the future will provide far more than what they typically do today: publicity, panelists, and venues. Instead they will be woven into the fabric of what we offer; for example:

- Instead of occasional collaborations, career centers will closely comingle and, in some cases, merge with other campus functions such as academic advising, financial aid, alumni relations, public service centers, leadership education, and development to create synergies and efficiencies around serving shared constituents and their interests. For example, in the future many career services units will greatly expand their partnerships with academic advising units, seeing them as much more than places to send students for course selection advice. It will become commonplace for staff in both units to join forces to help students navigate their way through their institutions and find pathways between academics and the world of work.

- While on-campus recruiting will still be important, the provision of experiential education will usurp its place as the hallmark of campus career services. Career centers will shift more of their resources to partnering with campus units, employers, and alumni to address the booming student interest in internship and externship programs.

- Student demand will drive campuses to centralize all online career content in one place. The campus "one stop shop" career web presence may be jointly owned by several campus units, and its student users will expect the content to be seamless, customizable, and optimized for mobile devices. The online career "one stop" of the future will include a workshop app that brings together career-related workshops hosted by any number of campus groups. Students can use the app to indicate which workshops capture their interest most and to provide information on their ability to attend them. In turn, campus units will use this data to inform decisions about workshop offerings and their timing in an effort to reduce duplicate events, ensure sizable audiences, and respond to immediate student needs.

- While many career centers today secure a grant here or there and generate revenue from a number of career fairs, most rely on a central campus allocation for the majority of their budget. To maintain operations, career centers of tomorrow will need to diversify their funding sources by entering into strategic campus partnerships. Along with sharing in campus and student registration fees, smart career centers of the future will increasingly integrate with academic departments that will underwrite portions or all of salaries and supplies for career services staff who will provide highly customized advising, resources, programs, and job development for their students.

Closing thoughts: Four ways to be a career services futurist

This essay presented a broad overview of external drivers impacting the future, the skills successful leaders of tomorrow will possess, challenges and opportunities they will face, how a national organization will provide support, and a vision for how leaders will integrate partners into their organizations to meet the needs and expectations of tomorrow's students and employers. While we feel our forecast is reliable, the only thing we can say with complete certainty is that the future will hold surprises. To help you stay one step ahead, we leave you with a few thoughts on how to integrate futuristic thinking into your work:

1. **Think big.** Set aside time from your immediate tasks to look at issues using a global perspective.

2. **Think long term.** While you do need to think about next term, reset your time horizon to think like a futurist. What will happen in 5, 10, even 20 years from now?

3. **Think possibilities.** Since no one knows what the future holds, don't get caught in a trap of thinking of one future or being beholden to how things were done in the past. Question the status quo and think in terms of different scenarios. Keep asking: "What if?" and "Why not?"

4. **Think beyond collaboration.** Campus departments, student groups, and external commercial vendors all want to be part of the career services sphere. A major role for our profession's future leaders is to figure out how to best integrate with these organizations to provide innovative and creative services for the students and employers of tomorrow.

References

Butler, Stuart M. The coming higher-ed revolution. *National Affairs*, Winter 2012, 10, pp.1-19.

Craighill, Peyton M. New polls value a college degree. *Washington Post Behind The Numbers Blog.* May 18, 2011. Retrieved from: http://www.washingtonpost.com/blogs/behind-the-numbers

Dey, Farouk, and Real, Matt. Emerging trends in university career services: adaptations of Casella's Career Center Paradigm. *NACE Journal*, September 2010, 71 (1), pp. 31-35.

Horowitz, Bruce. After Gen X, Millennials, what should the next generation be called? *USA Today*, May 3, 2012. Retrieved from: http://www.usatoday.com/money/advertising/story/2012-05-03/naming-the-next-generation/54737518/1

National Association of Colleges and Employers. "NACE's Future Initiative: Career Services and Recruiting—2015." Retrieved from http://NACEweb.org

IN 100 WORDS OR LESS...

Through various social media outlets and forums the following statements were provided by practitioners in response to the question: What is the best advice you could offer to a career services director?

With escalating changes in the career services field and in our ever-increasing relevancy to higher education, the work force, and the economy, my advice would center on two key things: 1) engage in as many aspects of the field and professional associations as possible while developing specialty interests and expertise, and 2) stay connected to the academic core of the institution you serve. No matter what division you are housed in, strive to meet with and support well-respected, experienced faculty, chairs, researchers, advisors, and deans. Gain a reputation for listening—for being concerned about the pressures and issues they face.

Denise Dwight Smith
Director and Liaison For NC Campus Compact
University Career Center for Work, Service, and Internships
University of North Carolina Charlotte

Your mission—if you choose to accept it—is Career Services Director. Your directions:

- The NACE Principles ARE your guide.
- Transformational leaders are transformed more than they transform.
- "Run flat" is better for organizations than tires.
- The moral is great but few people fish for their food nowadays.
- Social media is happening but no one cares what you ate for lunch.
- Ask yourself: If students learn at career services but no administrator "hears," did they actually learn?

This message and your career will self-destruct if these instructions are not followed!

Chaim Shapiro
Assistant Director, Office of Career Services
Touro College

Always keep in mind that the student is your customer and also the customer of the company recruiter. Both the career center and the recruiter exist to serve the same customer need...to help the student prepare for and make wise career decisions. With the focus on jobs and the cost of a good college education, more universities are realizing that a key differentiator for a parent and student in selecting one school over another is the quality of the career center. The career center should be the second place prospective students visit after the admissions office.

Steven Canale
Corporate Human Resources Manager
GE Global Recruiting & Staffing Services

I used to work for a director who would regularly send out job postings to his staff—not because he wanted people to leave, but because he genuinely wanted each of us to pursue any opportunity to develop professionally. As a director now myself, I encourage my staff to take on responsibilities that will fill holes in their resumes. When the head of our counseling team was tapped to start a new career services office at another institution, I mourned her loss—but delighted in her accomplishments. Develop the careers of your staff and their success will be your success.

Sharon Belden Castonguay, EdD
Director, Graduate Career Management Center
Baruch College Zicklin School of Business

While leadership is mostly episodic, followership is mostly constant. Career services leaders should know that followership is the subject of studies that aim to identify and define follower typologies and skills, since the interactions of leaders and followers can make the difference between success and failure in most endeavors. In the age of social media, "following" has become part of a shared vernacular, and followers are increasingly aware of their influence. Simultaneously, the leadership industry recognizes followership as an integral part of leadership studies, which is mostly contextualized within hierarchical power structures; self-aware leaders scrutinize their own status as followers.

Robert Thill
Director, Center for Career Development
The Cooper Union for the Advancement of Science and Art

Career services sits at the nexus of multiple, often conflicting stakeholders: students, parents, employers, alumni, fundraising/advancement, faculty, and student affairs. Sometimes, what we actually do is clearly understood by these parties—but not always. Sometimes, we are fully supported in what we do—but not always. Therefore, to be a good Director of Career Services, one must be the ultimate schmoozer, negotiator, advocate, communicator, and influencer, especially with those over whom we have no direct authority. There are two keys to success: communicating clearly, using metrics, graphics, and compelling stories; and always presenting our case in terms of how it benefits the other party.

Heather Krasna
Director of Personal and Professional Development
Fordham University Gabelli School of Business

"*Model* flexibility" is my advice to career services leaders. When faced with budget cuts, reorganization, and a challenging job market, leaders who adapt quickly and remain solution-focused demonstrate the professional skills that we aspire to impart to students and alumni. As we manage staff and programs and promote career services in our institutions, we often find expectations increasing as resources dwindle. Implementing creative ideas for change and creating a culture that supports that response to challenges can result in a happier work force, better service, and a useful model for professional life.

Elizabeth Burton
Director, Academic & Career Advising

Eastern Oregon University

Collaboration is important. Career services is linked to many key functions at a university. Establishing and maintaining collaborative efforts can go a long way to providing excellent service to students. Working with other offices such as admissions, advising, disability services, student activities, and academic departments can help students make the connection of what they are doing and learning in the classroom and how they will use this in their profession. Students can better understand how the decisions they make with processes such as admissions and advising will impact their professional options when career services is an integrated part of the process.

Tamie Eynon
Internship and Placement Coordinator
Stark State College

Look down your chain of supervision—these people matter. If you don't take the time and get to know them, you will never know how to lead them. You were not hired just to sign timesheets, arbitrate disputes, and attend meetings. You took this job because you wanted to be a leader and carry your vision to reality. To do this, you will need help along the way. These people won't be "your people" if you drop the ball and focus on the things that keep you from the true reason you were hired. Leaders lead people, plain and simple.

James E. Mitchell
Associate Director, Employer Relations and Recruitment Programs
Career Center
Ball State University

The best piece of advice I was given when I began my career as an advisor was "never get too comfortable, always keep your eyes open for the next opportunity." I have found that with every new opportunity comes new challenges. My transition from career advisor at a large public university to director at a small private university has now equipped me with advice to share: Take time to adapt to your new surroundings, do not try to "move mountains" in your first month, use the strengths of other staff on campus, and establish at least one to two mentor relationships with a seasoned professional in the field.

Kristin Eicholtz
Director, Career Services and Internships
DeSales University

We all recognize natural leaders in our profession—the ones who make leading a career services office look easy and professionally rewarding. To find a successful path, many aspiring leaders use model-based approaches to leadership. A supplement to leadership models is to understand and trust the natural ebb and flow of process and to integrate dynamic co-authorship into leadership practices. While this approach is not normally recognized as "capital L" Leadership, it is leadership without fanfare, trophies, or a focus on the top. The key is for leaders to let go of personal gain and instead focus on organizational gains.

Kevin Gaw, PhD
Director, University Career Services
Georgia State University

The best advice for a career services director is to have a sound method for getting to know the strengths and weaknesses of your staff. A career office's constituents are best served when employees are in roles that fit them best. Through numerous professional development opportunities, staff can enhance other attributes that are essential to an office's vision and growth, and a good director will use those effectively. And they should never forget to have fun every now and then!

Craig S. Wilkinson, M.A.
Career Advisor, The Career Center
University of Akron

Transitioning to the role of career services director is really about transitioning from practitioner to department manager, from being the strongest link to risk being the weakest (by building an exceptionally talented team), from being the person who gets it done to becoming the person who helps others get it done (by "managing up" and "coaching down" to reach higher performance levels), from being the student who aspires to teach to becoming the teacher who challenges students to become the next generation of leaders (by monitoring outcomes and modeling accountability). It's about taking the advice we've been giving to our students all along.

John Suarez, MA
Associate Director of Career Services
DeVry University - St. Louis Westline Campus

As a brand new career director, I knew I needed to connect with other career professionals and find a mentor with a history of success in career services. I was fortunate to find one who became a fantastic "go-to" for advice, materials, assistance with vendors, ideas to connect with faculty and parents, and even power points for my first few workshop presentations. My mentor even came to my university and presented on teaching portfolios when I had no idea what they were. The encouragement, guidance, and wisdom she shared with me that first year set the tone for what has become a most rewarding career. I am now a mentor through NACE and owe it all to her!

Amy Croft
Manager of Career Consulting
Colorado Technical University

While it can be a challenge for university career centers to work with college students with disabilities, the rewards are great. One of the best ways for career centers to work with such students is to focus on the skills (technical, communication, and interpersonal) these students can bring to a company. Once career centers have a better understanding of the skill set offered by their students, a next step would be to become familiar with some common accommodations in the workplace. With insight on both student skills and workplace accommodations, career centers can help educate employers about what students with disabilities can offer.

John Macko
Director, Center on Employment
National Technical Institute for the Deaf Rochester Institute of Technology

Have a clear vision and establish goals to help you plan and prioritize your efforts. Our vision was to make the office THE place for students, employers, and departments to go to for their career needs. We had four goals that were key to our planning process: centralizing services, providing specialized services and resources, reaching out to departments and offices, and our mantra, "Attract Believers, Build Allies and Form Partnerships." These four goals were the guideposts for our planning and operations. From a decentralized, fragmented campus, Stanford's career center has had great success achieving its vision through its planning process.

Lance Choy
Past Director, Career Development Center
Stanford University

"You work for them—not the other way around." Though I first heard this phrase on the path to becoming an officer in the United States Coast Guard, it has served me well in this field, as well. I find that I come back to it often and highly recommend this for any upcoming career center director. It is a crucial function of our jobs to make sure our staff members have the resources and support they need to get the job done. No matter how good we might be as a director, their success is essential to ours.

Hilary Flanagan
Director, Career Center
John Carroll University

At a recent career professionals workshop, in response to a discussion on tempering expectations of a new generation, a participant blurted out, "I feel like a dream crusher!" Fifty-nine of us laughed uncomfortably, but knowingly. We walk a fine line in career services, helping students articulate expansive career goals while encouraging realistic strategies in line with their education. And as pressure to provide positive metrics on first destination increases, so does the pressure to encourage students to get to the "realistic" part. My advice? *Garner clear institutional support and understanding for this duality so you can continue to offer the best possible career development experience!*

Kathy Douglas
Associate Director, Career Services
Yale School of Forestry & Environmental Studies

As an NACE MLI graduate, I was sure that I had the skills to take on the role of "Director" with confidence. While I still believe that to be true, there is no more valuable "director education" than that of coming to work every day. What I have learned:

- *Know thyself*: Before assembling a team or assigning tasks within that team, know where you and others excel. Allow everyone to shine in what they do best!
- *Allow and expect mistakes*: Mistakes are a part of growth. Without a few failures, success doesn't feel quite so wonderful.

Christina M. Whitney, MS, NCC
Director, SOM Career Services
Binghamton University

Engage in the best professional associations and be an *active* member. Attend two or three conferences a year (budget may dictate how many!). If you want to secure your ability to attend professional conferences each year, bring back a successful college-wide program that is a presidential "home run." Find ways to bring in funding to your program, like a community and corporate-sponsored etiquette dinner for seniors. Join a community civil organization like Rotary, Lions, or Kiwanis. Become a Chamber of Commerce member who actually attends mixers—you need to meet the influential individuals in your area. Help with your civic organization's fund raisers, and they will reciprocate when you need assistance. As you can see, if you follow this advice you will need to be off campus networking at least half the time.

Rol Walters, M.Ed
Director, Career Services Office
Ferrum College

Careers offices in the 21st century cannot operate in isolation. For your office to be perceived as a strategic advantage rather than a cost center to your institution, align your vision and goals with those of your university. Don't think you need to "go it alone." Often, you can expand your reach through partnerships with faculty, student peer advisors, or a "Career Community" of volunteer alumni and parents. You will, of course, need excellent leadership skills and the ability to shrewdly manage resources. But, for your students to find career success, you'll also have to understand employer needs, build relationships, and become orchestrators of opportunity.

Sheila Curran, SPHR
CEO and Chief Strategist
Curran Consulting Group

About the Authors

Emanuel (Manny) Contomanolis - Editor

Manny is the Associate Vice President for Enrollment Management and Career Services and Director of the Office of Cooperative Education and Career Services at the Rochester Institute of Technology. He has nearly 35 years of higher education experience and is active as a consultant, speaker, author, media contributor, and member of various boards and benchmarking groups. Considered one of the leading national and international experts in cooperative education and experiential learning, he has several research interests in this area, and is the author of various juried articles on the topic. Manny has represented the profession in a variety of roles internationally in Japan, China, Israel, France, and Australia.

Manny is a principal in TruMann Career Consulting and a Past President of the National Association of Colleges and Employers (NACE) as well as the Eastern Association of Colleges and Employers (EACE). He is the recipient of a Fulbright Award as well as a number of other outstanding professional service awards. He is a member of the NACE Academy of Fellows and an instructor with the NACE Management Leadership Institute and the Career Services Institute. Manny has chaired numerous national professional association committees and work groups in both career services and cooperative education and has provided leadership and expert opinion to a number of state government task forces, corporate and nonprofit entities. He was a key participant in the launch of the NACElink Symplicity partnership and resulting system application, and was a lead trainer in support of the launch of the NACE External Review Program. Manny has a Ph.D. in Educational Policy and Leadership from the University of Buffalo, a graduate certificate in Industrial and Labor Relations from Cornell University, an M.A. in College Student Personnel from Bowling Green State University, and a B.A. in History from the State University of New York at Cortland.

Trudy Steinfeld - Editor

Trudy Steinfeld is the Assistant Vice-President and Executive Director of the New York University Wasserman Center for Career Development and oversees 40 full-time and 25 part-time staff. Trudy has spent over 30 years in the field of career development, experiential education, and recruiting, and was selected to facilitate the training of external review consultants by the National Association of Colleges and Employers (NACE). Trudy is a contributor to Forbes.com and writes a column entitled Career Warrior. She has served as a consultant to numerous colleges and universities, nonprofits, and corporate recruiting organizations both within the United States and abroad. In addition, Trudy has been a presenter and keynote speaker at over 100 national meetings and conferences including NACE Annual Meetings, Career Services Institute (CSI), Universum, and Women for Hire, and, beginning in 2013, will be an instructor at the NACE Management Leadership Institute. She has chaired or served on several key committees, taskforces, and major conferences for the National Association of Colleges and Employers. In addition, Trudy has been a recipient of both NASPA and NACE Excellence awards.

Trudy is considered a national expert on the job market and employment trends and has been a frequent media contributor to major news organizations including The New York Times, Wall Street Journal, Business Week, CNN, PBS, and many others. Trudy earned her Bachelor's degree in American Studies and Education from Ramapo College and holds a Master's degree from the Graduate School of Arts and Science at New York University. She has also completed extensive doctoral level course work in Counseling Psychology from the NYU Steinhardt School of Culture, Education, and Human Development.

Marie Artim

Marie Artim is the Vice President of Talent Acquisition for Enterprise Holdings, supporting the Enterprise, Alamo, and National Brands. Marie is responsible for company wide strategies that involve marketing, branding, interactive media, as well as training and tools for more than 200 Enterprise recruiters.

Marie holds a Bachelor's degree from Purdue University and began her career in Enterprise's nationally recognized Management Training Program soon after graduation. Over the next several years, Marie worked her way up and assumed increasingly senior leadership positions in company operations, human resources, and recruiting. Marie took over global talent acquisition responsibilities in 2000 and now oversees one of the most respected and largest college recruiting programs in the country. Marie has been featured in several books, publications, and national media outlets including BusinessWeek, The Wall Street Journal, Forbes, and Good Morning America. Marie recently served as President of the National Association of Colleges and Employers (NACE) and continues to serve on the board and continues to be an important change agent in recruiting and career services.

Jim Beirne

Jim Beirne is the Director of External Relations for the Washington University Career Center, working on job creation via parents, alumni, and strategic recruiting organizations. He also works on branding campaigns to raise awareness the high quality of Washington University students and alumni in the employment marketplace. Jim joined Washington University in 2004 as Associate Dean and Director of the Weston Career Center. In prior roles, he led the Americas recruiting organization for Hewlett Packard and was Director of University Recruitment at General Mills.

Jim worked at the Wharton School at the University of Pennsylvania from 1985 to 1994, serving as General Manager of The Joseph H. Lauder Institute of Management & International Studies, and for seven years as Director of Career Services for the Wharton School, in addition to serving as Director of the Global Immersion Programs in Japan, Brazil and China. Prior to Wharton, Jim spent a decade in various management positions for International Multifoods, based as an expatriate in Venezuela, Brazil, and Canada. He holds a Bachelor's of Science from St. Joseph's University in Philadelphia and went on to earn his M.B.A. from the Thunderbird School of Global Management in Arizona.

Dan Black

Dan Black is the Americas Director of Campus Recruiting at Ernst & Young, a leading global professional services organization providing audit, tax, transaction, and advisory services. He works with a diverse team of recruiters, partners, and staff to solidify the firm's position as a market leader at colleges and universities throughout North and South America. Dan is active in several professional and philanthropic organizations including the American Institute of Certified Public Accountants, the National Association of Colleges and Employers (NACE), and the March of Dimes.

Prior to his current role, Dan served as the lead campus recruiter for the firm's Metropolitan New York Area practice. Before joining recruiting, Dan served a variety of financial services clients as a certified public accountant and senior audit professional. Dan earned his Bachelor's degree in Accounting from Binghamton University and his Master's in Human Resources from Fordham University. He is a member of the Board of Directors of NACE, and is a frequent spokesperson on recruiting trends in publications and media including the Wall Street Journal, Bloomberg BusinessWeek, CNN, and National Public Radio. In his spare time, he enjoys being involved in his community, playing and coaching sports, and serving as a volunteer firefighter in the Archville Fire Department.

Patricia Carretta

Patricia Carretta brings over 40 years of hands-on experience in higher education. As Assistant Vice President for University Life at George Mason University, her direct reports include University Life Assessment, Research and Retention, Career Services, Counseling and Psychological Services, Graduate Student Life, and Technology Integration. Before assuming her current role, Pat served as Associate Dean and Director of University Career Services at George Mason. Pat also worked at Career Services in several capacities at the University of Iowa. She is a member of the Council for the Advancement of Standards for Higher Education (CAS) executive committee and served on the CAS task force that revised the CAS learning domains and outcomes. She has presented frequently on assessment practices and student learning outcomes at CAS Symposiums, ACPA, and at NASPA Assessment and Retention Conferences. Pat is a recipient of NACE's Kauffman Award and is also a member of the NACE Academy of Fellows. She has served in several leadership capacities to NACE, EACE, MAPA, and the Virginia Association of Colleges and Employers in which an award was created in recognition of her contributions to the profession. Pat holds an M.A. in Counselor Education with emphasis on College Student Personnel and Higher Education from the University of Iowa and both an M.A. and B.A. in English from Binghamton University.

Andy Ceperley

Andy Ceperley has served on five university campuses during his 25 years as a higher education practitioner and leader. He joined the University of Melbourne in Australia in 2013 as Project Director for the university's re-envisioned Careers & Employment Services team. From 2003 to 2012, Andy served as Director of the Career Services Center at the University of California, San Diego. In 2011, he became the first Assistant Vice Chancellor for the UC San Diego Student Affairs Experiential Learning Cluster, a network of more than 100 Student Affairs professionals and student leaders across integrated student service areas, including undergraduate research; study abroad and international student/scholar programs; tutoring services; career and internship services; and employer engagement.

Prior to joining UC San Diego, Andy worked at the University of Virginia, the University of Texas at Austin, Santa Clara University, and the former May Company (Hecht's Department Stores, Washington, DC). Active in professional associations and benchmarking communities, Andy is frequently tapped to serve as a speaker, facilitator, and consultant. He has served on the faculty of the Career Services Institute as well as the NACE Management Leadership Institute, and he has conducted career services program reviews on campuses throughout the United States and abroad. In addition, he was awarded a grant from the Fulbright Commission to participate in a three-week seminar for career services practitioners in Germany and Poland and hosted the first team of Germans to visit the United States through the same program.

Andy has been a passionate NACE member throughout his career, contributing on the NACE Board from 2007 to 2010 and elected NACE President (2012-13). He is the first NACE officer serving the association from a university outside the United States.

Deb Chereck

Deb served in a variety of career services capacities for 35 years, most recently as the Director of the University of Oregon Career Center. While at the University of Oregon, she designed and taught several career-related courses and built a successful internship program. Deb also led several strategic planning processes and built an employer relations program that resulted in successful student outcomes. Deb served as President of both the Western Association of Colleges and Employers and the National Association of Colleges and Employers. Making contributions to the profession is a highlight of her career as well as the meaningful relationships she gained throughout her experience. She represented our profession in Germany with the Fulbright Commission, led a NACE delegation to Japan to sign a memo of understanding for the sharing of career services expertise, and delivered presentations at regional, national, and international settings. She is a member of two national benchmarking groups, the University Network and the National Career Services Benchmarking Group. Deb retired from the profession in 2012 and continues to support employer and alumni engagement for University of Oregon students.

Tom Devlin

Tom Devlin is the Director of the Career Center at the University of California, Berkeley. Before joining Berkeley in 1997, he was the Executive Director of University Career Services at Cornell University. Tom has appeared on the *Today* show and *NBC Nightly News* and has written numerous papers and articles, one of which received the *Journal of Career Planning and Employment* Award for "Most Outstanding Article of the Year." He has served as president of the Middle Atlantic Placement Association, and was president of the national professional organization, the National Association of Colleges and Employers (NACE) for 2009-10.

In addition to Tom's consulting work and speaking engagements, he has traveled to both Algeria and Rwanda to assist in establishing the first career centers there. He was in China during the summer of 2012 to address the first national Career Center conference. His work in the career services field has brought him recognition from his peers; including receiving the NACE Warren Kauffman Award and being elected to the prestigious NACE Academy of Fellows (2004). During his tenure at Berkeley, Tom has emphasized first-class customer service, leveraging technology, and developing partnerships to best serve students and employers. The Career Center has been awarded two national honors by NACE for producing the best publication for students and for the most innovative program in the country, and in 2009 Tom received Berkeley's Excellence in Management Award.

Tom's avocation is traveling, and he has visited more than 80 countries as well as traveling the world during a six-month sabbatical. He received a B.A. in History from the State University of New York at Geneseo and an M.A. in College Student Personnel from Bowling Green State University, Bowling Green, Ohio.

Joseph Du Pont

Joe Du Pont has worked in the fields of career services, external relations, corporate law and volunteerism for over 20 years and currently serves as the Dean of the Hiatt Career Center at Brandeis University. Previous to Brandeis, Joe was the Vice President of the Office of Career and Civic Opportunities at Teach For America, the national corps of recent college graduates who commit two years to teach in urban and rural public schools. Teach For America hired Joe in 2002 to design and implement its first national career development strategy for corps members and alumni. Under his watch, Teach For America was one of the first terms of service programs to create a robust network of graduate school and corporate partnerships to provide volunteers with opportunities after completing their corps commitment.

Prior to joining the staff of Teach For America, Joe worked at the New York University Office of Career Services. He has also chaired or served on several committees for the National Association of Colleges and Employers and currently serves on its Board of Directors. Joe also chaired the job development committee of the Liberal Arts Career Network. In addition, Joe has taught high school and practiced corporate law in New York City. Joe has his Bachelor's degree from Duke University in History and Religion, a law degree from Georgetown University Law Center, and an M.A. in Higher Education Administration from New York University.

Jeff W. Garis

Jeff is Senior Director for Career Services at Penn State University and is an Affiliate Professor of Counselor Education. Additionally, he is a licensed Psychologist in Pennsylvania. Jeff served as Director of the Florida State University Career Center from 1992 through 2011. He was also an affiliate faculty member of the FSU Counseling Psychology and Psychological Services in Education programs. Prior to his career at FSU, Jeff was associated with Career Development Services at Penn State University for over 20 years. He holds a Ph.D. in Counselor Education, a M.Ed. in Counselor Education, and a B.S. in Psychology; all from Penn State. He is co-author of a chapter addressing counseling services in Upcraft and Gardner's book, *The Freshman Year Experience* published by Jossey-Bass. Jeff also is the co-author of a book entitled *Handbook for the College/University Career Center* published by Greenwood Press. Jeff is the Senior Editor and chapter author of a book published in fall 2007 by Jossey Bass entitled *Emerging ePortfolios: Opportunities for Student Affairs.*

Jeff has been active in conducting program reviews and site visitations of university career centers. Recent reviews included Stanford University, University of Nebraska, University of Central Florida, Loyola Marymount University, and Florida Atlantic University. His international consultations have included University of the West Indies campuses in Jamaica, Barbados and Trinidad; University of Costa Rica-San Jose and Turrialba campuses; and the People's Republic of China National Ministry of Education in Beijing and Shanghai.

Marva Gumbs Jennings

Marva Gumbs Jennings is a 34-year plus veteran in the career services field and began her career working in with the disabled community on her home island of St. Croix in the Virgin Islands. Marva is Managing Director of Interdisciplinary Career Services Initiatives at The George Washington University Career Center. In this role, Marva is responsible for providing critical university-wide strategic coordination for a number of interdisciplinary initiatives designed to connect across schools/colleges, research centers, and administrative programs. Focused on key university priorities in sustainability, civic engagement and public service, entrepreneurship, and international programs, specific targets include veterans, international students, athletes, and students with disabilities. Prior to this position, Marva served as Executive Director overseeing strategic initiatives for a comprehensive center, providing career education and employer services, student employment and experiential education programs, and the technological, communications and event management aspects of the department. Prior to joining George Washington, Marva worked for a number of years with the Psychiatric Institute in Washington, DC, and the Division of Vocational Rehabilitation in St. Croix, USVI.

Marva received her graduate degree in Education from George Washington, and her Bachelor's from Rutgers University. She is active in the National Association of Colleges and Employers (NACE) and the Eastern Association of Colleges and Employers (EACE). Marva held the unique distinction of becoming the first elected president of EACE, a new organization formed with the merger of two professional associations. She served as president of the executive board (1997-98) and past president (1999) of EACE, as a member of the NACE Board of Presidents (1997-98), and on the NACE Board as Regional Director for EACE (2002-2004). Marva has served on several NACE national committees and task forces annually and is currently a faculty member of the Career Services Institute West. Marva is a well-known expert in the field of career development and has been featured in several media outlets.

Marcia B. Harris

Marcia B. Harris has over 30 years of experience in the career services field, having worked in three college career services offices. Marcia served as Director of University Career Services at UNC-Chapel Hill for 26 years. Marcia is now Partner/Co-founder of Career Dimensions NC. She provides career assistance to groups and to individuals and consults with career services offices around the country to help them improve their programs and services. Marcia was the project manager on NACE's initiative to develop a process and training for conducting external reviews based on the NACE Professional Standards for Colleges & Universities. She has conducted external reviews for over 25 colleges and universities. Marcia is co-author of the popular book for parents of college students, *The Parent's Crash Course in Career Planning*. Marcia has a Bachelor's degree from Vassar College and a Master's degree from North Carolina State University.

Marcia's many awards and accomplishments include her election to the National Association of Colleges and Employers' (NACE) Academy of Fellows, her two NACE Chevron Awards for Innovation, a NACE Award of Excellence in Technology, and a SACE Ajax-Griffin Award for Distinguished Service. Marcia was president of SACE (now SoAce) and a board member of NACE. She is also the recipient of NC ACE's Outstanding Professional Award and The University of North Carolina's C. Knox Massey Award for Distinguished Service. Marcia has been cited in ABC News, The New York Times, The Wall Street Journal, Time, CNN, USA Today, and NPR.

Richard (Rick) Hearin

Rick Hearin is the Executive Director of University Career Services at Rutgers University in New Brunswick, New Jersey. He leads and manages career services for a broad array of Rutgers academic programs, and maintains an extensive network of prospective employers seeking interns and new graduates from the ranks of the Scarlet Knights.

Before coming to Rutgers, Rick served as the Director of the University Career Center & The President's Promise at the University of Maryland in College Park, after having served as the Director of Career Services at

Miami University in Oxford, Ohio, for more than 20 years. He began his career as the Director of Career Development and Placement at Ohio Northern University.

A native of Detroit, Rick completed his Bachelor's degree in English and Psychology at Central Michigan University and his graduate work in College Student Personnel at Bowling Green State University and served as a Captain in the US Army in both domestic and international assignments.

Suzanne Helbig

Suzanne has nearly 15 years experience in university career services, including positions in management, marketing and communications, career counseling, and employer relations. She spent the last 12 years at the University of California, Berkeley Career Center where she helped set policies for the office as part of the management team and was responsible for many unit-wide initiatives, such as strategic planning, staff engagement, communications, and fundraising projects. During her time at Berkeley, Suzanne joined high impact strategic planning committees such as the Student Services Initiative charged with recommending sweeping changes for all academic and co-curricular student services units, the Advising Council that will align the delivery of all student advising across campus, and the Division of Student Affairs Strategic Planning Initiative team that will completely transform the student experience at UC Berkeley. Suzanne holds a Master's degree in Higher Education from the University of Arizona. In August 2013, Suzanne will join the University of California, Irvine's Career Center as its Director.

Ryan Herson

Dr. Herson has extensive experience defining and driving cost saving solutions to maximize performance and efficiency through human capital and organizational effectiveness strategies for select Fortune 500 organizations and government agencies. Well equipped to position services, Dr. Herson is accountable for collaborating with senior executives across a broad range of strategic initiatives in order to achieve results. He has contributed to the field in his formal research and as a thought leader in the industry, Dr. Herson has presented in academic and national symposiums on topics to include human capital strategy and transformational leadership. He is a respected colleague of Hofstra University, George Washington University, and New York University where he serves as a mentor and has presented in various seminars.

Dr. Herson currently works for PricewaterhouseCoopers (PwC) where he is accountable for leading engagement execution and business development initiatives, and trains consultants in several human capital domains. Prior to joining PwC, Dr. Herson was with Oracle, where he supported large-scale transformations and served as a lead in business development pursuits. Dr. Herson also worked in the branding industry with BBDO, Young and Rubicam, and Questus.

Dr. Herson earned his Bachelor's in Psychology with a minor in Communications from East Carolina University and even played a little football for the Pirates. He then went on to earn his Master's in Industrial Organizational Psychology and a Ph.D. in Applied Organizational Psychology from Hofstra University.

Gary Alan Miller

Gary Alan Miller, former Assistant Director for Social Media and Innovation with University Career Services and current Senior Assistant Dean with Academic Advising at UNC Chapel Hill, is an 18-year higher education veteran. He consults and delivers talks on communication strategy, technology use, project management, idea generation, and innovation. Gary received his Bachelor's of Science in Mass Communication from Middle Tennessee State University and a Master's of Science in Social Foundations of Education from Georgia State University. He currently serves on the boards of the Southern Association of Colleges and Employers and the North Carolina Career Development Association and is a finalist for the 2013 National Association of Colleges and Employers' Innovation Excellence Award in Research.

Catherine Neiner

Catherine Neiner is Director of Career Planning at Agnes Scott College. In 2006, she was one of six U.S. career professionals selected as a Fulbright scholar to study the emergent career counseling profession in Germany. She served for seven years with the Georgia Tech College of Management, first as Director of Management Career Services, then as Director of Communications. Catherine has held leadership positions at the state and national level in a number of professional organizations. She served as president of the Georgia Association of Colleges and Employers and Chairman of the Principles (Ethics) Committee of the National Association of Colleges and Employers. She was a founding board member of the MBA Career Services Council. She has been an invited presenter at numerous regional and national career conferences and frequently is invited to speak at leadership conferences. She has served on the faculty of the Auburn Women's Leadership Institute and the Entergy Advanced Leadership Program.

Catherine has published articles on interviewing, career search strategies, and strategic communications as well as contributing op-ed essays in the *Atlanta Journal-Constitution*. Her research focuses on the development of accurate expectations of first post-college jobs. In addition, she researches workplace issues that affect women's progression past mid-level jobs, and she consults to organizations on strategies to develop women in the workplace. Her clients have included Fortune 500 firms, and colleges and universities in the Unites States and Latin America. In addition, she provides executive coaching to mid- and high-level professionals.

Catherine holds a B.A. in Journalism from the University of Georgia and M.A. in Communication from Georgia State University.

Katherine Nobles

Katherine Nobles served as a Career Counselor for one year before taking on her current role as the Assistant Director of Social Media & Branding within University Career Services at The University of North Carolina at Chapel Hill. In her short time with UNC University Career Services, Katherine has presented at state, regional, and national conferences and is a finalist for the 2013 National Association of Colleges and Employers' Innovation Excellence Award for Research. Katherine earned her B.A. in Communication from Virginia Tech and M.Ed. in Higher Education Administration from The College of William & Mary, where she served as a Career Center Graduate Assistant.

Lindsey Pollak

Lindsey is a bestselling author, keynote speaker, corporate consultant, and recognized expert on next generation career and workplace trends. She is an official Ambassador for LinkedIn and the author of *Getting from College to Career: Your Essential Guide to Succeeding in the Real World*. Lindsey's advice and opinions have appeared in such media outlets as *The New York Times*, *The Wall Street Journal*, CNN, NPR, and NBC Nightly News. She is a graduate of Yale University.

Sam Ratcliffe

Sam Ratcliffe, holds a Ph.D. in Educational Leadership and Policy from Virginia Tech, a Master's in Counselor Education from James Madison University, and a B.A. from the Virginia Military Institute, where he is now Director of Career Services, as well as Academic Success Program Chair, and a faculty member in the Leadership Studies Program. Sam is a researcher, author, and frequent presenter on topics related to assessment and accountability, evaluation, and program review in career services. His highly regarded dissertation research was related to professional standards use by career services directors. Sam continues to conduct external reviews and consults for college and university career centers. Sam served as Co-chair of the ACES Presidents Roundtable and a national task force to conduct extensive research and develop recommendations related to certification and/or accreditation for career services practitioners and offices.

Sam currently serves as the Vice President College on the NACE Board and as a NACE representative to the Council for the Advancement of Standards in Higher Education (CAS) board. He has served NACE in multiple committee roles, including accountability, external review processes, leadership development, membership, professional advocacy, professional competencies for career services practitioners, professional outcomes assessment, professional standards for career services, and principles for professional practice. He has written several articles for the *NACE Journal* and is an instructor in the NACE Management Leadership Institute. A former president of both the Virginia Association of Colleges and Employers and the Eastern Association of Colleges and Employers, he has received the Distinguished Service Award from each organization.

Jack R. Rayman

Jack Rayman is Senior Director Emeritus of Career Services and Affiliate Professor of Counseling Psychology and Education at Penn State University. He received a Ph.D. in Counseling Psychology and Student Personnel Administration from the University of Iowa in 1974. He served on the faculty of Rajang Teachers College as a Peace Corps Volunteer in Sarawak, Malaysia, from 1967 to 1970, where he taught agriculture and English and designed and built the first 18-hole golf course in the country. His doctoral dissertation, "Sex and the Single Interest Inventory" was a groundbreaking effort to eliminate gender bias in interest measurement. It was the prototype for the Unisex Edition of the ACT Interest Inventory (UniACT), which is now an integral part of the ACT battery. He was Assistant Professor at Western Maryland College from 1974 to 1978 and during that time was a major architect of DISCOVER, the computerized career guidance system. From 1978 to 1983, he was Career Development Officer and Affiliate Associate Professor of Counseling Psychology at Iowa State University. He joined the faculty and staff at Penn State in 1983. He is the author of more than 40 journal articles and book chapters and has authored three books for career services professionals. He was elected to the National Association for Colleges and Employers (NACE) Academy of Fellows. In the early 2000s, he raised $9.5 million to build a new 44,000 square foot career services building at Penn State, which opened in 2002. Considered one of the most respected members of the profession, Jack remains extremely active as a consultant to national and international institutions. In his spare time, he writes poetry and has built a log cabin on the Allegheny Plateau.

Patricia Rose

Patricia Rose, a native of Ohio, is Director of Career Services at the University of Pennsylvania. In that capacity, she oversees career counseling and programming, graduate/professional school advising, employer outreach, and recruiting for all Penn undergraduates and graduate students in nine schools as well as post-doctoral trainees and alumni. She previously worked with

Wharton MBA's, and ran a program to help non-business PhDs make the transition to the corporate world. She holds undergraduate and graduate degrees in English, and, before embarking on an administrative career, she taught English at St. Lawrence University, and at Penn, where she did her graduate work.

Pat is a member of numerous professional associations, and speaks frequently to students, alumni, and business groups on career management topics and employment trends. She has a particular interest in the use of technology and social media in the job-search process. In 2001 – 2002, she was one of the original career center directors who joined with the National Association of Colleges and Employers (NACE) and the DirectEmployers Association to develop the NACElink system, which was launched during the summer of 2002.

Pat is involved in Philadelphia efforts to move from brain drain to brain magnet, and advises local groups working to make Philadelphia a region of choice for young professionals. She serves on the board of Philly Fellows, and on the School Committee of the Board of Trustees of Germantown Friends School. In her spare time, she roots for the Philadelphia Phillies and Eagles.

Kathy L. Sims

Since 1995, Kathy L. Sims has served as Director of the UCLA Career Center. For the previous 14 years she was Executive Director of The George Washington University Career Center in Washington, DC. Her 35 years in career services also include career counseling and management positions at West Virginia and Bowling Green State Universities.

Kathy is an active speaker and addresses numerous employer and college audiences on the topics of branding, marketing, campus culture, and the future of career services. She has appeared on the *NBC Nightly News*, ABC's *Good Morning America*, CNN, and French network television, and been interviewed for numerous regional and national print and broadcast media. Sims also serves as an international consultant, working with developing universities and industries in Japan, Mexico, China, and Algeria. Sims is a founding faculty member of the Career Services Institute, co-creator of the University Network (UN), a national benchmarking group for directors of selected large university career centers, and a founding partner in the development of NACElink™. At UCLA she serves in a variety of campus-wide leadership roles.

In 2000-01, she served as President of the National Association of Colleges and Employers (NACE). She was inducted into the Academy of Fellows in 2002, and in 2006 was named the recipient of the Kauffman Award for "leadership that significantly advanced the career services profession." She has been a faculty member of NACE's Management Leadership Institute since 2001. Kathy holds B.S. and M.S. degrees from West Virginia University.

Valerie Szymkowicz

Valerie Szymkowicz received her B.A. in Natural Science/Environmental Studies from New England College and her M.Ed. in Student Personnel from the Graduate School of Education at the University of Vermont. For over 20 years, she worked in higher education at both public and private, research, baccalaureate, and liberal arts institutions, principally in the areas of academic advising, experiential education, and career services.

Valerie joined the executive search industry in 1999 and has served as an associate with Spelman & Johnson (SJG) since 2002. With a strong belief in cultivating leadership potential among higher education professionals, Valerie helped established the SJG/NACE Rising Star Award and has been a guest presenter at the NASPA Region I Mid-Managers Institute, facilitating discussion on professional development priorities on numerous occasions. Valerie's current responsibilities as an SJG senior associate include search management, client and candidate relations, and new business development. Valerie and her family reside in rural Vermont, where she putters in her garden, takes an occasional schuss down snow-covered mountains, and thoroughly enjoys all four seasons.

Christine Timm

Christine (Chris) Timm received her Ph.D. and Master's degree in Education from the University of Nebraska-Lincoln (UNL) and her

Bachelor's in Speech Communications from Chadron State College. Chris has worked for the University of Nebraska-Lincoln for over 20 years. She began her work in Nebraska overseeing career guidance software and then moved into career services, serving in various roles including Assistant Director, Associate Director, and her current position of Interim Director. Her responsibilities include serving as liaison to the College of Engineering, office administration, career counseling, internship advising, assessment, and technology. She has served on campus technology committees including e-mail implementation, student information system administration, admissions software selection, and a number of committees related to student retention and success. Chris has been instrumental in the development of NACElink, was one of the original technology team members, and continued serving on advisory groups focused on system design, testing, and training. She also has served on many other NACE committees including annual conference and professional competencies, and chaired the Principles for Professional Practice committee.

Made in the USA
Charleston, SC
16 February 2016